This is the third volume of essays by actors with the Royal Shakespeare Company. Thirteen actors describe the Shakespearian roles they played in productions between 1987 and 1991. The contributors are Roger Allam, Simon Russell Beale, Brian Cox, Gregory Doran, Penny Downie, Ralph Fiennes, Deborah Findlay, Philip Franks, Anton Lesser, Maggie Steed, Sophie Thompson, Harriet Walter and Nicholas Woodeson. The plays covered include *Hamlet*, *Richard III*, *The Merchant of Venice*, *As You Like It*, *Much Ado About Nothing*, *Measure for Measure* and important theatrical rarities such as *Cymbeline*, *Titus Andronicus*, *King John* and the *Henry VI* plays in the Royal Shakespeare Company's highly successful adaptation retitled *The Plantagenets*. The result is a glimpse into the working methods of a major theatre company as well as a stimulating commentary on the plays themselves. A brief biographical note is provided for each of the contributors and an introduction places the essays in the context of the Stratford and London stages and of the music and design for the particular productions.

Players of Shakespeare 3

# Players of Shakespeare 3

*Further essays in Shakespearian performance
by players with the
Royal Shakespeare Company*

Edited by
Russell Jackson and Robert Smallwood

Published by the Press Syndicate of the University of Cambridge
The Pitt Building, Trumpington Street, Cambridge CB2 1RP
40 West 20th Street, New York, NY 10011–4211, USA
10 Stamford Road, Oakleigh, Melbourne 3166, Australia

First published 1993
Reprinted 1995

Printed in Great Britain at the University Press, Cambridge

*A catalogue record for this book is available from the British Library*

*Library of Congress cataloguing in publication data*

Players of Shakespeare 3: further essays in Shakespearian performance
/ by players with the Royal Shakespeare Company; edited by Russell
Jackson and Robert Smallwood.
p.    cm.
ISBN 0 521 36320 9
1. Shakespeare, William, 1564–1616 – Stage history – 1950 –
2. Shakespeare, William, 1564–1616 – Characters. 3. Theater –
England – History – 20th century. 4. Royal Shakespeare Company.
5. Actors – England. 6. Acting. I. Jackson, Russell, 1949–    .
II. Smallwood, Robert, 1941– . III. Royal Shakespeare Company. IV. Title:
Players of Shakespeare three.
PR3112.P555   1993
792.9′5′0942 – dc20    92–36175    CIP

ISBN 0 521 36320 9 hardback
ISBN 0 521 47734 4 paperback

CE

To the memory of our dear friend MAURICE DANIELS (1916–1993), who died while this book was in proof and whose work with the Royal Shakespeare Company did so much to bring academic and theatrical Shakespearians together and thus to make possible the *Players of Shakespeare* series, this volume is affectionately dedicated.

# Contents

# Illustrations

We are grateful to the following for permission to reproduce illustrations: The Shakespeare Centre Library: Joe Cocks Studio Collection for photographs nos. 2–7, 10–20, 25; Richard Mildenhall for 1, 21; Ivan Kyncl for 8, 9, 27, 28; John Haynes for 22, 23; Sarah Ainslie for 24; and Stephen Macmillan for 26.

# Preface

Explanations and excuses grow the more superfluous and transparent the more often one repeats the activity that originally provoked them. Readers of a third volume of RSC actors' essays on Shakespearian roles will thus no longer expect those responsible for bringing them together to account for their actions. This collection, like its predecessors, offers the actors' perspective on a series of roles presented in some recent RSC productions of Shakespeare's plays. The years covered by the volume are 1987 to 1991. The actors had all talked about their performances in courses at the Shakespeare Institute or the Shakespeare Centre in Stratford. As will be apparent, we have offered a cross-section of performances from the period covered, though with some attempt on this occasion to represent productions of rarely performed plays: *King John*, the *Henry VI* trilogy, *Troilus and Cressida*, *Titus Andronicus*, *Cymbeline*. As in preceding volumes, a brief biographical note on the contributors, with emphasis on their Shakespearian work, appears at the beginning of each essay; at the end of the volume we provide a list of credits for the productions covered. In spite of the likelihood of being accused of inconsistency, we have departed from the practice of previous volumes of keying quotations to the Riverside Shakespeare, which is not an edition much used by actors. The text issued to RSC players in the rehearsal rooms is the New Penguin, and all quotations and references are therefore to these editions; in the case of *Titus Andronicus* and *Cymbeline*, two plays not yet available in the New Penguin series, references are to the new Arden texts.

We are grateful to the editors of *Shakespeare Quarterly* for permission to repeat in the Introduction to this volume some material that appeared first in the pages of their journal. We are grateful too, as ever, to colleagues at the Shakespeare Institute, the Shakespeare Birthplace Trust, and the Royal Shakespeare Theatre for their help in the preparation of this book. We owe a particular debt to Sonja Dosanjh, the RSC Company Manager in Stratford, whose graciousness and efficiency do so much to create the appropriate circumstances for the friendly co-operation that exists between the Royal Shakespeare Company and Stratford's academic institutions.

R.J.  R.S.
Stratford-upon-Avon

# Introduction

## ROBERT SMALLWOOD

READERS of the third volume in a series have a reasonable idea of what to expect. The late Philip Brockbank was able to introduce the first of these collections as an innovation in publishing history, a book that was 'the first of its kind'. Seven years later it seems entirely unsurprising that we should be interested in the reflections of actors on Shakespearian roles which, over a six-week rehearsal period and a run of perhaps a hundred or more performances (not untypical for an RSC production), they come to know with a very particular intimacy.

The value of such intimacy was perceived at the beginning of this century by the critic whose work represents so decisive a stage in the educational establishment's appropriation for the classroom and lecture hall of Shakespeare the writer for the popular theatre: A. C. Bradley's introduction to his *Shakespearean Tragedy* advises his readers, generations of examination candidates over whom he cast so potent a spell, that the best way to understand the plays is to read them 'as if they were actors who had to study all the parts'. His next sentence, however, begins to drive that wedge between theatre Shakespeare and classroom Shakespeare which has been such a depressing element of the plays' twentieth-century incarnation: 'They do not need, *of course*, to imagine whereabouts the persons are to stand, or what gestures they ought to use; but they want to realise fully and exactly the inner movements which produced these words and no other'. The gestures, the position on the stage and in relation to other characters in the play, these and any other considerations of performance 'of course' do not matter; all that is significant for the study of Shakespeare is the *words*, their motives, their sources, their meaning. The reaction against Bradley, when it came in the 1930s, and most obviously encapsulated in Lionel Knights's essay of 1933 'How Many Children Had Lady Macbeth', was in no sense a reaction against this divorce of the words of the text from the performance of the play. On the contrary, Knights reinforces it, informing us early in his blistering attack on the Bradleyan critical

I

method that the only 'business' of the critic of Shakespeare is 'with the words on the page'. For a few more decades the academic establishment consigned Shakespeare to the classroom and library, and players of Shakespeare and teachers of Shakespeare were condemned to regard each other with mutual distrust, if not hostility, across an altogether artificial divide.

The bridging of that divide has been one of the principal endeavours of Shakespearian criticism over the last thirty or so years, discernible across a wide spectrum, from editors whose footnotes now spend much more time on matters of staging than on the questions of philology which used to obsess them to an enormous flow of criticism of the general 'text and performance' kind. There is undoubtedly a much greater awareness in current school and university Shakespeare teaching of the plays in performance. All this is healthy – healthy enough, indeed, to have itself been questioned (as all new orthodoxies quite rightly should be), though not, I think, seriously to be threatened. Though few have taken literally George Bernard Shaw's admonition that the 'simple thing to do with a Shakespeare play is to perform it' and that 'the alternative is to let it alone' – the world would not have been so pestered with Shakespeare books if they had – that typical phenomenon of a decade or two ago, the essay on Shakespeare in an academic journal, or an undergraduate work-file, without the faintest indication of the text's theatrical origin and destiny, is becoming, mercifully, a rarer event. For the comfortable enterprise of disquisition upon the significance of the 'words on the page' (supposing editorial scholarship has been able to decide what those should be) is immediately sabotaged by the process of giving those words to actors to speak. From the moment one sets out to cast the play (how old, for example, is the player one should be seeking for the majority of roles in Shakespeare: there is surprisingly little evidence on this from the words on the page) to the arrival at the last word of all Shakespeare's plays, the orthographically forgettable but theatrically potent (and frequently volatile) *Exeunt*, the enterprise is a constant process of choice among often equally persuasive alternatives.

That process of choice-making, the exploration of possibilities through rehearsal and the selection of what seems to work best in the present circumstances of acting relationships and concepts of set and design, forms an important element in the essays that follow. But preceding that endeavour, for most RSC productions at least, lie the larger decisions within which the rehearsal selection process must operate. The apparently limitless freedom of the rehearsal room, if not altogether illusory, is at least confined, for it is contained within boundaries on the one hand of playing space, set, and other directorial concepts which have already governed casting decisions – 'artistic' considerations in the broad sense – and on the other of available budget, audience expectation (and audience composition), choice of theatre – considerations that are economically driven and in a broad sense ultimately political. To take the choice of theatre first: the Royal Shakespeare Company, from the one large early 1930s auditorium in which it came into being when it was reconstituted at the beginning of the 1960s from the old Shakespeare Memorial Theatre organization, now operates in seven or eight regular playing spaces in Stratford, London, and Newcastle. Annually, or virtually annually, it also sends out a regional tour to distinctly irregular playing spaces, school and civic halls, sports arenas, even covered-over swimming pools. All these theatrical venues are represented in the essays in this volume and in them the huge influence over conceptual considerations and rehearsal procedures of the space for which the production is destined is, inevitably and properly, perfectly clear.

Why the space has been chosen invariably depends on box-office considerations. The RSC's first *King John* for nearly two decades was played in the studio theatre, The Other Place, because experience (even though limited by infrequency of production) remorselessly proved that *King John* is not a top-selling play; the 150 seats of the Other Place would therefore be easier to sell than the 1,500 seats of the 'main house', the Royal Shakespeare Theatre itself. The result of this externally imposed necessity happens to have been a happy one; Nicholas Woodeson, beginning his essay on the title role in the play, declares that play and place were 'made for each other', while the director of the production, Deborah Warner, already had an impressive record of artistic success in small and less formal theatre spaces when she began to add to that record with this production. One of those achievements had been with the RSC in the preceding season, when she made of that most neglected and contemned of Shakespeare's tragedies, *Titus Andronicus*, an overwhelmingly affecting and exhilarating theatrical experience. The venue on this occasion was the Swan, the RSC's newest auditorium, seating 450 spectators in horseshoe formation on three levels round a thrust stage in a relationship not altogether unlike that obtaining in an Elizabethan theatre. The play's success in that theatre, public and crowd scenes played out to actors inhabiting spectators' space, scenes of physical suffering threateningly, inescapably close at hand on the thrust stage, was, of course, a tribute to the skill of director and actors in exploiting the space which they had been assigned; but the assigning

3

process was no doubt largely the result of a not unsurprising belief that selling 1,500 seats per performance in the main house for *Titus Andronicus* might not be altogether easy.

The plays represented in main-house productions in this volume nearly all have a certain commercial safeness about them – as play titles that is, though obviously not, invariably, as particular productions. *Much Ado About Nothing, The Merchant of Venice, As You Like It,* and increasingly *Measure for Measure* (though this is a more recent phenomenon) are titles which can be relied upon to attract audiences from a wide range of the RSC's spectrum of potential customers – tourists in Stratford for a brief visit, the huge population of the adjacent West Midland conurbation, visiting school and academic groups, and so on. Productions of them, therefore, come round rather frequently in a theatre which is choosing half a dozen plays annually from the thirty-seven Shakespearian possibilities. It is no accident, therefore, that essays on roles from several of these plays are not appearing for the first time in a volume in this series. *The Merchant of Venice* and *As You Like It,* indeed, have figured in all three, *Measure for Measure* in two. That the same company should, every three or four years, be creating new productions of the same play on the same stage cannot but produce its pressures: the director and designer are almost always different, of course, there is rarely much overlap among the actors, and awareness of the work of predecessors is usually denied, but it is hard to imagine that some care not to be repetitive of earlier choices does not have to be taken, consciously or unconsciously. On the whole, Shakespearian playgoers should be able to regard this situation as a source of pleasurable anticipation rather than regret: the range of performance options (as recent Shakespearian criticism and scholarship in general, and these *Players of Shakespeare* volumes in particular, have insisted) is enormous; it would be absurd to suggest that one choice was in any absolute sense 'right' and exceedingly difficult to prove that another was altogether 'wrong'. That the economic and practical circumstances in which the RSC operates force it, through its constant re-examination of a limited number of play-texts, to explore across a wider range of those choices than any other theatre company, is perhaps not unhealthy, though like all systems of intensive cultivation it needs careful monitoring. My own experience, accumulated over thirty years of RSC-watching, is that the accusation, not infrequent, that production choices have been made solely for the sake of 'being different' is nearly always shallow and ill-judged.

The Royal Shakespeare Company, then, is a very particular and in many ways a rather curious organism. Some reviewers of earlier volumes in this series have said as much, and so criticized the editors for not spreading a wider net. The charge is understandable, and up to a point legitimate; that we here continue on the established lines may thus merit a word of defence. On one level this is inevitably pragmatic and personal. Our academic endeavours in Stratford-upon-Avon bring us into close and regular working contact with this theatre company in a way which is probably unique between any academic institution and a major professional company: these volumes are only one of several results of that co-operation. There are, however, less local and particular reasons: there has been a remarkable increase in recent years in companies concentrating on Shakespeare; no longer does the RSC have competition only from the National Theatre and an occasional local repertory or summer festival production, but such companies as Renaissance, Cheek by Jowl, the Peter Hall Company, and the English Shakespeare Company are enormously increasing the range of Shakespeare productions available to British theatre-goers. Nevertheless, the RSC remains by far the most wide-ranging, the most various, the most experienced, and, in terms of sheer volume of output, the most productive Shakespeare company in the world, employing a wider range of directors and actors than any other (including many who have previously worked for the other companies mentioned), operating in a range of locations and playing spaces as various as any other, and presenting productions which usually have longer lives than any other. A cross-section of its productions over a brief period may thus be said to offer a representative sampling of the current state of Shakespearian production in this country.

The essays in this volume, then, derive from ten RSC productions from the period from 1987 to 1991; these ten productions were the work of eight directors, six men and two women. They were designed for three playing spaces in Stratford (five for the main house, two for the Swan, and two for The Other Place), with one smaller-scale regional touring production that played a wide range of venues throughout Britain. Apart from this last, nearly all of them played for a year in Stratford, followed by a short season in Newcastle upon Tyne and a second year at the Barbican in London in houses requiring a considerable degree of set modification for the move, particularly so for Swan productions moving to the Pit studio theatre, which is considerably less than half its size. There is, then, no shortage of range in this small collection from the work of a single company over a comparatively short period. Some brief discussion of the main features of

1 'Main House' Shakespeare: a battle scene from *The Plantagenets*,
directed by Adrian Noble, designed by Bob Crowley, Royal Shakespeare
Theatre, 1988

each of these productions in terms of set and overall concept may be
helpful to provide a context for the more particular perspectives of the
essays that follow.

The four main-house productions of comedies from which the first five
essays derive present a quartet of representatively contrasted design
choices. Bill Alexander's *The Merchant of Venice* placed the play firmly in
the sixteenth century; Di Trevis's *Much Ado About Nothing*, though
looking occasionally reminiscent of earlier decades, was more or less
firmly contemporary; Nicholas Hytner's *Measure for Measure* made fairly
specific allusion to the inter-war years, perhaps to the mid-thirties; and
John Caird's *As You Like It* looked similarly thirtyish at Duke Frederick's court but energetically modern, in a non-specific sort of way, in the
Forest of Arden. Pilgrims to a 'royal' theatre in the town of Shakespeare's
birth, coming as if to a shrine or museum, not infrequently suppose
that they will be greeted by confirmation of all their doublet-and-hose
expectations. This by no means unrepresentative group of productions

makes clear how comparatively rare it is for those expectations to be satisfied.

Mark Thompson's dominating columnar set for Nicholas Hytner's *Measure for Measure* distilled all the most impersonal, alienating aspects of mid-twentieth-century architecture; its central pillars revolved to reveal, unsurprisingly, a prison beyond; only for the final scene did the back of the stage open up to give us a view of sky, and even of a tree, its unashamedly painted backcloth thus suggesting that escape from this remorseless urban world might, at least within the pretences of the theatre, be possible. Escape was never achieved, however; Isabella alone seemed to have the will for it, but, striding determinedly towards that backcloth open space in response to the Duke's final proposal of marriage, she stopped to look back at him before reaching it, and the lights faded on her uncertain glance as she stood poised and still between him and life beyond Vienna. The world of the city, with its silent and anxious civil servants around the Duke and later Angelo, its drug-pushers and rent boys hanging round the public lavatories of the suburbs inhabited by Mistress Overdone and the street-wise young delinquent Pompey, was an overwhelmingly modern, secular environment in which Roger Allam's Duke tried to face up to his own and his subjects' neuroses, sexual and political. The threatened violation of Isabella, though she wore a black headcloth and long black dress throughout, was of the woman more than of the nun, brutally physicalized as Angelo threw her across the desk from which he was allegedly dispensing justice, the corrupt white male in authority, tyrannizing over the defenceless black woman in subservience. Few productions could more vividly make the point that putting on a Shakespeare play is a matter of choosing among options: a whole critical (and to some extent theatrical) tradition of examining the play in the light of sixteenth-century Christian theology, with Vincentio as a sort of Christ figure, seemed to go out of the window to produce this sharp, intelligent, secular vision of *Measure for Measure*, centring on Roger Allam's worried, muddled, improvising, and altogether ungodlike Duke.

Also presenting a radical re-examination of the play's recent theatrical tradition was Di Trevis's modern-dress *Much Ado About Nothing*. The director clearly started from the premise that the society of Messina is rich, effete, selfish and unsympathetic, the opulence of its costumes, and the lazy decadence of its hotel-swimming-pool-patio society deservedly vulnerable to the misunderstandings which come close to destroying it. Mark Thompson's set presented Leonato's house in some late twentieth-century republic (Central American, perhaps) where the rich are very rich and the motives of the revolutionaries, even if led by the malevolent Don John, are perfectly understandable. The overwhelmingly lavish costumes (Beatrice and Hero never appearing twice in the same garments, and Hero's marriage dress putting *Tatler* wedding photographs to shame), the elegant sun-lounging furniture, the patio fishpools, the apparently shallow and superficial people with nothing to do, all combined to present an image of a society riding for a well-deserved fall. Don Pedro and his party arrived on stage (partly from above) to the sound of helicopters from a war (just out there in the real world) that has never seemed closer, one of those up-country flare-ups that explain why precarious governments need to keep ruthless standing armies. Press reviews of the production were on the whole energetically hostile – partly, no doubt, because its shock tactics had succeeded, but more seriously (where seriousness was discernible) because it was felt that little of new revelation of the play had emerged from the onslaught on accepted readings. The production's reappraisal of the play extended to Beatrice and Benedick, who were portrayed with a great deal more of an age gap than is customary between themselves and Hero and Claudio. They presented what seemed in many ways an ill-assorted couple and were given a perhaps harder task than usual to convince audiences that the growing evidence of their commitment to each other was anything more than a reason for laughter. That ultimately it was in fact much more emerges in Maggie Steed's description of her Beatrice's tentative and hesitant journey towards that final commitment.

Where Nicholas Hytner's *Measure for Measure* pushed religious issues into the background, Bill Alexander's *The Merchant of Venice* highlighted them – literally so, for on the back wall of Kit Surrey's set hung on one side an icon of the Madonna and on the other a Star of David, alternately lit according to the scene currently taking place beneath them. The play was treated primarily as a study in sectarian and racial hatred, its twentieth-century overtones not in the least diminished by its sixteenth-century costuming. In the trial scene, before Portia forbade the spilling of blood, Shylock prepared for the moment with prayers in Hebrew while the Christians prayed in Latin. Much offence was given to both religious communities by this aggressive depiction of the excesses of sectarian confrontation. At the end of the play, in that infinitely variable final *Exeunt*, the last two characters left on stage on this occasion were Antonio and Jessica, she searching for the little cruciform jewel, Lorenzo's first gift, which she had lost and which Antonio had found. Our last image was of his

8

holding it out to her, he the head of the Christian community, she the last survivor in the play of the Jewish community, and between them the symbol of her defection from her inherited faith, proffered yet withheld, reached out for but not grasped, as the lights went out.

The set for this production was Venetian throughout, a bridge (of sighs) spanning the stage and a wooden landing-platform in the foreground. Belmont had more elaborate floor coverings and curtains, but the basic playing space remained unchanged. Costumes were colourfully sixteenth century, Shylock in a flowing purple robe and multi-coloured turban, the Christians in ostentatiously wealthy dress, particularly Portia, whose silks and jewels were constant evidence of her having been 'richly left'. Shylock might, at a certain point, have had the ready money, but the Christians had the real wealth, and it seemed somehow fitting that the final moment of the production's exploration of racial tensions should crystallize around a jewelled crucifix. That this was held by the leader of Venetian society's dominant religious orthodoxy was complicated by the fact that Antonio was also presented as the leader of its subordinated sexual community, for Portia's victory over Shylock in the trial scene had also been a victory over Antonio's desire to die at Shylock's hand, as a martyr to his love for Bassanio. Antonio, presented as a depressive homosexual, aiming, through death, to achieve an unbreakable hold over Bassanio's emotional loyalties, needed to be defeated by Portia at least as urgently as Shylock if her marriage to Bassanio was to have the faintest hope of success; the grimly energetic determination of her expedition to Venice and her performance in the trial scene restored the dominant heterosexual orthodoxy at the same time as it was restoring Christian social and political supremacy. Again the choices made by the production were highly selective and partial, and the result intelligent, stimulating, and disturbing.

Deborah Findlay looks at the play from the point of view of its principal victor; in Gregory Doran's essay, on the other hand, we catch a rare glimpse of a Shakespeare production from one of those notorious 'bit parts' of which the plays are so full and which require such skill and commitment in the playing if the larger roles are to be properly sustained. Solanio, part of that male coterie attached to Antonio in this version, is not a large part, but its loyalties and affiliations chart the flow of prejudices which the production was highlighting.

Sophie Thompson came to the role of Rosalind at the RSC from a recent performance as Celia for the Renaissance Company, the complex inter-relatednesses of the roles thus asserting themselves in this third volume of

*Players of Shakespeare* as they did in the second. John Caird's Stratford production was designed (by Ultz) very much for the Royal Shakespeare Theatre, its set being a continuation of the decor of the theatre's auditorium and foyer to present an elaborate (some thought over-elaborate) gloss on the play's assertion that 'all the world's a stage'. The aim of the design was to blur and obfuscate the boundaries between our world and that of the play. One entered the theatre to encounter a replica of the highly distinctive foyer clock, telling the right time, dominating the stage; however early one got there the actors were there already, as at a court dance, their evening costumes in keeping with the 1930s design of the theatre itself, moving freely between stage and auditorium, theatre ushers and court ushers indistinguishable. Duke Frederick made his entry through the stalls and sat in one of the dress circle boxes for the wrestling while the theatre audience was required to stand, with the onstage court party, for the ducal anthem. (Did unwillingness to do so constitute inadequate surrender to the fiction, or, on the contrary, a thoroughly committed involvement leading to a very proper refusal to stand for the usurper?) Since all of these early scenes were set forward of the proscenium arch and played in front of huge wooden doors reproducing the panelling of the auditorium, it was not until Rosalind led the entry into Arden by pushing open one of these doors, that the play moved to what, when the theatre was opened in 1932, would have been thought of as the *stage*. And then, as the door swung open, breaking the great clock in two (for there is, of course, no clock in the forest) there was an empty (or virtually empty) space beyond, the magic world of Arden, alias a theatre stage, a place to play in. The role-playing games pursued in that space, and the discoveries and self-discoveries that come from them, are explored in Sophie Thompson's essay.

Two hugely contrasted styles in the production of Shakespeare's history plays are manifested in these essays. Adrian Noble's version of the first tetralogy (*The Plantagenets*) was on the grand scale of main stage ostentation; Deborah Warner's *King John* offered studio theatre simplicity at its most quintessential. Interestingly (and perhaps ironically), they played in Stratford and London simultaneously. In contrast to the massive cutting of *The Plantagenets*, Deborah Warner's *King John* played every line of the text – which seems likely to have been the first time such a thing had happened in the professional theatre since the play first saw the light. Court and battle scenes notwithstanding, the production confined itself to a 30-foot square in the centre of the tin hut which was the original Other

2 Studio Shakespeare: after the Battle of Angiers, *King John*, directed by Deborah Warner, designed by Sue Blane, The Other Place, 1988. (From left to right: Blanche (Julia Ford), the Bastard (David Morrissey), and Prince Arthur (Lyndon Davies))

Place, surrounded by its little complement of 150 spectators. Unlike *The Plantagenets*, with its historically coherent late medieval setting, costumes, armour, and heraldry, *King John* was shamelessly eclectic and anachronistic in its visual effects, its main piece of 'set' a collection of modern aluminium ladders for the siege of Angiers, its costumes mixing medieval chain-mail, Second World War greatcoats, First World War tin hats, and bits of Elizabethan style and patterning in some of the ladies' dresses. 'Commodity', it was clear, was not confinable to any specific period. Within this world, however, the naked struggle for power explored in the play was sharply and cuttingly conveyed. Hubert stood on the walls of Angiers like a spectator at a football match, munching on a baguette sandwich as he observed the warring armies in deadly conflict. John dodged round the battlefield, his crown chained to his money belt, and his sword of state much too big for him to handle. Even the Bastard, usually seen as providing some sort of moral centre to the play, was witheringly dismissed as a belligerent National Front bovver boy, draped in St George's flag. The constant alternation and juxtaposition of specifically modern with more timeless visual images as a setting to the careful, intelligent, and, for the most part, telling delivery of the complete text created a fruitful and provocative tension that left one wondering where the play had been all this while. Not that this was in any sense a 'definitive' production: its treatment of the Bastard made the play a meaner, a bleaker, a less intelligent thing than it has usually seemed to readers (or, perhaps, than it really is). But it was a production fully articulated in all its aspects, and at its centre was the penetrating performance of the title role by Nicholas Woodeson.

In contrast with the visual simplicity and textual fullness and directness of Deborah Warner's *King John*, Adrian Noble's production of *The Plantagenets* was, as a theatrical production, one of the RSC's more ambitious enterprises and in terms of textual cutting one of its most extreme. The creation of three play texts from the four plays of the first tetralogy (1, 2, 3 *Henry VI* and *Richard III*) is a theatrical enterprise by no means without precedent, of course: the English Shakespeare Company, indeed, was embarked upon a comparable project as Adrian Noble's began, and in 1963–4 John Barton and Peter Hall had undertaken a similar task for the newly created RSC (though with extensive new writing, which the Adrian Noble project ultimately – as described in Ralph Fiennes's essay – avoided). Again, commercial and artistic considerations seem to be deeply intertwined in provoking this approach: many would agree that the first part of *Henry VI* contains some of the least impressive writing in the Folio, and the urge to hurry its passing can be presented as artistically excusable. On the other hand, some of its events have a theatrical power that needs adequate time to be properly developed in performance, so the savage cutting that will create three plays from four has to be spread much more widely through the quartet, the process thus removing much that is poetically fine and potentially of great theatrical impact in the other three plays of the tetralogy. Behind the artistic dilemma, however, lie the economic imperatives: anything called 'Part 2' is by definition bad box-office, and 'Part 3' is obviously that much worse. Restoring the original quarto titles won't help much, either, since few potential customers have heard of them. The remedy of playing in a smaller auditorium, adopted for other less popular plays represented in this collection, is less accessible here, since the enormous casts of these plays, their big scenes of pageantry, or ceremonial, and of battle, all seem to demand the resources of a large stage and auditorium. That, at least, is clearly what they seemed to Adrian Noble to demand, and what they received. There was an unashamed assertiveness about the scenic elaboration and ostentation of the productions that provided the context for the three performances of the sequence's major roles discussed by their creators later in this volume.

The director–designer partnership of Adrian Noble and Bob Crowley is of long standing, accounting for many important productions at the RSC and elsewhere. The large scale of the project here necessitated an eighteen-week rehearsal period – not surprising arithmetically, the time being thrice the normal but the production being of three plays. The result, however, was something very unusual in RSC main-house productions – time to wait to finalize a design until rehearsals had done a good deal of exploration of the text. (The normal procedure, given the fact that workshops need about as long to build a set as the usual six-week rehearsal period, is that actors rehearse a play within the parameters of a design to which the production is already irrevocably committed.) The benefits were clearly discernible: design, music, text, action seemed to achieve that elusive organic coherence rather more assuredly than is sometimes the case. Bob Crowley's designs developed a pattern he has used frequently at Stratford, of exploiting the great depth of the playing space for certain scenes, but dividing it off, with traverse curtains or other barriers, to avoid monotony and to create more intimate effects. A perforated stage floor allowed light or smoke to pass through from beneath for battle-scene effects. A white floor cloth created the sense of interior scenes, or, spectacularly, of the snow field upon which the Battle of Tewkesbury was fought, later to be hauled up to the vertical, stained by the blood of the dying Prince Edward, as a backdrop to the slaughter of Henry VI and the final establishment of the Yorkist regime. The great golden sun of York, spiky rays emanating from it, hung behind the opening scene of *Richard III*, to be replaced later by its replica in black, circling across the stage in front of the backcloth in horrible imitation of the advance of Richard's power, a circular saw cutting down his enemies, perhaps, or a cog from a clock measuring the time to his defeat.

That sort of symbolic visual effect, suggestive without being heavy-handedly specific, pervaded the production. It was seen above all in the costumes: the pale green of Margaret's early youthfulness; the flaming gold of her dominance of Henry's court; the suave and sensuous black of her military leadership and embassy to France; the nondescript darkness of her final ruin. Henry in white throughout, crucifix at breast, was theatrically impressive, dominant even, in his political weakness. There was armour, gold or black, battle dresses and battle flags, heraldic and flamboyant, or ragged and mud-bespattered; there were scenes of genuinely impressive pomp, such as the great processional entry to the sound of Gregorian chant at the beginning, as Henry V's catafalque dominated the stage, dwindling to scenes of palpably phoney pomp as the struggle for power and self-assertion grew more frenzied. The visual register throughout, however, was firmly medieval. At much the same time as the English Shakespeare Company was making its point about the contemporary relevance of these plays through a succession of twentieth-century stage allusions and images, the RSC remained ostentatiously historical in its approach. The effect of the productions was indisputably spectacular, managing the plays' daunting succession of battle scenes through a variety of visual effects (and one of the largest casts of non-speaking actors that Stratford had seen for many years), so as to avoid the danger of monotony as successfully, perhaps, as may be. There were, indeed, memorable moments of war throughout the production, a constantly changing picture-scape of light, movement and colour. Whether the production avoided, or wanted to avoid, the charge of using actors as figures in a landscape painting remains a question; to remove something approaching a third of the words inevitably forces a production towards a cinematographic presentation of successions of images, and some watchers of the production (and no doubt some actors in it) might have found themselves muttering with Jonson about 'shows, shows, mighty shows'. There was undoubtedly some diminution of the plays' sharpness and radicalism of political outlook and analysis, though not, I think, as a result of the bold decision to make Richmond a genuinely courageous and politically blameless young man who, seriously believing God to be on his side, successfully defies the tyranny of Richard. Given current orthodoxies about the histories this was, in a sense, the most radical aspect of the production. Diminution came, perhaps, rather from the splendour of the staging and scenic effects themselves: theatrical spectacle on this scale inevitably makes its own statement about opulence and in the process tends to blunt the cutting edge of the texts' trenchant political vision. There is, clearly, an argument for the spectacular in productions of the histories, and some remarkable performances came to the foreground of the settings created by director and designer, three of them represented by essays in this volume; but in that struggle for an appropriate balance between word and image which is at the heart of all Shakespearian production, word was here, perhaps, on occasions a little neglected.

For his production of *Troilus and Cressida* at the Swan Theatre, Sam Mendes repeated the eclecticism of setting and costumes which had been offered in Deborah Warner's *King John* at The Other Place. Even more than The Other Place, the Swan presents a permanent challenge to the main stage. There is no down-market austerity about it as there is (comparatively speaking) about the studio theatre. Going there will still seem to any patron, however traditionally inclined, like 'a proper night out' at the theatre. Yet there the Swan sits, back to back with the larger auditorium, a constant reminder, in its vague Elizabethanness, that Shakespeare's plays were never meant for a proscenium-arch stage, yet its 450-capacity ensuring, in the present economic climate, that it will never be regularly used to stage plays that can confidently be expected to fill the 1,500 seats of the main house. *Troilus and Cressida*, however, is just the sort of play that the Swan was made for, and Anthony Ward gave it precisely the set that the space requires, simple, unfussy, and evocative. Tilted far upstage lay a huge, stone-coloured Grecian mask, cracked across, unsulliedly beautiful on one side, pitted and corrupt on the other. A simple playing area in front of it, divided by angled ladder-like bars across the stage which were used to suggest the entrance to a tent, or to Pandarus's house, seemed infinitely adaptable to Greek, Trojan, or battlefield locations. Anachronism of costumes and properties insisted on the timelessness of war: Grecian helmets, First World War khaki, medieval breastplates, Pandarus in elegant blazer and straw hat, the Trojans in the nattiest of white suits for their council

3  Swan Shakespeare: Cressida arrives in the Greek camp, *Troilus and Cressida*, directed by Sam Mendes, designed by Anthony Ward, Swan Theatre, 1990. (From left to right; Ulysses (Paul Jesson), Diomedes (Grant Thatcher), Agamemnon (Sylvester Morand), Cressida (Amanda Root), Ajax (Richard Ridings))

scene. And commenting on all their goings-on, their selfish, passionate, portentous, futile, goings-on, was the busy figure of Simon Russell Beale's Thersites, in his dirty old man's raincoat, his flasher's mac, beaky, scabby, gleeful at every evidence of human pettiness and folly, mediating the play's events to the audience.

The other Swan production represented in this volume also took a deliberately anachronistic approach to costumes and set. Deborah Warner's landmark production of *Titus Andronicus* was Roman only in the vaguest sense. It offered, like her *King John* a year later, that most unusual of theatrical phenomena, a textually uncut version of this rarely performed play. From Titus's first unforgettable entry sitting on a ladder borne by his captives, leading Tamora like an animal on a chain, his brows bound with laurel, in Roman breastplate and modern boots and trousers, the production flung together images from many periods with unashamed

16

energy and vigour. For the final Thyestean banquet, which was preceded by Titus's servants whistling a familiarly happy tune from *Snow White*, Titus appeared in tall white cook's hat, the founder of the feast, the host and *chef de cuisine*, to welcome his guests. Earlier, in string vest and with knotted handkerchief on his head, he looked like grandpa on the beach, playing at bows and arrows over the Emperor's garden wall. This succession of homely, evocative images, punctuating the potentially distancing excesses of the play's narrative and events, kept the audience's focus and attention steady and unflinching on the horrors and violence, offering no escape into laughter or disbelief. The exploitation of the space assisted this: we, the listeners and watchers in the auditorium, became the listeners and watchers appealed to by the rival emperors at the start of the play and the assessors of the cause of the survivors at the end; we might look away from the sight of Titus cutting off his own hand, or breaking his daughter's neck, but the sound made by these acts was inescapable; nor could we shirk our responsibility as participants in violence by pretending not to be excited by the final culmination of Titus's revenge on the loathsome Chiron and Demetrius as he cut their throats over his great blood-catching baking bowl. The utter simplicity of the set, the eclectic suggestiveness of the costumes, the insistence on the audience's participation in the play's events and contamination by its horrors through the production's success in sharing with us the whole of the Swan building – these things gave the play a level of seriousness and relevance that few critics had previously accorded it. It became a study in the source and effects of violence at both a social and a personal level, its energies driven by a man who, through the two women with whom we see him most connected, both inflicts violence and has it inflicted upon himself. That man's journey through the play is described in Brian Cox's essay.

If Deborah Warner's *Titus Andronicus* impressively exploited the space for which it was created, Roger Michell's *Hamlet* had to adapt itself to many spaces. Though all the productions discussed in this volume play in two or three regular RSC venues, the *Hamlet* is the only genuinely touring production of the collection. The annual regional tour has become a regular part of the RSC's pattern of work over recent years, taking a comparatively small company of actors with (usually) two plays on a tour of one-week stands at venues throughout the country. A portable 500-seater auditorium is transported (with the play sets) from venue to venue, and set up in school and sports halls, community and leisure centres, specifically in towns without regular professional theatres. In comparison with the RSC's main enterprise in Stratford and London, this is small-scale work, though the term is, of course, comparative: smaller groups of actors have been known to put on a Shakespeare play than the fifteen who took out *Hamlet* (with *The Comedy of Errors*) and smaller sets have served than the self-consciously theatrical gilded proscenium arch in front of which the *Hamlet* was played. But in terms of the normal RSC operation the scale was modest. To look through the RSC press archive is to become aware of the eager anticipation with which these productions are awaited in Burton and Bridlington, Tiverton and Truro, Belfast and Barrow, Macclesfield and the Isle of Wight, the speed with which they sell out, the enthusiasm with which they are received – the big, internationally famous company going out into the provinces. (No doubt closures of the London theatres in the 1590s, forcing the Lord Chamberlain's men on tour, produced similar effects.) Certainly, the *Hamlet* offered no exception to this eagerness of welcome. It is a typical choice for such a tour, of course, its box-office reputation utterly reliable, yet the play itself amenable to infinite variation of theatrical exploration. The metatheatrical slant of Roger Michell's production is clear from Philip Franks's essay; its Victorian-theatre setting, with a string trio constantly on stage beneath the arch accompanying the action, directed attention to the play's melodramatic qualities. It offered a further variation on the idea of anachronistic eclecticism evinced in other productions represented in this volume, juxtaposing straightforward Jacobean costumes within the Victorian theatre set and contrasting a number of challengingly modern properties: a flashlight camera, briefcases, umbrellas, plastic coffee cups, and so on. It made a feature of its lighting – splendidly effective, and utterly undisguised, so that the arrival of the players at Elsinore, with their rickety lighting equipment, nicely pointed the irony of one group of travelling players joining another. That idea of the play slightly detachedly watching itself was carried through to the title role: the ironic sense of humour which struck many reviewers of the production is among the aspects of the part which Philip Franks discusses.

Harriet Walter's essay on Imogen in *Cymbeline* appears last in the volume because we follow the Folio order, and the Folio editors printed *Cymbeline* among the tragedies – mistakenly, of course, for the play ostentatiously fulfils the most fundamental requirement of comedy that it achieve a happy ending, one so replete, indeed, with revelations and reconciliations as to flirt with self-parody, and providing notorious problems of tone in performance which Harriet Walter discusses in her essay.

Bill Alexander's production of *Cymbeline* is the second of The Other Place productions represented in this collection. The choice of The Other Place is altogether unsurprising for a play distinctly low down in the Shakespearian box-office league, and presenting interpretative problems to director and actors which might well benefit from the greater experimental freedom of small-space presentation. The production exploited and even increased the intimacy of the space from the start, reducing the playing area to a small semi-circle, with the seats crowded around the actors as if drawn round a fireplace for the telling of a story. This sense of gathering round to hear a wonderful tale was enhanced by placing actors in front-row seats among the audience for the initial narrative-setting scene, and repeating this on occasions throughout the evening, as it were in response to the story-telling mode which is very much part of the play's technique. A vaguely pagan sun decoration on the back wall was the only vestige of a set. The space dealt splendidly with the play's main narrative sequence of direct emotional conflicts, but the battle scenes were more awkward and for the inset masque with the descent of Jupiter the bright light and voice-over solution seemed to offer an inadequate impulse of theatrical energy for that great gear-change in the play's narrative drive. Overall, however, the simplicity and plainness of the production and the directness and immediacy of confrontation created by that tiny semi-circular playing space permitted a vigour and speed of approach that was highly effective in releasing the energy of the play's sequence of intimate, emotionally confrontational scenes. Musical accompaniment was provided by the players themselves, striking, ringing, rattling, or twanging a series of drums, bells, gongs, tubes, and the strings of a skeletal piano, all visible behind the audience. The costumes were simple, vaguely Jacobean, though with occasional manifestations of earlier, more primitive motifs. (Cymbeline, for example, wore a plain, halo-like circle of gold to identify his kingliness.) Colours were muted: jerkins of buff, brown, russet – an autumnal range in plain, homespun materials and leather, though for the scenes in Rome the mood shifted, with brighter colours, cigarettes, whisky and one (wildish) woman to create a mood of decadence and cynicism for Iachimo's wager. Within this carefully understated milieu, then, with everything focused intensely on the work of the actors, a difficult play, at times seemingly wilful in its eccentricities and incredibilities, was allowed expression. The mutual commitment of actors and audience, intimacy between them already inevitable given the nature of the space, was greatly intensified by the production itself. Laughter at the play's extremes of surprise and coincidence was part of the treaty – actors encouraged it, audiences were not abashed to indulge it – but in no way undermined the fullness of imaginative commitment that the production demanded. This was, then, a 'chamber production' in the full sense of the term and it is against the background of its success in concentrating the play's emotional power that Harriet Walter's essay on its principal role has to be read.

To sketch in something of the background to the performances remembered and discussed in the following essays is to sense yet again the foolishness of trying to describe briefly what a theatre production was like for those who did not see it. Theatre is (as has been said with quite appalling frequency) an evanescent art, and a volume of this kind is in a sense a monument to the futility of attempting to resist that fact. Yet every production contributes something to a play's critical and cultural inheritance; once over it may in one sense be finished and irretrievable, but in another it becomes part of the accretion of the play's journey through history. It would be technically impossible for a volume of this kind to be genuinely 'topical': productions are generally over in much less time than it takes to get a book into print, so a volume such as this will always be concerned with the past. Fortunately, however, the effort to make it topical would also be foolish, since this collection of essays, and the earlier volumes in the series, exist to catch at the evanescence of past performances in the attempt to hold on to and record something of what was distinctive, unique, and perhaps valuable in their responses to the plays they sought to illuminate. Because of these productions – eccentric or traditional, well or ill received, recent as this book is published, less so during its library shelf-life – our awareness of these plays is altered, our understanding of them adjusted, slightly or more considerably as the case may be, but perceptibly and illuminatingly. To provide that perception and illumination 'the actors are at hand . . .'.

# The Duke in
## *Measure for Measure*
### ROGER ALLAM

ROGER ALLAM played the Duke in Nicholas Hytner's production of *Measure for Measure* at the Royal Shakespeare Theatre in 1987 and at the Barbican Theatre the following year. During the same seasons he played Brutus in *Julius Caesar* and Sir Toby Belch in *Twelfth Night*. He first appeared with the RSC in 1981 in *All's Well that Ends Well* and *Titus Andronicus* and in 1983 (on the regional tour) and 1984 (in Stratford) was Theseus and Oberon in *A Midsummer Night's Dream* and Mercutio in *Romeo and Juliet*, contributing an essay on the latter role to *Players of Shakespeare 2*. In an earlier production of *Measure for Measure*, for the Contact Theatre, Manchester, in 1979, he had played Angelo and for the same company he also appeared as Macbeth. He was in the first cast of *Les Misérables*, playing Javert in 1985–6 at the Barbican and later in the West End. His most recent RSC roles were Benedick in *Much Ado About Nothing* and Trigorin in *The Seagull*, at Stratford in 1990 and the Barbican in 1991.

All Shakespeare's great roles only truly come to life when they are set in relationship to other characters in a production that creates some kind of consistent world for them. However, because of our theatre history, certain characters, of which Hamlet is the most famous, can separate themselves off from their plays and become almost like icons. They are seen as 'peaks' that are 'conquered' in turn through the ages by a succession of star actors. One of the means by which this takes place is the soliloquy. The character/star/icon comes downstage centre and goes over one or two problems with us. We inevitably start to see the play through his or her eyes. The Duke, although one of the longest roles Shakespeare ever wrote, is manifestly *not* one of these. He soliloquizes twice, briefly, and not in a manner which is self-revelatory. He has a murky stage history, and has been played in completely opposite ways: as a Christ-like figure taking on the sins of the world, and as a cynical manipulator of power. It is Angelo and Isabella who reveal to us their torments of mind through eloquent soliloquies. How the Duke is played relies, even more completely than usual, on an interpretation of the whole play. In a way the Duke is the cement of that interpretation. No wonder he has not appealed to the great star actors.

In 1979 I played Angelo at the Contact Theatre in Manchester. The production was influenced by Jan Kott's view of the play, and showed the state as an instrument of total repression. To this end the Duke, excellently played by Simon Molloy, became the arch-manipulator and machiavell, totally ignoring Isabella's feelings of revulsion for his proposed marriage to her, in his display of ultimate power in the fifth act. Also to this end we cut the 'be absolute for death' speech to shreds. It seemed, within this context, over-repetitive. I always thought this a shame, for no very articulate reason, but because I thought it a speech of great beauty. I read through the speech many times, long after we finished our run, and in doing so it came to represent to me an embodiment of utter despair. It was from that time that I began to develop hazy notions of a different interpretation of the Duke, and of his reasons for leaving Vienna at the start of the play. It was also from this point that the Duke became a part I passionately wanted to play one day. I did not, however, expect to play it in the 1987 season at Stratford, considering myself, at thirty-three, too young. Luckily for me, the RSC were having great difficulty casting it, as it is one of those roles traditionally considered by actors to be a complete pig. Also the director, Nicholas Hytner, being young himself, had no difficulty imagining the role played younger than usual, and so, to my great and lasting joy, I was cast.

In initial discussions with Nick, he spoke about the two separate worlds of the play, the government/court versus the street, and of how these worlds seemed irreconcilable. I spoke of my hunches as to why the Duke left, which was that he seemed to be in the midst of a deep personal crisis about the value of life itself. This seemed a useful starting-point, as it linked the public and private worlds in a dilemma of fragmentation. This was in January 1987 and we did not start rehearsals until August. In the meantime I opened in *Julius Caesar* playing Brutus, another play which deals with tensions between public and private life. For Brutus I dipped into various books recommended to me by friends who worked in education: Richard Sennett's *The Fall of Public Man*, a brilliant book which ranges through history examining the diminution of all forms of public life, and rigorously exposes modernity's obsession with the self. Also, Quentin Skinner's excellent study of *The Foundations of Modern Political Thought*, which covers the thirteenth to the sixteenth centuries, the decisive period of transition from medieval to modern political theory, and concentrates particularly on the concept of the state. I wish I could say that I made an exhaustive and meticulous study of these books. However, I tend to use material like this in a quite dilettantish way to stimulate my imagination, and provide me with ideas that can set off my own trains of thought. So – I dipped. Much of this reading was, of course, invaluable for the Duke as well.

Nick had asked me if I wanted to be in on some of his discussions with Mark Thompson the designer. *No* director has *ever* asked me to do that before, so I leapt at the opportunity. They had decided to set the play in the twentieth century, but not in a particular period, something of which I very much approved. If you shift the period of a classical play, the danger is that the production can become about how clever you are in your re-creation of the detail of that period, rather than releasing the meanings of the play itself. Mark side-stepped this problem quite brilliantly. He and Nick had already developed the two massive towers that referred to the confident public architecture of the nineteenth century. These they had then deliberately spoiled by adding to them the odd twentieth-century junction box and air-ducting unit. For the street scenes the towers turned around and inside out revealing the inner workings of postmodern disintegration in a plethora of ducting and brightly coloured piping that made Richard Rogers look restrained. The costumes equally strongly contrasted the formality of court dress and the anarchy of the streets.

It is significant that much of the play is set in a prison, the ultimate embodiment of the state's desire for control. None of us, fortunately, having actually experienced prison life, we arranged a visit to Pentonville. The prison service, being anxious for better public relations, do guided tours of various prisons, and so Mark, Nick, and I, and a large group of local government officials, spent an entire afternoon being shown round Pentonville by a prison officer who took a ghoulish delight in the history of the place. 'Crippen's buried there,' he announced with relish, pointing to an inoffensive-looking flowerbed. From our point of view it was perfect. Michael Ignatieff, in his fine book *A Just Measure of Pain*, a history of the penitentiary in the industrial revolution, says of Pentonville that it 'represents the culmination of a history of efforts to devise a perfectly rational and reformative mode of imprisonment'. Its architectural design is based on Jeremy Bentham's panopticon, a central observation tower with wings going off it. Under this system, punishment became about the prisoner's isolation from the world and his fellow convicts, and the vigorous ordering of his day around work, prayer, and meals – a punishment seeking control of the mind rather than wreaking vengeance on the body. Rules governed every detail of existence; personal identity was reduced to a number. To walk round Pentonville now is to see that system in complete breakdown. The terrifyingly small cells, which in 1842 used to contain running water, a proper lavatory, and perhaps a loom for one prisoner, now contain two prisoners, and no water, lavatory or work occupation. Later that day we had tea with one prison officer and a young female graduate assistant prison governor.

To hear them speak, they could have been anyone currently working for a public service, a teacher, nurse, doctor or railwayman. They complained of lack of funds, so that prisoners had to be locked up twenty-three hours a day sometimes, as there wasn't the staff to supervise work. They talked with a kind of fatalism about the impossibility of prisoners actually reforming under the present conditions, and of how negatively they experienced the service being made into a political football. By chance I had a friend who had recently spent a few weeks at Her Majesty's pleasure in Pentonville. From him I heard stories of how many prisoners subverted the system of punishment. He told me how they brewed up lethal alcoholic concoctions; of the breathtaking quantities of drugs they smuggled in; of how one of them had stolen a phone which, when doing odd jobs around the prison, he plugged in and called his wife. Indeed our prison officer recounted similar stories to us, almost with a kind of pride in the prisoners' inventiveness at avoiding regulations.

While I was up in Stratford that summer, Michael Ignatieff's splendid series *Voices* was being shown on Channel Four. Each week he and two guests would explore different aspects of the problems of modernity. I remember Saul Bellow speaking of the 'moronic inferno' of modern culture and Christopher Lasche on the 'culture of narcissism'. A constant theme was the fragmentation of society into sectional interests and the decay of the public realm. Ignatieff summed up one programme in a way that was particularly pertinent to *Measure for Measure*. For Aristotle, 'a human being cannot become a human being in full, until he becomes a citizen and shares the collective life of the public realm. That is the tradition we start from, the tradition that haunts us. The modern self, since Freud, poses acute questions to that classical political tradition. We are no longer producing selves capable of realising the Aristotelian vision.'

This was the varied soup of thoughts and experiences I brought in at the

4  Roger Allam as the Duke and Escalus (Mark Dignam) at the start of
*Measure for Measure*

start of rehearsals to begin the more practical task of finding some sort of
character for the Duke.

The Duke's first speeches in Act One, Scene One I found difficult to
understand because of the complex and involved sentence structure. He
constantly repeats and qualifies himself, trying to pin down his meaning
more precisely. He is reductive of his own worth and ability to govern in
comparison with that of Escalus:

> your own science
> Exceeds, in that, the list of all advice
> My strength can give you.                    (lines 3–5)

Even though he says he has elected Angelo to be his deputy 'with special
soul', he twice asks Escalus what he thinks of the idea, betraying his lack of
confidence in it.

'Lent him our terror . . . ': this struck me as a fortuitous double meaning.
'Terror' means both the Duke's temporal power of government, and also
literally his own fear. Perhaps fear is driving him from the court: fear of

government. When Angelo enters, the Duke again goes into complex and self-deprecating arguments about Angelo's inherent virtue and his public use of it:

> Thyself and thy belongings
> Are not thine own so proper as to waste
> Thyself upon thy virtues, they on thee.
> . . .
> for if our virtues
> Did not go forth of us, 'twere all alike
> As if we had them not. (lines 29–35)

The implication is one of self-criticism by way of praising Angelo. Once he tells Angelo of his appointment, he becomes far less repetitive in his haste to leave. He clearly hands over to Angelo the power of judgement:

> Your scope is as mine own,
> So to enforce or qualify the laws
> As to your soul seems good. (lines 64–6)

In Act One, Scene Three we learn not only the Duke's reasons for leaving, but also hear an interesting self-description:

> No, holy father, throw away that thought;
> Believe not that the dribbling dart of love
> Can pierce a complete bosom
> . . .
> My holy sir, none better knows than you
> How I have ever loved the life removed
> And held in ideal price to haunt assemblies
> Where youth and cost a witless bravery keeps. (lines 1–10)

The last sentence is a variant on a sentiment he expresses in Scene One; not exactly self-deprecating here, in fact a rather rarified opinion of himself as being somehow above life, or certainly above ordinary human existence.

He then admits to having made a complete mess of governing

> We have strict statutes and most biting laws
> . . .
> Which for this fourteen years we have let slip. (lines 19–21)

'Fourteen years', no less. A long, slow, process of decay. When criticized by Friar Thomas for not carrying through the difficult political task of unloosening 'this tied up justice', he expresses guilt at what he has done and fear of the consequences of putting it right. He makes interesting use of 'I' and 'we' throughout the scene.

26

> *I* do fear, too dreadful.
> Sith twas *my* fault to give the people scope,
> Twould be *my* tyranny to strike and gall them
> For what *I* bid them do: for *we* bid this be done
> When evil deeds have their permissive pass ...
>
> (lines 34–8; italics mine)

Perhaps this shows how enmeshed his own personality has become with his public office. This is something Angelo does later in Act Two, Scene Two when he identifies himself with the law. The Duke overrides any misgivings Friar Thomas may have about his disguise plan, and ends the scene with a description of Angelo as being inhumanly certain:

> Stands at a guard with envy, scarce confesses
> That his blood flows.                    (lines 51–2)

The last line seems to suggest that the Duke is testing Angelo in some way:

> Hence shall we see,
> If power change purpose, what our seemers be.        (lines 53–4)

He then disappears for a long time.

I could only begin to make sense of this seemingly contradictory picture of the Duke by looking at Act One, Scene Two, in which he does not appear. Here we see the direct results of fourteen years of non-government, and also the immediate effect of Angelo's rule. We move from the court into the world of pimps and whores, a public street-life teeming with vitality, but one that is corrupt. We stressed this very strongly in our production. The grey cut-away coats and knee-breeches of the court gave way to outrageous cycling shorts and Doc Marten boots. Most of our whores were rent-boys, run by Pompey, working a gents' toilet that rose from the floor. This was our attempt to de-anaesthetize the clichéd presentation of prostitutes in Shakespeare's plays, and thus shock and awaken our audience anew to the meaning of the scene. Jeremy Sams's jazz-rock music helped enormously here. The brothels are being closed, we discover, although a 'wise burgher' seems to have bought up those in the city.

The public parade and imminent execution of Claudio focuses the issues. It is Angelo's first act as deputy. An example is going to be made, not of a prostitute or pimp, but of someone who, as Escalus says, 'had a most noble father'. A fundamentalist and prescriptive government is making its intentions clear. This scene helped me get a sense of how massively the Duke has failed. I began to form a picture of a man who was a recluse, an intellectual, and a celibate; a man with a rapid mind, but who has, in a sense, thought himself into paralysis and inaction. We tried to get this idea across, at the beginning of the play, with the Duke transfixed, staring into space, while around him civil servants were trying to get him to sign important papers. Only Escalus could wake him from his trance, and even then his hand trembled so he could barely sign his own name.

The Duke has to do something drastic before he ceases to function altogether. Flight seems the only solution. The disguised ruler who seeks true knowledge of his world is an old story that Shakespeare refers to and makes revolutionary use of. Above all things the Duke lacks certainty. Angelo, on the other hand, seems absolutely certain of how to live and govern. Perhaps fourteen years ago the Duke was certain too.

> Hence shall we see,
> If power change purpose, what our seemers be.      (I.iii. 53–4)

Does the experience and responsibility of power change your belief in how to live, even if you seem absolutely certain? The line relates to the Duke as much as to Angelo. He needs to discover how power has changed his own purpose. The only way he can do so is by becoming someone else. Angelo is used because he seems certain, not because he is suspected of being a hypocrite. But above all the Duke is testing himself. The Duke constantly uses other people, Angelo, Claudio, Isabella, even Lucio, as a means of self-knowledge. The breakdown in the state is reflected by a breakdown in the Duke himself. This also ties in with the sense of self-importance he betrays to Friar Thomas in Act One, Scene Three. Having a nervous breakdown is quite an egotistical thing to do. The pride is concealed but none the less is there.

The next time we see the Duke, in Act Two, Scene Three, so much else has happened that we almost need to be reminded of his existence. Like Angelo, he equates sexuality with sin: 'Repent you, fair one, of the sin you carry?' (line 19). This scene always felt like the descent into Hades, as lines of prisoners were being signed into the prison.

'Be absolute for death' seemed not only the Duke's nadir, but also the nadir of the whole play. Life itself has become utterly valueless, sex and procreation are equated with sin and death. Angelo rejects sexuality and sentences people to death for it. He can only conceive of his own desires as bestial. The Duke at this point seems to agree, and becomes passionately articulate as never before as he equates life with all that is worthless, foolish, base, and ignoble:

> Thou art not *thy self*.
> For thou exists on many a thousand grains
> That issue out of dust. Happy thou art not,

28

> For what thou hast not, still thou striv'st to get,
> And what thou hast, forget'st. Thou are not certain,
> For thy complexion shifts to strange effects,
> After the moon. (III.i.19–25)

These seemed to me the central lines of the speech. I found that if I related the lines to myself as much as to Claudio the speech was unlocked for me, and a central part of the Duke's character fell into place. His sense of self has fragmented into 'many a thousand grains' of dust. Certainty about how to live is therefore no longer possible, as wants and desires are affected by something as arbitrary as the moon. I found again and again that it was more fruitful and dynamic to try to say the words as if the ideas were being discovered for the first time. In a sense the purpose of the Duke's journey through the play so far is to realize completely his own sceptical fatalism. But somehow this can only be expressed through someone else's situation. The Duke is therefore using Claudio to realize something about himself. For the Duke at this point, life equals being dead but having to live.

The revelation of Angelo's utter hypocrisy is a complete bombshell. Rape is the very last thing the Duke expects of him. This, and hearing Claudio passionately express an opposite view of death and life, is the turning-point for the Duke:

> The weariest and most loathèd worldly life
> That age, ache, penury, and imprisonment
> Can lay on nature is a paradise
> To what we fear of death
> . . .
> Sweet sister let me live. (III.i.132–7)

'Let me live' could easily be the Duke's motto from now on. The problem here is how to view the Duke's knowledge of Mariana and Angelo, as it seems to suggest that the Duke has always thought Angelo a hypocrite. Nick encouraged me to tell Isabella the story very much in the present tense, almost discovering it on the moment. Doing it this way, Angelo's corruption becomes a vital new factor that makes it possible completely to reinterpret his previous behaviour towards Mariana. The Duke then seizes on Angelo's failure with enormous relief and 'this well-*seeming* Angelo' became a line expressing delight. Isabella's predicament becomes a straw that the Duke clutches at to haul himself out of his own crisis. Revealing his true identity is not yet possible – he has no actual legal proof as yet, but somehow, more importantly, he is not ready. Being a Duke would still mean paralysis, whereas as the Friar he has become someone who can use his intellect to solve problems, make judgements, and act upon them immediately whilst responding to events as they occur. He is, as it were, living. He is also speaking prose rather than verse.

'It is a rupture that you may easily heal' (line 236). Perhaps he senses dimly that his 'rupture' could be something more all-embracing than just bringing to book a corrupt deputy. The 'rupture' certainly applies as much to himself as to that between Angelo and Mariana. The stakes are very high. Everything hangs by a thread: 'If you think well to carry this, as you *may*, the doubleness of the benefit defends the deceit from reproof' (line 256).

'If' is one of the most important words in the play.

> ISABELLA: If he had been as you, and you as he,
> You would have slipped like him; but he, like you,
> Would not have been so stern. (II.ii.64–6)
>
> Go to your bosom,
> Knock there, and ask your heart what it doth know
> That's like my brother's fault; if it confess
> A natural guiltiness such as is his,
> Let it not sound a thought upon your tongue
> Against my brother's life. (II.ii.136–41)

In Act Two, Scene Two Isabella asks Angelo to consider an alternative course of action, and to put himself in Claudio's place. He rejects this even when he admits his 'guiltiness' to himself. Although Isabella is in some ways as 'absolute' as Angelo in her attitudes, she is able to consider alternatives, and to take them, both through necessity and through a more generous spirit. The ability to do this on her part and on behalf of others like the Provost is crucial in the play's movement towards a fragile optimism.

> The evil that thou causest to be done,
> That is thy means to live.
>
> . . .
> Say to thyself,
> From their abominable and beastly touches
> I drink, I eat, array myself, and live. (III.ii.18–23)

The Duke may now have taken on a more positive attitude towards life, but the problems of exactly *how* to live are still as present as ever – except of course for Pompey and Lucio, who represent for the Duke everything that fourteen years of non-government have produced. The scene with Alex Jennings's Lucio was always great fun to play. Throughout the run of more than a year we would always give each other notes on how it had gone, during the interval. The Duke is flustered and angered by Lucio's scandalous descriptions of him; at the same time he is provoked to begin reconstructing his view of himself: he becomes humanized by being the object of humour. It amused me very much that the insult which really works and upsets him is not his supposed lechery, but his lack of wisdom: 'A very superficial, ignorant, unweighing fellow' (III.ii.132). It is this that makes the Duke let rip in his own eloquent defence. This seemed to be a further clue to the strange sense of pride the Duke has in his own seriousness of purpose. He is almost proud of his nervous breakdown. He somehow wants credit for giving himself a very hard time.

We had taken the decision not to stress the Duke's disguise in any physical way. Having been such a recluse, he would only be recognized when wearing the outward trappings of dukedom. The only person who would recognize him under any circumstances would be Escalus, so I took great care to cover my face with my friar's hood in the scene with him. Escalus was beautifully played by the late Mark Dignam, who effortlessly gave the sense of the older, easy-going, senior civil service man. He had played the Provost in Tyrone Guthrie's 1934 production, and also in Peter Brook's 1950 production, and was heard to remark close to opening night that our effort had 'got to be the best since Brook's'. He was of course biased – but it did boost my confidence.

ESCALUS: What news abroad i'th' world?
DUKE: None, but that there is so great a fever on goodness that the dissolution of it must cure it ... There is scarce truth enough alive to make societies secure, but security enough to make fellowships accursed.  (III.ii.211–16)

The last line was rendered more effective by our decision to remain in the prison for this scene. This is a wonderfully compressed speech which I found useful in the way it shows how the Duke has been observing the particular betrayals of Pompey and Kate Keepdown by Lucio, and making connections between them and the state of things in general.

ESCALUS: One that, above all other strifes, contended especially to know himself.
DUKE: What pleasure was he given to?
...
ESCALUS: ... a gentleman of all temperance.  (III.ii.222–7)

The Duke desperately needs to hear a more positive view of himself than Lucio's. I used to clasp Escalus's shoulder with relief and then whip it away in case I got recognized – which got a nice laugh.

31

If his own life answer the straitness of his proceeding, it shall become him well; wherein if he chance to fail, he hath sentenced himself. (line 244)

Here is further evidence that a plan is forming in the Duke's mind of how to use Angelo's failure to heal the rupture of which he has spoken to Isabella. I tried to suggest on the line that the Duke is literally imagining Angelo sentencing himself.

> He who the sword of heaven will bear
> Should be as holy as severe. (lines 249–50)

This is one of the two short soliloquies the Duke has: the more I did this speech, the more I became convinced that in developing a critique of fundamentalism, the Duke is questioning the validity of bearing the 'sword of heaven' at all: 'Craft against vice must I apply.' Practical, political 'craft' must be used against 'vice' rather than some abstract heavenly notion of absolute virtue. A big 'if' hangs over the Duke's 'craft', however, for his plan relies completely on Mariana agreeing to it, and also on the Provost's assistance:

> The best and wholesom'st spirits of the night
> Envelop you, good Provost. (IV.ii.70–1)

The Duke is breezy and confident on his return to the prison, as Mariana has agreed to the plan. David Howey's world-weary Provost, wearing an old cardigan over his breeches and clutching a mug of tea, was a great help here.

> PROVOST: What comfort is for Claudio?
> DUKE: There's some in hope. (lines 74–5)

The Duke almost enjoys the Provost's lack of hope in the knowledge that Claudio's reprieve will come. He feels in control, until Angelo's further betrayal destroys it. Once again he clutches at straws and comes up with the Barnardine plot: 'O, death's a great disguiser.' In his desperation, death has become a useful 'disguiser' rather than something to be absolute for.

The Provost's unwillingness to commit himself almost forces the Duke to reveal his identity. Instead he shows him the letter he has written to Angelo announcing his return:

This is a thing that Angelo knows not, for he this very day receives letters of strange tenor, perchance of the Duke's death, perchance entering some monastery, but *by chance* nothing of what is writ. (lines 192–6)

32

I felt strongly that if Angelo had *not* proved a hypocrite the Duke would never have returned to Vienna. He would either have entered 'some monastery' or, remembering the despair of 'be absolute for death', would have committed suicide. The only reason this is not happening is 'by chance'. A series of chances and 'ifs' has occurred to pull the Duke back from despair. I tried to achieve this in the speech by allowing brief reflective moments, although the main objective is the persuasion of the Provost: 'All difficulties are but easy when they are known' (line 198). Again, I tried to realize this as an all-embracing statement as well as an explanation to the Provost.

The Duke is very up at this point, his mind is racing and he is making connections on many levels about himself, at the same time as explaining what has happened to the somewhat dazed Provost. Phil Daniels, as a marvellously sleazy Pompey, is now practically running the prison, handing out drugs with the books from his mobile library unit. The realization of these scenes and the attitudes of the prisoners, Provost, and guards was directly influenced by our visit to Pentonville.

The Barnardine sequence is central in the working out of the life and death themes in the play. Here is someone who has spent nine years in prison, is a convicted murderer and yet somehow is absolute for life. He *refuses* to die, and will live whatever the circumstances. He also refuses to be controlled, and with Gordon Case's massive physique as Barnardine, it was believable that he *could* resist. Barnardine, Pompey and indeed all the prisoners embodied a spirit of resistance to all control and an affirmation of life which may be corrupt but is positive.

The following scene, with Isabella, provided the most difficult problem concerning the detail of the Duke's behaviour. Why does he not tell her that Claudio is alive? I hated the idea that *he* was somehow going to teach *Isabella* about mercy, rather than the other way round, but at first the scene seemed to force one down that path.

We looked very closely at the scene just before it, with the Provost. He now knows the Duke's true identity and they are working as a team. The Duke seizes on the Ragozine solution, but the Provost makes him consider the difficulties:

> PROVOST: But Barnardine must die this afternoon,
> And how shall we continue Claudio,
> To save *me* from the *danger* that might come
> If he were known alive?
> DUKE: Put them in *secret* holds
>
> . . .
> You shall find your *safety* manifested. (IV.iii.81–8)

33

Also the Duke's line when the Provost is taking the head of Ragozine to Angelo:

> Make a swift return,
> For I would commune with you of such things
> That want *no ear* but *yours*.        (IV.iii.101–3)

The situation is very dangerous; it is of the utmost importance that no one other than these two should know of the Duke's plan to 'enter publicly' at the city gates and 'proceed with Angelo' 'by cold gradation and well-balanced form'.

It satisfied me intellectually that we could pursue this interpretation without bending the text. It was, however, difficult to make clear in playing, as it happens so quickly. One further thing helped us. Almost by accident, we ignored the editorial exit for the Provost after his line 'I'll make all speed' (line 103) keeping him on and therefore allowing him to hear Isabella's offstage 'Peace, ho, be here.' This meant I could do the following speech as a shared problem:

> The tongue of Isabel. She's come to know
> If yet her brother's pardon be come hither.       (lines 105–6)

That has, yet again, to be solved very quickly on the hoof: 'But I will keep her ignorant of her good.' Then, in a desperate attempt to make a virtue out of necessity – 'To make *her* heavenly comforts of despair / When it is least expected' (IV.iii.108–9) – just, in a sense, as *she* has done for the Duke. A hasty solution from a desperate man, who then has to face the awful consequences of telling Isabella that her brother is dead. I tried in performance to show how difficult and agonizing this was for the Duke and was greatly helped by the emotional honesty and directness which Josette Simon brought to Isabella:

> If you can, pace your wisdom
> In that good path that I would wish it go.       (lines 131–2)

'If' again. The plan still relies on Isabella being prepared to confront Angelo in public:

> For my poor self,
> I am combinèd by a sacred vow
> And shall be absent.       (lines 142–4)

Josette used to fling her arms round me in desperation at the prospect of the Friar not being there to support her. Throughout the play the Duke has used Isabella's crisis as a means to solve his own. His desperation borders on ruthlessness, and I think at times he realizes quite how much he has put Isabella through. In Act Three, Scene One he says to her 'It lies much in your holding up' (line 263), and indeed here he is relying on her again. In exchange he offers her

> Grace of the Duke, revenges to your heart,
> And general honour. (lines 134–5)

His gratitude and guilt are transferring into love, and a nun and a friar are clasped in each others arms:

> LUCIO: Good even, Friar. (line 148)

Of course it got a huge laugh, Alex doing the line in his most suggestive manner. The Duke is still totally flustered by Lucio, and as we played it, Alex forcibly detained me to pour yet more filth in my ear.

I loved playing this scene, as it shows the wonderfully varied and daring way in which Shakespeare uses his material, constantly undercutting pathos with farce, and sustaining a thriller-like quality.

Act Five seemed a minefield of problems in rehearsal, but never in performance, as the working-out of the story seemed to take over. At the start we know the Duke intends to 'proceed with Angelo ... by cold gradation and well balanced form' (IV.iii.98–9). The public nature of the plan is all-important and is something to which the Duke ironically refers in his opening speeches to Angelo:

> we hear
> Such goodness of your justice that our soul
> Cannot but yield you forth to public thanks,
> Forerunning more requital. (V.i.5–8)

In Act Four, Scene Five he has said to Friar Peter:

> And hold you ever to our special drift,
> Though sometimes you do blench from this to that,
> As cause doth minister. (lines 4–6)

He is aware that although he may be in possession of more information and therefore one step ahead of Angelo, that still does not put him in complete control; things could go wrong. For me, then, his entrance was powerful and impressive but shot through with nerves.

The first problem he encounters is Angelo's claim that Isabella is mad. Indeed, she seems hysterical in the public context, using extreme language to describe Vienna's most famous puritan. She calls him 'a murderer', 'an adulterous thief', 'an hypocrite', and 'a virgin violator'. The Duke has to seem to dismiss her until she argues more rationally. Even so, when she later calls Angelo 'this pernicious caitiff', the Duke has to warn her 'That's somewhat madly spoken.' Through the first section Angelo has several opportunities to confess, and I used to make small pauses to give him the chance to speak; before

> Away with her. Poor soul,
> She speaks this in th'infirmity of sense.            (lines 46–7)

after

> Many that are not mad
> Have sure more lack of reason.            (lines 67–8)

and after

> If he had so offended,
> He would have weighed thy brother by himself,
> And not have cut him off.            (lines 110–12)

This was a delicate balance to strike, as both with Sean Baker and John Shrapnel, who played Angelo in Stratford and London respectively, we did not wish to give the impression that he in any way suspected the Duke.

The other problem is Lucio, whom the Duke at first triumphantly enjoys silencing:

> It may be right, but you are i'the wrong
> To speak before your time.            (lines 86–7)

Later, however, he does annoying and unpredictable damage to the Duke's plan.

In 'Be absolute for death' the Duke has encouraged Claudio to 'reason thus with life', in a completely negative way. Now Isabella asks the Duke to put his 'reason' to proper use:

> but let your reason serve
> To make the truth appear where it seems hid,
> And hide the false seems true.            (lines 65–7)

Her line describes a crucial change that has taken place in the Duke since 'Be absolute for death.' Throughout the scene I kept my eyes very much on Angelo. The Duke is half convinced that he will break down and confess. When he does not, the Duke is forced to arrest Isabella to prevent her disappearing in the crowd, and also to get her to name Friar Lodowick as her accomplice: 'Who knew of your intent and coming hither?'

LUCIO:   My lord, I know him, 'tis a meddling friar.

. . .

A saucy friar,
A very scurvy fellow.                                    (lines 127–36)

The Duke is again flustered and thrown off course by Lucio. He needs to
hear a more favourable view of Friar Lodowick from Friar Peter, not only
to suit his plan, but also because he simply cannot bear Lucio's constant
slander of him, whether in disguise or not. Also, there is a slight element of
truth in 'a saucy friar', as he was found in rather compromising circumstances with Isabella.

Come, cousin Angelo,
In this I'll be impartial. Be you judge
In your own cause.                                      (lines 165–7)

This is the point the Duke has been leading up to since 'if he chance to fail,
he hath sentenced himself' (lines 239–40), at the end of Act Three, Scene
Two.

After the Mariana section Angelo is convinced that Isabella and Mariana
are involved in a plot against him, but thinks he may be able to avoid the
consequences:

ANGELO:     Let me have way, my lord,
            To find this practice out.
                        . . .
DUKE:       think'st thou thy oaths,
            Though they would swear down each particular saint,
            Were testimonies against his worth and credit
            That's sealed in approbation.                (lines 236–43)

There is much concealed anger towards Angelo in the bitter irony of the
Duke's reply, and disbelief that he is prepared to go so far in denying his
guilt.

It always amused me that the only excuse the Duke can think of to leave
the stage to change is simply, 'I for a while will leave.' I used briefly to
pause, panic-stricken, before the line, trying to think of a good reason, and
then just rush off. It got a nice laugh.

My business in this state
Made me a looker-on here in Vienna,
Where I have seen corruption boil and bubble
Till it o'errun the stew. Laws for all faults,
But faults so countenanced that the strong statutes
Stand like the forfeits in a barber's shop,
As much in mock as mark.                                (lines 314–20)

The Duke wants and needs to say these things publicly – 'Stay, sir, stay

37

awhile' – and clearly has more to say, by way of leading up to an impressive revelation of himself, but, once again, Lucio messes things up.

'Like doth quit like, and Measure still for Measure' (line 408): obviously the Duke cannot actually have Angelo executed, as then how could he reveal that Claudio was alive? I felt that he wants to put Angelo through exactly the kind of despair and anguish that Claudio went through whilst facing death. 'Measure *still* for Measure' then suggests that there is still more judgement to be meted out. Perhaps, also, it is a kind of gift of revenge to Isabella, as he promised her in Act Four, Scene Three:

> And you shall have your bosom on this wretch,
> Grace of the Duke, revenges to your heart,
> And general honour.
>
> (lines 133–5)

This means that he *still* cannot tell her that Claudio is alive. I resisted the notion that the Duke teaches Isabella about mercy in this scene. It can be played that way, but we rejected it and in doing so did not have to bend the text. We felt strongly that Isabella is a positive character. Her wish to be a strict nun may be naive, in some ways, but on the other hand a life of contemplation praying for the world is a noble aspiration. The play questions living life by absolute abstract values, but in the end the absolute value of mercy, which Isabella embodies in her plea, is celebrated:

> Thoughts are no subjects,
> Intents but merely thoughts.
>
> (lines 450–1)

She has the great generosity of spirit to take the curse of guilt off Angelo, and in doing so teaches the Duke one final lesson. At the start of the play people are sentenced to death for sex, the act of procreation; after Isabella's plea the Duke sentences everyone to life, even Barnardine who 'apprehends no further than this world', and especially Angelo, who 'craves death more willingly than mercy'.

For me then, as the Duke, Isabella's plea was an astonishing unlooked-for event. When Mariana first begs her to plead, I played a moment of horror that yet more should be asked of her. Then, on Mariana's second speech, I half hoped that she would plead. On 'He dies for Claudio's death', I thought that she couldn't, and was returning to the original scheme of taking Angelo to the brink of death. The Duke's plan has become a quest for resolution, an attempt to heal the public and private ruptures of himself and the world; a quest for a happy ending. Isabella's plea achieves it in unimagined ways. Marriage represents a happy ending in the comedy form, but in *Measure for Measure* the ending is deliberately

5   The Duke's proposal to Isabella (Josette Simon): 'Give me your hand
and say you will be mine' (*Measure for Measure*, v.i.489); in the background
the Provost (David Howey), Juliet (Kate Littlewood), and, in prison
uniform, Claudio (Hakim Kae-Kazim)

ambiguous. Isabella says nothing to the Duke's proposals. I stammered
hesitantly on the first one, and Josette used to look at me in disbelief at the
Duke's crass timing. It got a wonderful laugh on 'but fitter time for that',
but I was trying to show the Duke's realization of the anguish and pain he
has put Isabella through. Marriage for Angelo, and for Lucio, is double-
edged. They have to live with the consequences of their actions. But
marriage has a large meaning. Many things have to be married in order that
life may go on in a better way and with more honesty than it has in the past.

In the closing speech I used to look at Isabella between each sentence,
trying to summon up the courage for another attempt:

> Dear Isabel,
> I have a motion much imports your good,
> Whereto *if* you'll a willing ear incline,
> What's mine is yours, and what is yours is mine.    (lines 531–4)

A last, final, big 'if'. Josette gave me a long appraising stare, and still did not consent. The play stops rather than ends, leaving many possibilities in the air. Shakespeare often writes characters who refuse resolution in his comedies – Malvolio, Jaques, Shylock, Antonio – but here he uses the device for the whole play. Connections have been made between *Measure for Measure* and the Romances, and indeed there are similarities. But the Duke has no magic like Prospero, and there is no statue to come to life. We are left at the end with a number of meanings and possibilities, and a number of new stories about to start. The possibility for Angelo resides in the crucial figure of Mariana. Because she has remained faithful, Mariana has somehow made sexuality and desire all right. Perhaps hope for them resides in what happened in Angelo's 'garden house'. Perhaps it was an intensely erotic experience.

In our production we tried to show this open, unresolved ending by putting a wordless coda after the text has finished. In Mark Thompson's set the huge city gates had been drawn up to reveal a kind of idyllic pastoral never-never land beyond. The people of Vienna were behind crash barriers at the back. The Duke is left standing between them and they reach out over the crash barriers to shake his hand. (This was in the London version; in Stratford they used to surround me, but this was constantly misunderstood as threatening.) They go, leaving Claudio, Juliet, and their new baby on one side of the stage, Angelo and Mariana on the other. Isabella goes towards the pastoral scene at the back, stops, and turns back towards the city and the Duke as the lights go down. People often used to ask me whether they married or not, annoyed at our denying them a happy ending, or suspicious at our being over-optimistic. We thought probably they did, but only after a very long conversation.

Peter Brook has likened Shakespeare's plays to planets. At certain points in history particular plays orbit closer or further away from the earth. *Measure for Measure* seems close to us now because it examines questions of the unresolved tensions between public and private worlds, and it looks at these tensions through the prism of sexuality. We could only have come up with our particular view of the text at our point in history, that is, post-feminist, post-Aids, and post-Thatcherism. Fifteen to twenty years ago, in the first flush of sexual liberation, productions of the play often revolved around whether or not Isabella was a sexual hysteric. Post-feminism and post-Aids, Isabella has become a much more sympathetic character. Fifteen to twenty years ago many people viewed the state and its public institutions as corrupt, or useless, or repressive. After all the Thatcher privatizations, many of those same people look back with nostalgia and regret to those times of greater consensus. Productions of *Measure for Measure*, a play which deals so directly with these very issues, will inevitably reflect these changes.

> if you'll a willing ear incline,
> What's mine is yours, and what is yours is mine.     (v.i.533–4)

The play's refusal to end neatly throws these questions back at us. It almost seems to open its hands and shrug to us, as, like Isabella, we are asked to consider the possibilities. It leaves me with the sense that life is all there is, so we might as well live it as best we can; that being human is not a given but something we have to strive for. That the reason we are here is to live and that this involves making many difficult judgements.

The role of the Duke was the most difficult, rewarding, and varied that I have undertaken. Whenever I got stuck on matters of individual motivation, it was usually thinking about the whole play and the direction it seemed to be taking that unlocked the character for me.

# Beatrice in
# *Much Ado About Nothing*
## MAGGIE STEED

MAGGIE STEED played Beatrice in Di Trevis's production of *Much Ado About Nothing* at the Royal Shakespeare Theatre in 1988. She had appeared for the company the previous year on the regional tour, playing Adriana in *The Comedy of Errors* and Gertrude to Philip Franks's Hamlet. Previous roles for the RSC in London had been in *The War Plays* and *Crimes in Hot Countries*. Earlier work included Livia in *Women Beware Women* at the Royal Court and Mrs Driscoll in *Small Change* at the National. More recently she has appeared in *Whale* at the National and *Lady Windermere's Fan* at the Bristol Old Vic. A wide range of television work includes *The History Man*, *Brideshead Revisited*, and *A Year in Provence*.

I heard that I was to play Beatrice only ten days before rehearsals started for the new Stratford season, and was at the time performing Gertrude and Adriana in Truro, on the last leg of the RSC's regional tour – one of the happiest jobs of my life. For a few days a dangerous euphoria set in.

What followed over the next nine months was complex. I did not emerge from an acclaimed production to write this – for many reasons work was left undone during the rehearsal period and we performed this domestic play in a vast, pillared setting (which dwarfed the actors) and wore a series of glossy costumes over-indicating wealth and an obsession with style which I know confused many audiences. However, the solid work that *was* done during the rehearsal period was always our bedrock and it was from this that the developing life of the play and our playing came. The main bonus of this rehearsal was a precise examination of the text, and the form in which it is written.

*Much Ado About Nothing* is mainly a prose play, switching to verse as Shakespeare swings it towards tragedy. People often say how 'difficult' this mix is; how unsatisfying; a broken-backed play. It is sometimes easier, I think, to see the comedy as sub-plot and the serious as the main thrust of a play, but this attitude always undervalues comedy and, besides, Shakespeare was much more skilled and anarchic than this, and in *Much Ado* he really throws the cat among the pigeons by making us think we are in a comedy and therefore perhaps safe (as indeed do most of the characters in the play: after all the war is over and it is time for parties and tricks) and then plunging us all into catastrophe in our own front rooms. I like this. The world is a dangerous place, and the audience and the characters are all caught out laughing at awful moments, and both have to work hard to come to the resolutions. It is properly difficult.

So, the text told us that we were in the household of Leonato, the Governor of Messina, who has a daughter Hero, and niece and ward, Beatrice. The household must be large and rich: it can entertain Don Pedro and his returning retinue to large feasts and parties; indeed, they are to stay for a month. We don't know how they usually spend their days because the first news we receive is that Don Pedro is returning from a triumphant war, and that no men of any note have been lost (no noblemen that is). The action of the play before we begin has been offstage at war, not here in this household. And the action from now on is to entertain these men. However, we have to know how this household works, and I had to find Beatrice's place in it before I could begin to know how and why she operates in the way she does. That sounds very linear, and rehearsal processes are not like that, but I knew I wouldn't really get started until then.

There she is, an orphan, adopted into this rich household by Leonato, her uncle. There is no evidence that she has money of her own, a crucial lack in this society:

CLAUDIO:   Hath Leonato any son, my lord?
DON PEDRO:   No child but Hero; she's his only heir. Dost thou affect her, Claudio?
(I.i.274–6)

Beatrice doesn't figure on this market; Hero is the rich daughter – all is invested in her. Hero doesn't have to win affection or approval and her continued position in the household remains assured so long as she remains chaste – truly an unopened casket of riches. No wonder she remains mostly silent: what does *she* have to win or prove? In private she may be very spirited, but in this public context of money she has only to 'be'. Beatrice, on the other hand, talks a lot and is renowned for it. How does she talk?

The only scene in the play that features the whole family without the presence of the visitors is at the beginning of Act Two, Scene One, after the

6   Maggie Steed as Beatrice with Don Pedro (David Lyon) (II.i); in the
background Leonato (Antony Brown) and Hero (Julia Ford)

great supper and before the dance. Antonio, Leonato, Hero, Beatrice and
other members of the household enter from the supper and wait for the
revellers to come with their masks. Beatrice seems to 'hold the floor'. In
rehearsal, we spent much time examining her speech rhythms. Repeatedly,
she uses a rhythm almost characteristic of the stand-up comic – setting up
an idea, expanding on it, and then capping it, throwing it away. For
example: 'Too curst is more than curst' – statement; 'I shall lessen God's
sending that way, for it is said, "God sends a curst cow short horns"' –
expansion; 'but to a cow too curst he sends none' – punch line (II.i.19).
This is crude methodology, perhaps, but illuminating. Another example:
'Lord, I could not endure a husband with a beard on his face' – statement;
'I had rather lie in the woollen' – punch line (II.i.26). At home, I found I
could break the whole scene down in this way. Beatrice expands her jokes
imaginatively, leading her listeners into unexpected corners, employing
the sort of clever inevitability that a good raconteur delights in. More
interestingly, I think, she does this with the help of Leonato. He acts

almost as her stooge, egging her on, and feeding her her next passage. When we were rehearsing this became very evident and, in the context of the family, with Leonato at its head, it appears that he is allowing her to be confident and outspoken, for all his seeming disapproval of what she is saying, and at the same time is colluding with her in her role as family entertainer. It seemed to me that here was an interesting combination to look at: that Beatrice is greatly loved and unthreatened inside the arms of this family, but, as an orphan adopted into the family, the role that she has found for herself is that of clown – still the outsider, 'singing for her supper'.

Reading and watching the rehearsals of the men's scenes, I could recognize similar patterns in their relationships: Benedick is a gentleman, not a count or a prince, but it was almost as though these princes were saying, 'Thank goodness, here comes Benedick, now we can have a laugh.' After the scene in which they are challenged by Leonato and Antonio they do in fact turn to Benedick with obvious relief – 'See, see; here comes the man we went to seek' (v.i.109) – and ask him to joke with them about these old men and take away their feelings of unease.

There is a mythology amongst my friends that I am a joker, and it occurred to me one day what a tyranny it is to be always the entertainer, providing the laughter in other people's lives. They can simply look to you for that and never know anything more about you, especially when that is the only picture that you provide for them. The space I occupied when younger was always the clown rather than Vivien Leigh, and this ability, when well developed, becomes a very efficient defence against the dangerous things of life: pain, betrayal, etc. I started not to believe what Leonato says of Beatrice 'There's little of the melancholy element in her, my lord' (ii.i.317). 'Oh really?' I thought. 'Perhaps that's just what *you* think.' So, at the same time as discovering her *esprit*, I was starting to sniff out how 'well-defended' Beatrice is and against what.

She speaks very quickly, on an equal footing with the men. Her ideas come quickly, with no time for reflection, and all of a piece into her mind. She listens to other people very hard, picking up their words and throwing them back with another shade of meaning immediately. This girl is definitely living on her wits:

BEATRICE I may sit in a corner and cry 'Heigh ho for a husband!'
DON PEDRO Lady Beatrice, I will *get* you one.
BEATRICE I would rather have one of your father's *getting*.
Hath your grace ne'er a brother like you? Your father *got*
excellent husbands, if a maid could come by them. (ii.i.294–300; my italics)

45

This is the language of men, not simply in the sexual innuendo, but also in the warmly combative, almost packaged way that Beatrice lays her cards on the table. When Hero sends Margaret to find her, she says:

> run thee to the parlour;
> There shalt thou find my cousin Beatrice
> Proposing with the Prince and Claudio.                    (III.i.1–3)

She is definitely not sewing in her closet. In fact, when she is joking with Leonato in Act Two, she looks forward to the time when St Peter 'shows me where the bachelors sit, and there live we as merry as the day is long' (II.i.41). It required great mental energy to be on top of the speed of her thoughts, and while rehearsing this energy made me feel that she must find the company of men exhilarating and enjoyable. It's fun to think so quickly; I envied her the ability.

Benedick's energy is also in his ideas and delivery. His invention tumbles out of him in the scenes with the men, sometimes five examples when three would do. (Beatrice has about half as many lines as he does! Some comics would say that less means more – but perhaps this is what Beatrice would say of him: she does call him the Prince's jester.) When we started to rehearse the first exchange between them (there are few in fact in the play), even a first reading showed us that they are obsessed with each other. Each listens precisely to the other, immediately picks up a word, turns it on its head and uses it in another context to invent a different insult. They are really having fun, whether they show it or not; it is like a fast, sexy fight. It was impossible to play this in an unengaged way; in fact the effort went into trying to hide the interest they have for each other and in keeping the energy in our minds. I have always felt that in the midst of the insults they couldn't help congratulating each other on the quickness of the other's thought. More fun – and very revealing about them. However, the verbal form this interest takes is the insult, repeated in different ways in each scene they have with each other, before they are tricked. And sometimes the jokes aren't even that good, though the rhythms are nevertheless pleasurable: 'It's not what I say, it's the way I tell them.' It is probably obvious to everyone else that these two people have the best time when they are together.

Within this direct, humorous headtalk that Beatrice uses she is sending other messages. This was very difficult to fathom. On the face of things it seemed obvious. For goodness sake, this woman goes on and on about men, their faithlessness, their feet of clay, their foolishness, and how uncomfortable they must be to sleep with when they have beards (she doesn't mince words either). She also makes jokes about how no one will marry her. There are, however, no references by anyone else to her being unattractive; she is obviously loved in the family; Don Pedro calls her 'a pleasant-spirited lady'; and Benedick never insults her beauty, only her sharp brain and competitive tongue (we immediately realized that she keeps the final word and upper hand in most of their exchanges). Her first words in the play are asking for Benedick and she refers to him constantly. Finally, the energy that I had discovered when she was with him and during the party scenes indicated that she is very excited, firing on all cylinders. Very contradictory . . . She is indeed well defended; it took me a long time.

She makes only two references to her history. In a conversation with Don Pedro in Act Two he remarks 'to be merry best becomes you; for, out o' question, you were born in a merry hour'. She replies: 'No sure, my lord, my mother cried; but then there was a star danced, and under that was I born. Cousins, God give you joy!' (ii.i.306–7). Those famous words! The director, Di Trevis, and I had been working on the text, walking round and round the room one day. She was bullying me to find the way to deliver Beatrice's ideas whole and complete in the way that they occur to her. I came to these lines and managed to say 'No sure, my lord, my mother died' and as I started to say 'But then there was a star danced' I knew I was going to cry (all sorts of things happen in rehearsals). It is so concise, touched on for only a moment, not an excuse for a long pronouncement, and is then followed by another tiny sentence: 'Cousins, God give you joy!' 'Crying' and 'joy' with so few words between them. I felt then that her mother had indeed had a painful story, not only the pain of childbirth, but that her marriage had been unhappy, that she had probably been betrayed, and that Beatrice had been marked for ever by this history. Of course, this wasn't new intellectually – there are enough footnotes that speculate on this bit of text. But what I mean is that the precision of the phrasing, the smallness of it, took me inside the character. This was terribly important; for me, it opened a chink into her feelings and I knew that I had to find a way to let that truth be seen for a moment and covered again. Actually, as in our own lives, everyone else with her is aware of it; it's only Beatrice who thinks she has covered it up. The other important thing that I discovered with that tiny speech was that, for me, the 'star' that had danced is Leonato, the loving uncle who has taken her into his home and family. How lucky she is! This fed later into the church scene when the world is crashing about her ears and it was sometimes as awful to see this man so terribly upset as it was to look at Hero weeping on the floor.

The other reference to her past is more 'packaged'. Don Pedro says: 'Come, lady, come; you have lost the heart of Signor Benedick.' She replies: 'Indeed, my Lord, he lent it me awhile, and I gave him use for it, a double heart for his single one. Marry, once before he won it of me with false dice, therefore your grace may well say I have lost it' (II.i.253–8). It is the only reference anywhere in the play to the possibility that these two might have had a close association. It is difficult to imagine what this might have been, but I was tending to think that she keeps herself so close that it would have needed only the smallest opening and the smallest disappointment for her to scurry back into the security of her own brain. She does put Benedick down, though, implying that he couldn't cope with her large heart, and covers it in another way, implying that he was false to her. In performance, we gradually came to play this more and more easily and directly (she does seem very at home with Don Pedro) and even though she jokes a little, he hears it. Then, one day, I was sitting and listening to a music rehearsal; the words of Balthazar's song came through loud and clear:

> Sigh no more, ladies, sigh no more,
> Men were deceivers ever
>
> . . .
>
> Then sigh not so, but let them go,
> And be you blithe and bonny.               (II.iii.60–5)

Sensible advice for women: sigh no more.

On the first day of rehearsal, Di Trevis had said something that had stayed with me all the time: that hovering around the play was the perilousness of falling in love, and the perils to ourselves if we refuse to. How far down that perilous road of refusal has Beatrice gone and how can she turn back? When she is spying on Hero and Ursula in the gulling scene she hears many uncomfortable truths about herself, the most vivid and shocking for me being 'her spirits are as coy and wild / As haggards of the rock' (III.i.35–6). We found that a haggard was an untamed adult female hawk, having passed the age when it was tameable: a frightening and lonely prospect for Beatrice perhaps. She certainly returns to the image in her speech at the end of this scene:

> And, Benedick, love on; I will requite thee,
> Taming my wild heart to thy loving hand.               (III.i.111–12)

I discovered that it was supposed that the only way a hawk could be tamed was, indeed, with love.

This speech is ten lines of verse. It is her first speech in verse and she speaks it alone on the stage. I read a lot of notes on it, some very unhelpful, but I read that Ellen Terry had said of it: 'Very difficult words for an actress; not very effective, but charged with the passion of a strong, deep heart!'. I always felt very relieved by this statement, because these line *are* hard. She doesn't speak first of the news that Benedick loves, but of how she is condemned for contempt. It seems to take a while to be able to speak even to herself of the possibility of his love. It then very quickly becomes triumphant:

> If thou dost love, my kindness shall incite thee
> To bind our loves up in a holy band.                    (lines 113–14)

She ends with a quiet, half-serious jest to herself:

> For others say thou dost deserve, and I
> Believe it better than reportingly.                    (lines 116–16)

It always felt to me that this combination of hesitation and humour indicated what a big risk she knows she's going to have to take with herself if she is finally to declare her love.

In the next scene we see her with the women of the house, the only such scene in the whole play. She seems very agitated. She has a cold (convenient for us, since on our bare stage I had been forced to hide in a small pool to overhear the girls in the gulling scene, which takes place the evening before, and which meant that she emerged at the end of the scene bedraggled as well as chastened). She manages to summon up only a couple of stabs at defending herself against the mockery of the others who know that they have indeed 'caught' her. We played her already dressed for the wedding as though she has been up for hours, while the others are still fussing over their petticoats.

When I knew that I was to play Beatrice, it was the church scene that made my jaw drop. It is only in the midst of so much pain that she and Benedick manage to lower their defences and declare their love for each other; and the scene is so short. In the space of about a page their relationship is potentially over! Again they both speak in short dense sentences and in rehearsal it was very difficult to utter them. This seemed right, because they are still employing metaphors, protecting themselves with little jokes, and directness only flashes in and out. There is an urgent plea in her 'Will you not eat your word?' (II.i.274) and it is his insistence on his love that finally *forces* her answer out. Then she says 'I love you with so much of my heart that none is left to protest' (line 282). It took me ages to say this line in one rehearsal and we returned to that treatment in perform-

49

ance because it felt so human, with the audience laughing and sighing with recognition and relief (or so it seemed). 'Kill Claudio', of course, is fraught with danger – not so much in the well-worn worry about whether the audience laughs: sometimes they do and sometimes they don't; if they do they soon realize what a tactless mistake they have made and I think this problem is good for them. It is dangerous *inside* the play, particularly for Claudio and these two. Of course, the significance of this statement is that it is a test of his love, but it seems that running alongside the joy and relief of their love is so much pain and anger in her that she has no alternative but to venture 'Kill Claudio' in response to his 'Come, bid me do anything for thee', and she must know that she risks losing him. Indeed she does lose him in his reply and is actually leaving on 'You kill me to deny it. Farewell' (line 288). When he stops her the rest of the scene tumbles on from her cry of 'There is no love in you' and out comes all the underside of her jokes throughout the play about men being made of clay. Even Benedick cannot stop her outpourings of pain, anger, and frustration at being an intelligent, passionate woman with no power to act against the cruelty of men. Her final line, 'I cannot be a man with wishing, therefore I will die a woman with grieving' (line 317) seems to me an echo of her mother and a quiet and tragic defeat. The fact that all this is what moves him to promise to do what she asks is an enormous surprise, an awesome gift. And all in two pages!

When they meet again, after Benedick has challenged Claudio, they are still joking, but the joking has a different quality. Together now, their supposed cynicism is revealed as a humorously realistic view of how hard this world is. She says little, but there is a feeling of security in the fact that she can join him in his quizzical view of the world while still admitting to him that she is 'Very ill' (v.ii.83). He says 'Serve God, love me, and mend' – what a fella! We found it hard to discover the right note for this scene. The last thing we wanted was to do them the disservice of falling into sentimentality.

In their final scene, after the revelation of the truth about Hero, they speak together in verse. She can now play with him securely and there is wonderful collusion with the audience who have already heard her say how full her heart is with him, when here she can claim that she loves him 'no more than reason', an echo of her old ways. The celebration is circled still with references to the fragility of love and the faithlessness of men and women; I hope that in our production people were left with the feeling that these two were in for a stormy, robust, and loving ride. Truly an adult relationship!

Like Beatrice, I think I had a bumpy ride. It was always hard to find the

7 Maggie Steed as Beatrice with Benedick (Clive Merrison): 'I do suffer love indeed' (v.ii.61)

lightness of touch, to let her be easy and direct with her humour, and to hold to the rhythms of the text while still retaining her inner stillness. I was no doubt sometimes too much of the clown, or too excited, or too tragic, and most of the time some of the play worked at the expense of some of the rest. Audiences were nearly always warm and responsive, which encouraged us to feel that we were speaking the play to them, even if only in a truncated form; but it was after my admired friend Paola Dionisotti came to see the show one chilly summer afternoon that I began to feel that I might have a chance of doing Beatrice justice. By that time we had been playing on and off for about four months and I had discovered a lot. She slipped me a note: 'I think you could afford to stop playing the character as much.' This little gem was enough to make me relax, to rely on the speed of playing and the fact that all the work was somewhere about me. After that I felt more free to think and play Beatrice as mine in this production. Perhaps, in Beckett's words, I 'failed better'. As the run came to an end I felt I wanted to play her again and again – partly, no doubt, because of the wish to have such a man as Benedick beside me when the chips are down!

# Portia in
# *The Merchant of Venice*

## DEBORAH FINDLAY

DEBORAH FINDLAY played Portia in Bill Alexander's production of *The Merchant of Venice* at the Royal Shakespeare Theatre in 1987 and at the Barbican the following year. In the same season, her first with the RSC, she was Olivia in *Twelfth Night* and Prudence in Jonson's *The New Inn*, roles to which she added Olga in *Three Sisters* in the Barbican season. Earlier Shakespeare parts had included Mariana in *Measure for Measure* and Lady Macbeth, and among other notable roles had been Mary Warren in *The Crucible*, Mrs Linde in *A Doll's House*, Martirio in *The House of Bernardo Alba* and the title role in *Hedda Gabler*. More recent work has included Rosalind in *As You Like It* and Goneril in *King Lear* for the Oxford Stage Company and Beata in *Once in a While* at the National. Among a number of television appearances are *Shroud for a Nightingale*, *What if it's Raining*, *Ladies in Charge*, *Top Girls*, *Anglo-Saxon Attitudes*, and *Natural Lies*. On film she played the role of Claire in *Truly, Madly, Deeply*.

I think of my time spent playing Portia – about eighteen months and more than 150 performances – as a journey of discovery, about the play *The Merchant of Venice*, the character of Portia, and myself as an actress. It is a role that never ceased to fascinate me, every night a challenge to get a little nearer to the vibrant, excellent person that she is, though sadly I came to feel that I was in a production which ultimately misplaced and under-valued her role in the play. My appreciation of her and of the subtleties of the play grew over the eighteen months. Let me begin at the beginning and tell you about the journey.

Portia was my first role with the RSC. I really jumped in at the deep end and had a lot to learn about playing a big space like the main stage at Stratford or the Barbican, since my experience of theatre had been mainly small intimate spaces. What reads in a small space goes for nothing for somebody far away in the upper circle, so I had to learn how to send my thoughts and feelings winging their way to 1,500 people without becoming too demonstrative or two-dimensional. I also had to learn how to use my voice. I worked a lot in rehearsal with Cicely Berry (the RSC voice teacher) and apart from getting to understand the verse structure and the marvellous juxtaposition of words, I also learned a lot about projection. Each theatrical space is different, but she taught us that enunciation and intensity of thought carry better than shouting. Particularly at the Barbican I had to learn how quiet I could be and still be understood in order to develop a suitable range and not speak everything in a loud monotone. This practical knowledge allowed me to share my deepening awareness of Portia – something I really only discovered in performance.

In my first meeting with the director, Bill Alexander, we talked about the general notions of the play and of Portia in particular. He wanted to present two opposed cultures, mutually exclusive, Christian and Jewish, both alien to a twentieth-century audience. He talked of wanting to create a situation where the audience's sympathies would be always shifting, where they would constantly have to assess and judge the characters on their actions and beliefs and presumably in so doing reassess themselves. I felt that this linked up with an idea I had of the nature of the Elizabethan man and woman. I remember reading a court ambassador from Spain or Italy of that period who wrote home about this passionate, volatile English nation. He spoke of our forebears in terms which we would reserve, suppressed as we now are by Puritanism and Victorianism, for the hot Latin temperament. It was my ambition to catch some of this full-bloodedness and for us all to embrace characters who could hate and love, and feel joy and sorrow, passionately. It takes great generosity of spirit to do this and I fear too often we slipped into violence and harshness in the attempt.

Bill also wanted to create a society in which it was possible to believe that someone would be allowed to make the flesh bond and carry it through. There had been several recent productions of this play using a Victorian setting, and while these served the legal overtones in a Dickensian sort of way, it is hard to imagine a Victorian society countenancing such brutality. It seemed that Renaissance Venice was, after all, the ideal setting. As a city based on 'trade of all nations' it had evolved a highly complex legal and political system to override personal conflict. And yet we felt that beneath this labyrinth of rules lay a welter of passions that could erupt at any moment. Our trial scene, for example, was set outside. It had an *ad hoc* atmosphere to it and violence was constantly breaking the surface. Bill wanted the idea of a legal system in the making. In our research we discovered that an Elizabethan audience would probably have been well versed in the law and would have been excited by the legal jugglings.

The set underlined the dangerous nature of the production. A big wooden jetty formed the main playing area connected to the wings by ramps and a bridge and, under this, light rippled as on water giving a feeling of shifting. The back wall was crumbling plaster broken away to reveal the brickwork beneath, and on that wall were two images of religious conflict: an ornate shrine for the Madonna and a Star of David daubed in yellow paint. The Venice scenes were dimly lit through smoke to suggest danger and decay. By contrast the Belmont scenes were lit brilliantly. We set all the Belmont scenes, apart from the last, in the casket room – a room set aside expressly for the ritual of the caskets – to which Portia is drawn constantly and obsessively to ponder her fate. The three caskets appeared and disappeared from a hole in the floor downstage and were little houses, miniature Belmonts, set on shifting scales which mirrored the shifting light of Venice. A great golden and blue carpet covered the floor, and the luminous quality of Belmont should have been completed by a curtain of light: tiny jets of water creating a fine mist through which light shone were to create a magical curtain and allow people to appear and disappear through it; most importantly, this would have cut out the two warring images on the back wall of Christian and Jew. The machinery for the light curtain never materialized in Stratford and when it finally appeared in London tiny jets dripped and everyone got wet so the idea was abandoned, leaving the Belmont image incomplete. I saw an understudy run of the play in London, and only then was I able to see, as an outsider, how much the image of Belmont was marred by the presence of the back wall: by not having the two warring images removed, there could never be a true sense of peace.

I wanted to make Belmont a real place and imagined it to be a great estate some twenty miles down the coast: 'For we must measure twenty miles today' (III.iv.84). I thought of it as opulent and lush with fields and groves running down to the sea and a feeling of clean sweet air. There would have been a great number of people to run the household and to look after the estate and these retainers made their appearance in the song in Act Three, Scene Two when Bill Alexander brought the whole cast on in disguise to sing the song as Portia's household. We felt it important to show that she had great wealth and that she and Nerissa are in charge of a large establishment. They are at ease, therefore, with money, power, and responsibility. My costume was ornate and spoke of money, leisure, and feminine charm. It was designed, as is so often the case, before the first day of rehearsal and I was wary of its artificiality, but I thought that on the big stage, big statements were necessary in terms of costume and that the dress would take care of certain ingredients of her character – her status and wealth – leaving me free to develop the extraordinary person within. We all agreed that she should be blonde-haired. There are so many references to her golden locks and it seemed fitting that the centre of this light-filled, shimmering Belmont should herself be golden. There was a pay-off to this costume. Generally people said that I looked like a large woman but a small boy, which underlined the transition period when she assumes men's clothing. In a man's world (i.e. outside Belmont) she can, as a man, rely only on her wits. The world proves to be a frightening place and she can expect no concessions or chivalry, neither can she compete physically. I thought that her journey to Antonio's trial was probably the first time she had been to Venice, maybe the first time she had set foot outside Belmont. She comes to the trial with her notions of morality and ethics learned in the seclusion of her home and through the process of the caskets with their lessons about bonds, choices and the consequences of decisions. For someone brought up in the security of a country estate, our Venice was a terrifying place. Portia sees obsession and violence there for the first time and it proves to be a cathartic experience. But more of that later.

Bill used broad strokes to create a fast-moving, intensely dramatic production that focused on the racial issues of the play. This was his reason for creating two alien cultures and for playing the Christians with a vindictive power which highlighted both the racial conflict and the Christians' assumption of religious and moral superiority. This play more than most has subtly shifted ground through history. Some believe that because of the Holocaust it should not be performed. I think Bill wanted to show that although there are anti-Semitic characters in the play, the play itself is not anti-Semitic. So he made the characters of Gratiano and Antonio, and, indeed, all the Christians, violently racist in order to expose them for what they are.

But where does Portia fit into all this? She is undoubtedly a Christian, and a rich white one at that. In a production which highlighted racism, a large-spirited rich white Christian seemed to be an anomaly which had to be sat on to fit in with the scheme of things. Is she a rich bitch, the flower on the dunghill of a corrupt society; carelessly racist – 'let all of his complexion choose me so' (II.vii.79) – and ultimately no better than

Gratiano with all his cant? It was the logical Portia to fit in with this production and I was encouraged to take this line and did so to begin with. I was asked to hit my servants, be calculating about money, beady about Antonio. All these things came from a misunderstanding of her true worth. They were all rejected when I realized that her place is above and beyond this pettiness and that because she is rich and has all the natural confidence that wealth can give she is not necessarily 'a bad thing'.

I believe now that racism is an element of the play, but not the main one. It is encompassed by the broader debate about mercy and justice, about commitment and loyalty, about the nature of choice and its consequences, and most broadly about how we should treat each other. It is when you see the play from these points of view that Portia's role becomes clearer, because she addresses herself to the philosophical problem of how we should lead our lives. That is why the play doesn't stop after the trial scene in Venice, as there is far more to resolve than a court case.

What I realized, and what I beg anyone who is reading this and who might play Portia to consider, is that she is never mean. Any choice you make about motivation for this character has to be made with all the generosity of spirit that you can muster. She is as loving, as intelligent, as witty, as brave, as compassionate, as everything as you can make her. That is why it is such a challenge every night. You never annexe part of yourself and say that is Portia. She's all of you and more! But I learned all this on the way. Here's where we started out.

Bill took as his starting-point for Portia the principle that what is said about dead people in Shakespeare is true. So that Nerissa is being truthful when she tells Portia 'Your father was ever virtuous, and holy men at their death have good inspirations' (1.ii.26). If Portia's father was a well-intentioned man, it follows that he must have had good reason to devise the lottery of the caskets and that Portia must have seemed to him like a headstrong girl who, left to her own devices, might very well have chosen the wrong man to be lord of the Belmont estates. We felt that it was probably after seeing her go weak at the knees at the sight of Bassanio (when he comes to Belmont with the Marquis of Montferrat) that Portia's father decided to devise a lottery that would exclude fortune-hunters like him from his daughter's marital horizon. It is thus a delightful irony that the man who on the surface seems to be the least suitable candidate ends up choosing right.

The idea of a headstrong nature is borne out in the first scene in Belmont. Portia describes herself as 'a hare ... madness the youth' skipping over 'the meshes of good counsel the cripple' (1.ii.19–20). Her first speeches are full of references to blood (sexual appetite), to hot temper, and to the will of a living daughter. Immediately you are given the image of tremendous vitality and passion trapped by the sobering constrictions of a dead father. Bill was very anxious for Portia's first line to denote trapped energy rather than ennui. It would be easy to moon over 'By my troth, Nerissa, my little body is aweary of this great world' (1.ii.1), but since she criticizes the County Palatine for 'unmannerly sadness' (1.ii.47) it was obvious that she had no time for melancholic turns. Her first scene reveals a tremendous will to survive. She is in limbo, trapped, and despite her wealth and intelligence she can do nothing until her fate is decided by the caskets. I felt this transition from passive to active state very strongly – particularly as Bill put the interval before the casket scene with Bassanio. So the first half was Portia bound and the second Portia unleashed.

The play is constructed so that you are introduced to Venice and Antonio first and hear about Portia from Bassanio. He seems to be a bounty-hunter, nothing more. Then there is a brief glimpse of Portia and Nerissa before the action returns to Venice. In our production this was especially so because Bill put the two Morocco scenes together, so it was not until after the elopement of Jessica that we returned to Belmont. The first Belmont scene was thus crucial to establish Portia and Nerissa and to keep them in the minds and hearts of the audience. We had quite a fractured rehearsal period because a number of shows were being rehearsed at the same time. So I didn't have my Nerissa (Pippa Guard) or my Bassanio (Nick Farrell) for much of the rehearsal period. Because of this I thought: 'Well Portia treats Nerissa like a servant; they have secrets from one another. We'll just have to have a servant–mistress relationship.' And that is basically how we started out. But a wonderful chemistry that sometimes happens between actors happened between us and although the basis remained a servant–mistress one it was infused with warmth and humour – very much a double act and one which I found very supportive. Nerissa doesn't say very much, but she is there in every scene with Portia, almost as her alter ego. She is more worldly and down to earth than Portia; this is seen in their love-lives too, so that in Act Five Gratiano and Nerissa seem to express the sexuality of both pairs of lovers. Pippa and I felt that Portia and Nerissa developed through the experience of Venice into true and equal friends, so that in Act Five they are working together to educate their men.

In that first scene Nerissa seems to be guardian of the caskets and upholder of the father's wishes. We decided that neither Portia nor Nerissa knew the answer to the caskets, that many suitors had come and stayed and eaten all their food, but that none of them had been brave enough to chance choosing. The conditions after all are very tough – complete secrecy, immediate dismissal, and total bachelorhood for the rest of life. The joke about the German and the glass of rhenish wine on the contrary casket is no more than a joke at which Pippa laughed dutifully every night. The decision makes for a more dramatic progress of the casket scenes. Portia learns through the two scenes that there is a logic and validity to the riddle of the caskets. She is enlightened by the verses in the gold and silver caskets and only learns by a process of elimination which is the right one, so that when Bassanio comes, although she is in love with him, she cannot cheat and tell him because he has to prove himself – she is hooked on the caskets.

After the darkness of the first Venice scene, I think the audience was pleased to get the lightness of Belmont and a chance to laugh. I loved playing that first scene. It is very satisfactory to make people laugh at the wit of Shakespeare and Portia's descriptions of the suitors really are very funny. In rehearsal we devised rather a complicated story about what the two women were actually doing here. We imagined that Nerissa had come in to tell Portia that the suitors had decided to leave, but when Portia seemed so moody Nerissa decided to have a game with her and pretend that there was an imminent possibility of one of them actually trying to choose the right casket. It was rather complicated and although it was a starting-point it proved redundant in performance. The scene is actually about Portia making herself and Nerissa and the audience laugh. Through the run I introduced more and more sadness into the scene so that there was a feeling of laughing through adversity, that if Portia and Nerissa didn't keep their spirits up they'd sink into despair. How much she is exaggerating the faults of these men one will never know. We felt that it was a game of wit that the two women played to amuse themselves, so we gave them licence for exaggeration.

Some people say that this scene and the next two casket scenes show Portia as xenophobic. Given the emphasis on racism that was in our production, I think the audience may be forgiven for taking this attitude. But rather than racial politics I think the scenes are about sexual politics. She is completely at the mercy of these men. Bassanio is called a soldier and a scholar and we felt that the casket scenes preceding his arrival in Belmont showed the separate qualities and their weaknesses. Both Morocco and Arragon want to dominate Portia, Morocco by machismo and Arragon by a patronizing approach. We felt that Morocco would treat a wife as his property, appropriate her physically, so there was a bit of manhandling in the scene which Portia reacted against. This may have been seen as reacting against his colour but it is much more to do with being treated as a sexual object – an interesting conundrum: who is the oppressor?

Bill and I discussed the notion of Portia as consummate actress. This is a very important side to her. She plays the part of a male lawyer totally convincingly. She also plays the part of religious, devoted wife in Act Three, Scene Four and of wronged wife in Act Five, and we felt that she dramatized and mythologized her life in moments of crisis (e.g. III.ii.53–62). So in the casket scenes too she is playing a role. You have to remember that she might end up marrying one of these suitors, that however much she might despise them her future might be bound up with them. So she is very polite to each of them while satisfying her wit in a private way. 'Yourself, renowned Prince, then stood as fair / As any comer I have looked on yet' she says to Morocco (II.i.20–1), when the audience has heard her discount all previous comers. She has a passive role in these scenes and yet I felt there was a vitality lurking there that would not be repressed. So at the end of the Arragon scene when he has chosen wrong and by a process of elimination she knows that the lead casket is the answer, there is an upsurge of joy:

> O these deliberate fools! When they do choose,
> They have the wisdom by their wit to lose.      (II.ix.80–81)

And this is doubled by the news of the arrival of 'one that comes before / To signify th'approaching of his lord'. Could this be Bassanio?

The last casket scene shows Portia in a new light. In the first act of our production, she was oppressed but self-contained. Now she enters in quite a desperate state, because now someone has come to gamble on the caskets whom she wants to win. The speech to Bassanio at the beginning of Act Three, Scene Two is full of urgency, though Portia never loses her capacity for humour. In playing it the audience's reaction turned from laughter to concern through the scene.

> But lest you should not understand me well
> . . .
> I would detain you here some month or two
> Before you venture for me.      (III.ii.7–10)

'Should he lose, my eye shall be the stream / And watery deathbed for him' (lines 46–7). Bassanio and Portia don't know each other. They have met briefly. Obviously some spark is there between them but it is not really until the last act that this attraction turns to love and respect, certainly in Bassanio's case. So we talked about them being two gamblers seeing the quality of each other. For the moment, winning and the game are all. As I said before, Bill wanted the idea of self-dramatization in this scene. Portia brings all of her estate on to witness this cataclysmic event in her life:

> the Dardanian wives,
> With bleared visages come forth to view
> The issue of th'exploit. (III.ii.58–60)

They also sing the song.

Is the song a clue? I think it has to be. This is as far as Portia will go to help Bassanio while not cheating her father. Bassanio was isolated downstage with the caskets while Nerissa, Gratiano and I moved upstage away from him while he made his choice. Portia's aside when he has chosen the lead casket is a wonderful moment when time stands still. A moment of sheer joy quietly expressed before the great cheer from the household on 'What find I here? Fair Portia's counterfeit' (line 114).

The next section of the scene Nick and I developed in performance. Both characters have been so intent on winning the game that they have allowed their passions and fears to speak out. Having won they are now confronted with each other: this is my husband; this is my wife. What do you say when you have achieved what you most desired? I am going to spend the rest of my life with this stranger; how do we begin this life together? Having been so free physically and emotionally with each other, there is a formality in this next section that had to be placed. Bassanio is speechless – and says so, very eloquently! Portia's speech ('You see me Lord Bassanio where I stand' (line 149)) is much more rooted. At the beginning I was encouraged to stress the contractual nature of the speech and there is that element to it. She understands that winning means responsibility and she wants to make him understand too, and bring sense to his giddiness. He has won her, her lands, her servants, her wealth, and she gladly gives them all away; but he must take care of all these things, not least of her. Powerful as she may seem, she is in many respects naive and vulnerable – 'an unlessoned girl'. So the ring theme of loyalty and commitment, which has its resolution in the last act, is set up here. But again there is a warmth and generosity which we both found as the run progressed which makes the contract a very joyous, loving act.

Even though she gives away all her worldly goods, she cannot lose the habit of wealth. We noted that almost in the next breath she reappropriates

8   Deborah Findlay as Portia with Bassanio (Nicholas Farrell) and the leaden casket, *The Merchant of Venice* (III.ii)

her money. Bassanio, a poor man, has no concept of being as rich as Portia. She has to teach him. To him, 3,000 ducats seems a fortune. To her it is 'a petty debt' (III.ii.307). This is Portia's first act as a woman freed from the bondage of the caskets and she delights in solving her husband's problem. At this point in the security of Belmont she believes that money and love can cure all. She has yet to meet the fanaticism of Shylock.

I felt that Portia decided to go to Venice herself *after* this scene. Again I think the decision to do this comes from a tremendous surge of released energy. For her life is now golden, she can do anything, and there must be a doubt that Gratiano and Bassanio will be successful armed with only money. We wanted to show, too, how much of an adventure the trip to Venice was for Portia: as well as wanting to free his friend, Portia wants to see what Bassanio's life is like. No longer will she be passive: she won't stay at home and wait for the outcome; she wants to take an active part in life. It is a journey of discovery and in our production Venetian life outside Belmont was certainly an education for her. We set Act Three, Scene Four once more in the casket room, but this time the caskets were being packed

9   Portia disguised as Balthazar (IV.i)

away in a chest and the golden carpet had been rolled up. The casket room was no longer of use. Portia's description of the sort of boy she will be is very perceptive. From her experience of a long line of suitors she has a pretty shrewd idea of the foibles and arrogance of young men. I used this as a basis for my Balthazar. We wanted an image of a young David 'come into the court' and felt that Portia's androgynous quality as a boy would lend her a psychic power. She sees the violent world of men from a different angle and as a man can teach these men how they should behave. So my judge was not a shrouded clerk but a confident raunchy boy. Because her life has turned to happiness she believes in the power of mercy and that people do behave decently towards each other. The mercy speech is thus an act of faith. How prepared is she when she comes into court? This was an area that I changed completely in performance and is the most telling example of underselling Portia in rehearsal.

The trial scene is the only time that Shylock and Portia meet and yet each character and the actors who play them affect the other greatly. My Shylock was Antony Sher, an actor of great power and presence who created a very striking Turkish Jew and who was mainly concerned with the racial issues of the play. By the time he came to the trial Tony's Shylock had moved through grief at the loss of his daughter to an immovable fixation on revenge amounting to a religious crusade. He was certainly a force to be reckoned with. Bill and Tony wanted an idea of a ritual sacrifice in the trial scene. Bill wanted an image of Antonio strung out on a cross, highlighting the Christian–Jewish conflict, and Tony wanted to enhance the drama of the scene by having Shylock perform an improvised ritual before he kills Antonio. The ritual included spattering blood on a sheet before Antonio's prostrate body and he suggested that this would be a marvellous way for Portia to get the idea of 'no drop of blood'. I didn't understand the scene sufficiently to counter these suggestions and so I tried to accommodate them into my motivations. This meant playing the scene in a bewildered state, buffeted by the events and grabbing onto the solution in a last desperate attempt. This may have been dramatic and therefore a very attractive interpretation, but I came to think that it was completely wrong and I had to change what I did. Portia is in control of the scene from the moment she enters: again, the power balance.

I thought initially that it would make for a more dramatic progression if she had to learn on her feet, so I started out thinking that Portia is naive enough to come into the trial with only the conviction that she can convince Shylock to be merciful. After that fails she is acting on her wits. She conceives the notion expressed in her final sentence – 'If it be proved against an alien / That . . . he seek the life of any citizen' (IV.i.346–8) and so gets Shylock to condemn himself by his rejection of the surgeon. But the pound of flesh is pure inspiration. Portia herself has not visited her uncle Bellario; there was no time for that. She had instructed her servant to get the lawyer's garments, and any information that might be of use from Padua, and to meet up with her at the 'common ferry / Which trades to Venice' (III.iv.53–4). So to a large extent she is working on her own. I thought at first that she got drawn into the violence of the scene and proved to be more vindictive than any of them. After all, she stops Bassanio from giving Shylock the money and reduces him to a heap. She draws out the torture of unknowing for Antonio when she could come into the court and deliver salvation straight away. It seemed initially that she got more spiky after Bassanio's declaration of love for Antonio. Does it actually cross her mind to let Antonio die? Does she get caught up in the general blood-lust of the scene? All these elements were in the initial playing, but as I got to know Portia better I realized that this was to undervalue her. I think now that she *does* have all the alternatives when she comes into the trial. Rather than being fed the solution by Shylock *she* runs the scene. I suppose it is the challenge of becoming in a way superhuman while not being precious or boring that I had to learn to take on. Far from being vindictive, she follows a simple rule of thumb: mercy, or justice. Having learnt about the nature of choice and its consequences from the caskets, Portia brings this wisdom to the trial and seeks to educate everyone there. It is her only option. She certainly can't compete physically and she is incorruptible. She has only that logic and her wit to see her through. She holds scrupulously to the letter of the law, since that is what Shylock has chosen. I felt it important, therefore, to disengage myself from Gratiano's outbursts. Now he *is* vindictive, and he and Portia provide a counterpoint of justice and vengeance, particularly between lines 302 and 338 – for example, 'He shall have merely justice and his bond' . . . 'A Daniel still say I, a second Daniel' (lines 336, 337).

Portia gives Shylock as many chances as she can to choose mercy, but once he has made his choice (for me when Tony produced his knife) she follows the consequences through to their final terrible conclusion. Hers is an act of strict impartiality, explaining the law to everyone present. If you reject human mercy then there is only the implacable face of justice to fall back on. If you seek to pervert that, chaos follows.

I found the imposed ritual almost impossible to sustain. I watched Shylock, sometimes feeling pity for this man so set on revenge, sometimes feeling horror and disbelief. The ritual seemed to break the rhythm of the scene and to stop the momentum of Portia's logic. It also made her seem very cruel to have Antonio spread out like so much meat before delivering the mercy blow. And you don't stop someone with a knife by saying 'Tarry a little.' As Olivia in *Twelfth Night* in the same season I stopped Sir Toby Belch fighting Sebastian with 'Hold, Toby! On thy life, I charge thee hold!' (IV.i.44). 'Tarry a little' is an undercutting line, part of a thoughtful, logical progression still offering the choice to Shylock, though the room for manoeuvre gets smaller and smaller. I had to shout the first line and deliver the speech in a more aggressive fashion than I think it merits, but the company was hooked on the dramatic tension and I was not man enough to cut this away. What I tried to do was to portray that notion of teaching and impartiality as much as I could within the context of the existing structure.

I felt increasingly that the outcome saddened her. It isn't a pleasant victory. She has heard herself betrayed by Bassanio and had her notions of humanity knocked. Almost in desperation she asks if Antonio has any mercy. I was rewarded with cold comfort from my Antonio (whom John

Carlisle played as a vengeful, fanatical Christian) as he spat out his conditions. We swapped the lines round here so that 'He presently become a Christian' (IV.i.384) concluded the speech, as the last and most shocking of Antonio's conditions, rather than being less conspicuous in the middle of it. Thus positioned it was clearly the worst thing that could happen to Shylock.

We felt that Portia saves Antonio as much for her own happiness as for anyone else's. There was a strong element of homoeroticism in this production. It was obvious that Antonio was in love with Bassanio and if he couldn't have him as a lover then he wanted to die for him. There seemed to us to be similarities in the Portia/Bassanio/Antonio relationship to that portrayed in the Sonnets. Portia will not tolerate the martyrdom of a former lover hanging over her marriage to Bassanio, so she condemns Antonio to life:

> He is well paid that is well satisfied
> And I delivering you am satisfied. (lines 413–14)

Portia and Nerissa are sickened by the experience and return to Belmont wiser people. The ring test seemed to be a whim sparked off by Portia's witnessing of Bassanio's behaviour at the trial.

I used to enjoy the little moment between Portia and Nerissa after the trial. We set it on the jetty where they are waiting for the ferry. Both are in contemplative mood, reliving the past moments. Portia suddenly realizes that they've forgotten to get Shylock to sign the deed of gift. It is a moment of friendship that shows how far the two women have travelled and also their last moments of freedom in the guise of boys.

When they are next seen, they have reassumed female attire and are again in contemplative mood. This time it's that wonderful feeling of coming home: 'That light we see is burning in my hall' (v.i.890). It used to make me think of all the songs I'd ever heard about homecoming – a marvellous sense of peace after a storm. For they have been through a nightmare and now Portia can see Belmont in a new light: 'Nothing is good, I see, without respect' (line 99). That whole section for me was Portia realizing the true worth of her home and her life – 'a good deed in a naughty world' (line 91). She has seen the world of Venice, the world of malice and vengeance, and returns to the calm of her old life with a new maturity and understanding. Whether or not this reading of this section would be endorsed by others I can't tell, but this is what it felt like playing it every night. At the sound of Bassanio's arrival Nerissa and Portia prepare for action. This time they are working together, no secrets any more, and both are prepared to teach their husbands a lesson. This is the last great role that Portia plays – the wronged wife. This act is a comic interlude, but beneath the humour a very serious point is being made. Both Pippa and I felt that Nerissa and Portia are enacting a psychodrama for their husbands on the subject of fidelity and in its way this is as important a trial as that which takes place in Venice. Although a man's life is not at stake, the same issues of loyalty and commitment are in debate. Rather than the extraordinary issue of the flesh bond, what is being looked at here is the day-to-day betrayals or loyalties that make or mar our lives.

Having concentrated so much on the racism in the production, it was difficult to place this scene. Here are the men who spat at Shylock and knocked him to the ground; here is the ruling class at play. Are we expected to forget their atrocities and be charmed by them? There was worry that the Jewish element would be forgotten in the welter of froth, and so we introduced a final image of Antonio dangling the cross above Jessica as if to say 'you're not really one of us'. But I maintain that this act isn't just froth and that the game-playing has a serious function.

Portia mirrors each of Bassanio's reasons for giving up the ring and shows how hollow they are. When he talks about blind honour making him betray her, she says that blind honour will make the doctor her bedfellow. She takes on all the colours of the cartoon wife – adoring, trustful, hurt, vengeful, vacant – until finally she gets from him a commitment that she can believe. I was struck by the similarities of the final oaths of Shylock and Bassanio: 'By my soul I swear / There is no power in the tongue of man / To alter me' (IV.i.237–9); 'By my soul I swear / I never more will break an oath with thee' (v.i.247–8). Antonio puts the finishing touches to Portia's mercy and I felt that she won both men in the end. Rather than alienate the former lover she very wisely accommodates him and so diffuses his threat.

Having forgiven Bassanio and given him the ring I always felt that last twist to the ring joke was inspired. Bill and I talked about her taking everything to the limit and it seemed that she couldn't resist the wickedly funny pay-off: 'I had it of him' (line 258). Portia has forgiven Bassanio and so this has to be said for the fun of it, I think. This is one step too far, however, and Gratiano's violent reaction at the thought of being a cuckold triggers off the revelation of the disguise. Portia says that Nerissa and she will answer all things faithfully, while Gratiano talks about keeping safe Nerissa's ring – sexual meaning much in evidence. So the marriages will be conventional after all. But we felt that it was in this scene that Bassanio finally realized Portia's true worth, so that they start their new life together with genuine love and understanding.

The play is termed a comedy. One has to consider this in the playing of it. Too often the play is seen as the tragedy of Shylock. Bill compromised happily and called it a drama, so combining the elements of tragedy and comedy. For the comedy keeps bubbling up. Even in the trial scene there is that surprising laugh on, 'Your wife would give you little thanks for that / If she were by to hear you make the offer' (IV.i.285–6). It is moments like these that put the whole piece into perspective. The point being made by Portia is a serious one, with serious consequences, but it has an edge of humour to it. It diffuses the madness and violence and is a pointer to more sane and rational behaviour.

The great bonus of doing a play such as this with the RSC is the length of time you spend with the part. With other companies in an average run of six weeks you would not be able to distance yourself sufficiently from the choices you made about your character in rehearsal. With Portia I was able to put all those choices to the test. A play in performance is a living, changing thing. Particularly with the great Shakespearian roles, I believe that there is no such thing as a definitive reading. That is why they are so endlessly fascinating. And as I discovered, a performance can develop within a run. Certain decisions are taken in advance, guidelines for the character to follow, but the route to these pointers may change every night. Through my time spent with Portia I was able to build up layers to this marvellous character so that what may have been on the surface at the beginning became subtext and what was subtext came towards the surface. Portia started off (perhaps as I did myself at the beginning of a new job) a little defensive and suspicious. Over the run she opened up to become much more loving and generous. My Portia, I think, grew up.

# Solanio in
## *The Merchant of Venice*
### GREGORY DORAN

GREGORY DORAN played Solanio in Bill Alexander's production of *The Merchant of Venice* at the Royal Shakespeare Theatre in 1987 and at the Barbican the following year. In the same season (his first with the RSC) he was Octavius in *Julius Caesar*, Don Mathias in Marlowe's *The Jew of Malta*, Beaufort in Jonson's *The New Inn* and Rider in Shirley's *Hyde Park*. Earlier performing work had been in theatre seasons at Nottingham, York, Harrogate, and Leeds. He has wide experience as a director, particularly as Associate Director at the Nottingham Playhouse. His Shakespeare productions include *Romeo and Juliet*, *The Winter's Tale*, and (in New York) *A Midsummer Night's Dream*. He has also directed, at the Young Vic, *The Book of Sir Thomas More*. He was assistant director at the RSC in 1989–90 and returned to Stratford in 1992 to direct Derek Walcott's *The Odyssey* at The Other Place.

> No! I am not Prince Hamlet, nor was meant to be;
> Am an attendant lord, one that will do
> To swell a progress, start a scene or two.
>
> (T. S. Eliot, 'The Love-Song of J. Alfred Prufrock')

Someone once said there are no small parts, only small actors. That may be true. Nevertheless, there are some pretty small parts in Shakespeare, and no matter how thorough and dedicated the actor, they can be fairly unrewarding. In fact I've played what must be the smallest part in the canon: Pacorus in *Antony and Cleopatra*. You would have to be pretty hot at Trivial Pursuit to identify Pacorus. Amid all the to-ing and fro-ing between Egypt and Rome there is one little scene set in Syria, among warring Medes and Parthians. Soldiers enter carrying the dead body of the son of King Orodes: that's Pacorus.

There is no great challenge in tackling Pacorus, apart from not breathing; the problems start when you come to play parts a little larger, parts with lines. And that's not an entirely flippant remark. As much deliberation and heartache, radical re-evaluation, and detailed experiment can go

68

10 Gregory Doran as Solanio (right) and Salerio (Michael Cadman)

into the creation of an attendant lord as any of the more exalted characters from Shakespeare's crowded pantheon.

I played Solanio in Bill Alexander's production of *The Merchant of Venice*. Solanio is not a large part. The 1619 quarto mentions three characters: Solanio. Salerio, and Salarino. They are known as the Salads, or, I suppose, the salad roles. Salarino is generally regarded as a mere reduplication of Salerio and unless it is felt useful to have an extra salad dressing the stage, he is generally amalgamated. Imagine trying to isolate and characterize a printing error!

To be honest, I suppose the Salads are often regarded as a bit of a joke. At least their Danish cousins Rosencrantz and Guildenstern have had their very insignificance celebrated by another major playwright. You sometimes feel that when directors come to cast the Salads they wonder what on

69

earth to do with the two of them, and in despair clad them with directorial concepts, making them lisping gondoliers, or yuppy stockbrokers, or Laurel and Hardy. They've sometimes been played as a sort of Italian Tweedledum and Tweedledee, implying that they are more or less inter-changeable. They're not – or at least I don't think they are. During rehearsal Bill, Michael Cadman (playing Salerio), and I began a search to find out who the Salads are, to identify them, flesh them out, and put them into the context of the play and the production: part man-hunt, part wild-goose chase.

A basic problem when playing parts of this size is the level of characteri-zation to apply. Sometimes these roles need to be particularized indi-viduals in a specific social context, with attitudes and aspirations, with identifiable opinions and real emotional resources to draw upon; some-times you suspect, as the old actor-manager said, that they should just 'say the lines and bugger off left'.

What about the Salads? They set the scene; they make up numbers in Lorenzo's masque; they are insatiable gossips, and as such they fulfil their primary function of bringing the audience up to date by recounting offstage action. They are useful as messengers and as sounding-boards and they reflect the central relationship between Bassanio and Antonio. It's a fascinating relationship. It seems clear that Antonio is in love with Bas-sanio. For me, Antonio is the voice of the Sonnets which were, after all, probably written about this time: a man struggling with the love of a younger man, racked with jealousy, obsession, devotion, and passion. Antonio begins the play in a melancholy humour which those close to him can't understand. (So does Romeo, another great lover.) Solanio, with bare-faced cheek, hits the nail straight on the head: 'Why then, you are in love' (1.i.46). Antonio dismisses the suggestion with a terse half line: 'Fie, fie!'.

Later, when the Salads are gossiping together, Salerio recounts Anto-nio's farewell to Bassanio, as the latter left for Belmont. He relishes every detail of the scene:

> And even there, his eye being big with tears,
> Turning his face, he put his hand behind him,
> And with affection wondrous sensible
> He wrung Bassanio's hand; and so they parted. (II.viii.46–9)

Solanio has clearly diagnosed his malady correctly. Somewhat wistfully he muses: 'I think he only loves the world for him' (line 50).

The Salads are parasites, Venetian Venticelli. They seem to live vicariously through the lives of other people and to have little function on their own. By making them lovers we paralleled the central relationship and pointed up the way the two follow its vagaries, hang upon its changes of mood, and thereby fuel the cold embers of their own affair. At one point we had the sentimental Salerio attempt to kiss his young toy-boy. It seemed a valuable moment, neither gratuitous nor provocative – but it was hell on schools' matinées.

We decided to push them a little further and explore the seedy, decadent underbelly of the world of Venice which they inhabit and which Bassanio, away from it all in Belmont, comes to realize is all 'outward show'. In researching the period I discovered that the young Henry III of France had visited Venice on his way back from Cracow, where as a young general he had won the throne of Poland. When he returned from Venice, however, he was a different man. The court was stupefied to see him caked in powder, hung with precious stones, and surrounded by a flock of parrots and little dogs. He began to hold fêtes in the royal parks, decked out in a pink damask dress embroidered with pearls, emerald pendants in his ears, diamonds in his hair, and his beard dyed with violet powder. Such was the civilizing effect of La Serenissima.

Adreana Neofitou, the costume designer, drew the line at the violet beard powder, but created a very dashing outfit for Solanio, in russets and umbers, with a splendid orange panache, and for further ornament I added an ostentatious pearl rosary, commas of rouge on the cheeks, kohl on the eyes, and a pickadevant beard and moustache. All this gave plenty of scope for Solanio's 'outward show' to fall apart as the first half progressed, and pull himself together by the trial.

The search for supplementary detail can become an obsession when one is playing these parts. I remember playing Octavius Caesar in Terry Hands's production of *Julius Caesar*. It is tempting to flesh out Octavius's few lines with reference to the character he later becomes in *Antony and Cleopatra*, or by returning to the source for inspiration. I found out that Octavius had famously found Rome brick and left it marble, but couldn't think of any way of playing that, so fell upon Cassius's gibe:

> A peevish schoolboy, worthless of such honour,
> Join'd with a masquer and a reveller.    (v.i.61–2)

'Ah,' said Terry, 'enemy propaganda!' You don't have a problem distinguishing truth from libel with the Salads, as nobody ever talks about them at all. In fact no one even calls Solanio by name. Nevertheless, the

Stanislavskian search for detail goes on, the tentative extrapolation of arguable subtextual hints into quintessential radix traits; forgetting the fact that in a play of some 3,000 lines, Solanio only has fifty-seven of them. It's easy to become so involved in the search for character that your perspective becomes distorted. Even the attempt to discern a through line can be deceptive. I don't really think Shakespeare thought in those terms. These characters work from moment to moment; there is little psychological progression discernible. But you can lose a sense of proportion, and start playing your discoveries, colonizing the text with generalizations and irrelevant attitudes. So wrapped up do you become that you forget the audience's primary concern is the story itself, not particularly how it affects your character. Barry Kyle tells the story of a rehearsal of *Equus* by Peter Shaffer when a young actor playing one of the horses, champing and snorting away, was asked to cross downstage on a particular line: 'Oh no,' he said, 'my horse wouldn't do that!'

How you retain a sense of perspective is, I suspect, largely through listening. After all, with few lines, that is what you spend most of your time on stage doing. The quality of that listening, the concentration on what is being said, can be difficult to achieve, especially over a long run, but I suspect that it is finally the secret of good ensemble playing.

In Bill Alexander's production of *The Merchant of Venice* Solanio and Salerio had another important function. They became representative of an attitude within the whole community. The Salads acted as a funnel for the bile of anti-Semitism flooding throughout that society. The universally topical theme of racism was one which this production brought right to the fore. Generally the play is viewed from the Christian perspective. If we forced the audience to witness the violent and unholy racism of the Christian Venetians with their apartheid regime we might adjust that perspective. After all, Shylock says he is frequently spat upon, spurned and kicked as a matter of course. When the play is transposed to a more genteel period, to a more polite society such as the Victorian or Edwardian era, it is difficult to convey the routine violence of this racism.

Antony Sher had chosen to play Shylock as a Levantine Turk. There were apparently three different racial types among the Jewish population in the Ghetto: German/Italian Jews, the Ponentine Jews, who had escaped the Inquisition in Portugal, and the Turks. Making Shylock an Ottoman Turk allowed the two opposing communities to have distinct cultural differences which the production could heighten. Thus the segregated Jewish quarter might resemble a Byzantine bazaar, with the money-lenders squatting in the street clicking abacuses, while the Christians strut about in doublets and lace collars, with swords strapped to their thighs: two societies, far apart from each other, irreconcilable opposites. A shrine to the Madonna was juxtaposed with a yellow Star of David, daubed on the back wall of the set, underlining this tension.

One of the challenges of playing Solanio is the speech where he mimics the distraught Shylock, after the abduction of his daughter. In the confusion following the flight of the lovers the Salads are apparently separated. Shakespeare tells the audience what happens next in the manner of the tabloids: 'Venice in uproar', 'Rich Jewish heiress kidnapped. Father on rampage.' The Salads exchange their snatches of news with the relish and inventive authority of hack journalists. We played this scene as if the events they describe had just happened and they are reeling with excitement, intoxicated both by the alcohol and adrenalin upon which they seem to thrive. Solanio takes enormous pleasure in the terrible suffering of Shylock, raging through the streets, bereft both of his daughter and a large portion of his wealth. He launches into his cruel diatribe with gleeful relish. Under the tuition of Joan Washington, Antony Sher had mastered a Turkish accent, which I tried to copy: 'ducats' became 'dockets'; 'Christian' became 'Chreestian'; and 'Justice' 'Jostice'. As we rehearsed his stride became deeper, his stance took on a broader base, and my script became full of scribbled sketches; diagrams of headslaps, swinging arms, pounding fists, and a barrage of rude Turkish gestures supplied by Jondon Gourkan, one of the RSC stage managers: plenty to work on there. Even if playing small parts gives no real understanding about how to play large parts (the only real preparation for playing large parts is playing large parts somewhere else), at least it affords you the opportunity of watching actors you admire at close range.

The Salads' description of Shylock's distraction provided the cue for his entrance into the next scene. The boys of Venice chased the Jew on stage, mocking him and pelting him with stones. It was a brilliant device which propelled Shylock straight into enemy territory. Apparently this scene is sometimes played with the Salads sipping chocolate and nibbling wafers, like Henry James at the Café Florian. Bill had something more active in mind, bringing the central theme of racism into sharp focus.

Sher arrived on stage like a whirlwind, bruised and bloodied from the street boys' catapults, dazed with grief. The Salads, bored with each other, and tetchy, fall upon this new distraction like vultures on a rattlesnake. We taunted and sneered at the Jew, shoving him between us, and knocked him

11   Solanio and Salerio goad Shylock (Antony Sher) (III.i)

to the ground: 'You knew, none so well, none so well as you, of my daughter's flight' (III.i.22). Even Shylock knows of his assailants' reputations. The Salads are proud of their part in the scam, and brag about it, gloating over Shylock's misery. We prodded him with a stick, as if he were a poisonous scorpion, until he scuttled out of reach. Solanio enjoyed himself giggling and poking, but Michael's Salerio suddenly lost control and blurted out: 'There is more difference between thy flesh and hers than between jet and ivory' (line 34). But suddenly he recovers and asks instead if Shylock has heard whether Antonio has had any losses at sea. It is an extraordinary thing to do, reminding the Jew indirectly about his bond. Surely it is mischievous. It may be that Salerio wants to provoke Shylock with possible further losses. If Antonio loses his ships, his bond will be forfeit, and Shylock will lose all his money. No one anticipates him actually exacting his penalty. If this is Salerio's motive it misfires horribly, for Shylock, at the depth of his pain, cruelly beaten by the Christians, replies that Antonio had better look to his bond.

At this point Bill Alexander introduced a haunting sound cue. Out across the foggy lagoon a bell tolled, signalling perhaps some terrible wreck at sea.

It seized attention for a second. We had arrived at Shylock's famous tirade, 'Hath not a Jew eyes?' (line 53). It is always difficult to approach purple passages in Shakespeare. You almost prefer no one to mention their fame or notoriety, so it can be regarded as simply another part of the debate of the scene. We played it many ways in rehearsal; as an extension of the bullying, with Shylock escaping their attacks, and once even torturing the poor man by holding him out precariously over the canal. But the bell had introduced a new dynamic; it hushed the scene. Salerio asked quite quietly, with implied menace, what good a pound of flesh would be to Shylock, advancing slowly upon him. In order to deflect further violence, Sher's Shylock made light of it, joking 'to bait fish withal'. Confronted with Antonio's sudden storm of anger in the third scene Sher had done the same thing; thrown up his hands to protect himself from the blow, and surrendered at the same time, nodding with nervous grins and submissive chuckles. Here it gave Shylock a moment's breath to recover and begin his attack: 'If it will feed nothing else, it will feed my revenge' (line 48).

Solanio is confused; he keeps the Jew at bay with his stick – at once a weapon and a defence. Sher began to grow; stalking the sycophants, his anger began to rumble and rise, ravelling out the injuries that Antonio has done him. And for what reason? Suddenly, with flashing eyes, Shylock erupted: 'I am a Jew.' He blasted his anger, white hot, into the air. He seemed to tower with ferocity, fuelled with all the suffering of the Jewish nation. Exasperation hit 'fed with the same food' and tears of frustration seemed to well in his eyes, checked as suddenly with furious contempt. The Salads quiver; there is silence, and with chilling irony Shylock pushed his bleeding hand into Solanio's face: 'If you prick us, do we not bleed?'; with icy derision – 'If you tickle us, do we not laugh?'; with outraged impotence – 'If you poison us, do we not die? And if you wrong us ...' – suddenly grabbing Solanio's stick, and with a terrible howl – 'Shall we not revenge!' (lines 58–61). As Antonio's servant called the Salads away, they beat a hasty retreat, lobbing a final gob of rheum at Tubal as he appeared over the bridge and shrieking the final word 'Jew' in angry chorus as they vanished.

After tumbling off the stage, I would always stay to watch the rest of the scene in the wings, as Shylock wiped the spittle from Tubal's gaberdine, screamed with fury at his daughter's loss, gasped and panted with disbelief at news of Antonio's misfortunes, and then beat the air with his fists, hurling his righteous thanks to God. Amid this tempestuous vacillation between despair and vengeful delight, Tubal tells Shylock that Jessica has exchanged a ring for a monkey. Suddenly Sher sank to the floor, as if mortally wounded: 'It was my turquoise; I had it of Leah when I was a bachelor' (line 110). In one line Shakespeare paints in Shylock's youth, his courtship, his days of love, and at once recalls the loss of a beloved wife: a whole history.

When Sher rose, we understood the depth of Shylock's pain, the tensile steel strength of his resolution, the righteousness of his cause, and as he sends Tubal for an officer, we feared the consequences: 'Go, Tubal, and meet me at our synagogue; go, good Tubal; at our synagogue, Tubal' (line 118). With eerie distraction he dismissed Tubal and, seated at the end of the wharf, rocked back and forth, muttering a silent prayer as the lights faded, and a dismal bell rang out over the water.

Solanio doesn't actually appear in the trial scene according to the Quarto, but we had him there, weeping on Salerio's shoulder, glowering at the Jews, and fiercely telling his rosary. As the Jew is finally triumphantly ejected from the court, and Bassanio and Antonio are reunited and leave for Belmont, the Salads are left alone. Having tucked away his rosary, and eyed up the pretty young clerk, Solanio seized upon Shylock's knife, and pocketed it as a souvenir.

I don't know whether these details ever really registered to the audience. In the end it doesn't really matter. Perhaps someone noticed them; perhaps they contributed to the general life of the world we were depicting. I hope so. I hope they didn't pull focus, or ever distract from the main action. After all, Solanio and Salerio are not the main course; they're only side salads.

# Rosalind (and Celia) in
## *As You Like It*
### SOPHIE THOMPSON

SOPHIE THOMPSON played Rosalind in John Caird's production of *As You Like It* at the Royal Shakespeare Theatre in 1989 and at the Barbican the following year. It was her first role with the RSC. She had previously played Celia in Geraldine McEwan's production of the play for the Renaissance Theatre Company in a season in which she had also appeared as Ophelia in *Hamlet* and Margaret in *Much Ado About Nothing*. Earlier work had included Perdita in *The Winter's Tale* and a range of roles for Bristol Old Vic, the Cambridge Theatre Company, the Chichester Festival, and others. On television she has appeared in *A Traveller in Time*, *Secret Orchards*, *Bomber Harris*, and *Sherlock Holmes*. She returned to the RSC in 1992 to play Helena in Sir Peter Hall's production of *All's Well that Ends Well* at the Swan Theatre.

To play Rosalind at Stratford so soon after playing Celia for the Renaissance Theatre Company gave me an interesting dual perspective on *As You Like It*. In the production that Geraldine McEwan directed for Renaissance we didn't explore so many of the perhaps slightly frightening, black or melancholy aspects of the play – a side that I didn't really see then. The forest was generally a jollier environment. The 'deer song' (Act Four, Scene Two), for example, was rather lyrical, with Amiens wandering across the stage singing, followed by Jaques; in the Stratford production all the men ran on with their faces smeared with blood, having just killed the deer. We didn't sit down at the beginning and discuss a 'concept' for either production, although with the Stratford one the audience seemed to sense a definite angle. What happened tended to evolve from things we discovered along the way, without the director starting off by saying 'This is where we're going.' The Renaissance production used Edwardian costumes: the Stratford version was unspecific. It started in the 1930s, but shed that early on. Ultz, the Stratford designer, wanted a change of seasons, so we got wind and snow in the first half, but in the Renaissance production it was

77

late summer or early autumn all through, much warmer and sunnier. In Ultz's designs the court characters were seen to begin with at a glamorous party in what looked like the art deco foyer of the theatre itself; when they got to the forest Rosalind, Celia and Touchstone were stripped of their finery; as the stage itself broke up, so we found ourselves wearing fewer clothes, making the forest a place of revealing – except for Hugh Ross as Jaques: he kept his overcoat on, and appeared not to have given in to the forest and its liberating qualities.

Playing Celia means doing a lot of watching and listening. I did find myself wanting to interrupt at times: there are moments where you want to react but there aren't any lines for you to do so and you have to find ways of translating this into actions or stillness. You begin to feel that Celia is a sort of mouthpiece for the audience as well, a representative up on stage, joining with them in watching what's going on. Rosalind gets rather carried away, and Celia has to try and keep up in her own way. In the second scene of the play – and our first – she realizes after Rosalind has met Orlando that her friend has fallen in love, and that is a breach between them. Previously they have had only each other, and it is not until Celia meets Oliver in the latter part of the play that Rosalind becomes the observer for the first time since they were at court where Celia was in charge.

The ending of the scene where Celia meets Oliver is tricky. In Geraldine McEwan's production we started with a version in which Rosalind fainted again as they were leaving the stage and had to be carried off. Then we realized that it was better without that extra faint, particularly if, when she says 'Will you go?' (IV.iii.181) Rosalind is noticing that Celia and Oliver are interested in each other. In the Stratford production we made a lot of changes as we worked on the scene. The key we had found in the earlier production was that the situation gave us a reversal – a reflection – of the meeting between Rosalind and Orlando. Whatever you think the situation to mean, we found we had to try to keep the energy up in a *different* way now that the game and the deception are coming to an end for Rosalind. The faint felt like the end of that process – a physical manifestation of spent adventure. In the RSC production Rosalind came down the steps at the front of the stage – towards the audience, that is – and stood watching Celia and Oliver for a moment. Then she said 'Will you go?' just as they were about to kiss, recalling the 'Will you go?' that Celia says when Rosalind and Orlando first meet.

That first meeting between Rosalind and Orlando is difficult to do from a staging point of view. As Rosalind I found I had to leave Orlando talking to himself and do a lot of 'pretending to be going off' acting. At Stratford the stage is big, and getting the distances right is hard. Gillian Bevan (who played Celia) and I thought up some business about Celia being rather irritated that I had given away my only necklace to a man who didn't even say thank you! So she stayed looking at him rather beadily as Rosalind left. In the Renaissance production things were simpler because the stage was very much smaller, both in the studio at Birmingham Rep and on tour, but we had a lot of discussion about whether Celia stays offstage (and calls to Rosalind from there) or lingers at the edge. As it is one of those pivotal moments – the moment where we see Rosalind and Orlando fall in love – although the text is sparse, each syllable feels tight to bursting. And like a lot of staging problems, it has its source quite deep in the texture of the play.

In the next scene Rosalind defies the Duke: he accuses her of being a traitor, and he gives as his reason that she is her father's daughter. She refuses to accept the logic of this, or the imputation that her father was treacherous:

> Treason is not inherited, my lord,
> Or, if we did derive it from our friends,
> What's that to me? My father was no traitor. (I.iii.59–61)

She has never said anything like this before. As we played it at Stratford, when he said 'Thou art thy father's daughter, there's enough' (line 56) all the anger welled up in her. She had started by pleading ('I *beseech* your grace' and '*dear* uncle' (lines 43, 48)): now she was shaken. The Duke and his bodyguard were going off and she stopped him in his tracks – 'So was he when your Highness *took* his dukedom' (line 57) – there was nothing tentative about it. It became white, clear anger in the sight of supreme injustice, with no fear, and she shocked herself. As we played this scene, Celia was very isolated, but her determination grew out of this. She takes positive steps, *doing* where Rosalind was *done to*. Rosalind was very broken, down to the last speech in the scene, and Celia said 'Now go we in content' (line 135) to stop me crying again. Rosalind has the idea of disguise, but at this point I felt very like someone who's feeling down and decides that if they do a lot of cooking or decorating they'll feel better. The next time we see the two women, Rosalind is a 'man' and playing at being in charge and it is Celia who is doing the sobbing and needing support. As for the forest, Rosalind knows about it as a fairy-tale place, and we tried to mark this in the Stratford production in the way Oliver and Charles talked about it in the first scene, conjuring it somehow with their attitude to it.

12    Sophie Thompson as Rosalind enters Arden; Celia (Gillian Bevan) and Touchstone (Mark Williams) hesitate, *As You Like It* (II.iv)

When we got to the forest, in the Stratford production, it wasn't a nice cherry-tree grove with deer. It always had an edge to it. We had begun in a grand state room, then the floor was broken up by the exiled Duke's followers, who dismantled it and stacked it at the sides of the stage. By the time Rosalind, Celia, and Touchstone came to the forest, there was just a big wall with a clock on it: Rosalind pushed against the middle of the wall and it swung open like a pair of high doors; there was a deep, ominous musical chord and what we found was a frightening void, with swirling smoke and wind and nothing remotely resembling a tree. Geraldine McEwan's production was altogether different. Jenny Tiramani had designed a silk canopy that hung over the opening scenes of the play, like a sort of ceiling, but was swept away as the three of us reached Arden. Leaves fell slowly from the roof and there was gentle piano music – and all the colours were warm and autumnal.

I found it was important when I played Rosalind to remember that she doesn't go into the forest *in order* to meet Orlando. When she does meet him everything changes – she pivots in a moment, as she discovers that it has all linked up. Something that was born in court, in a life blasted apart before her very eyes, is here. She's not just a displaced princess having a laugh, finding extraordinary poems on trees, bouncing about with a fool. In the Stratford production, when Orlando met Rosalind in the forest, Celia did a lot of 'significant' looks and pointing, as though it was possible – even likely – that he would recognize Rosalind. As actors you have to forget that you know the end of the play, that you will have another scene together, and I had to try to let the audience see me decide, as Rosalind, to go further, forging the deception before their eyes. I think the audience should see clearly that Rosalind doesn't know what will happen. But she does see that she has undreamt-of opportunities – and suddenly it all comes flooding into her mind. She's playing a dangerous game: not only can she discover things about his love, but about her own as well, and what it all means. All the outrageous things she says – 'love is merely a madness' (III.ii.383) – seem to spring from an instinctual source that speaks through her (sometimes at great length) and believes that romantic love of the kind Orlando follows needs a bit of knocking about. This could never happen in the court because the forest has something special. It isn't just a big park or a nice bit of countryside. It's a magic place.

Rosalind knows about her double nature – as Ganymede and herself – but Orlando is operating on one level, playing a game with a young bloke who seems at times to be taking it all a bit too seriously perhaps. The

13   Rosalind and Orlando (Jerome Flynn) in the wooing scene (IV.i)

costume allowed me to be fairly sexless. I only 'acted' in a fairly corny 'manly' way when I was with Silvius and Phebe, being affected. With Orlando I didn't change my voice or 'act' like a man unless I felt she panicked somewhat, and she tended to when she lost her way a bit. He kissed me in the speech about orators – 'Very good orators, when they are out, they will spit, and for lovers lacking – God warn us! – matter, the cleanliest shift is to kiss' (IV.i.68–70). We were up against the left-hand side of the proscenium arch, and we wanted it to be somehow dangerous, with Rosalind cornered and her cover in jeopardy. In a lot of places I felt I could react directly as Rosalind rather than as 'Ganymede', having established Orlando's belief in him. When he told me he had to go to attend the Duke at dinner I was speaking as Rosalind when I made it difficult for him – 'Ay, go your ways, go your ways. I knew what you would prove ... ' (IV.i.168) – and Rosalind really meant it.

By the time we get to the 'howling of Irish wolves' scene, Orlando has said that he can 'live no longer by thinking' (V.ii.48). It's the end of Rosalind's being able to do all the things she has been able to do as a man, and it's heartbreaking that he is so unhappy. There is an element of relief, but from then on a whole aspect of her personality has to be cut away, like a boat set adrift. She has come from a man's world, turned into a man, done what a man can do and a woman shouldn't, has gone on this voyage of discovery, and now she has to go back to doing things for real. His love and hers have been tested. I don't think this is a 'pretty' moment, as if she were thinking, 'I'll put a frock on and everything will be lovely because I love him and he loves me.' She has found out what was in her head and her heart, she has an idea of how bloody love can be, and she knows that you can't be sure of anything. I was in a dress at the beginning, then I found a new kind of freedom – if there had been a tree on the set I could have climbed it – and now as we move towards the ending I have to go back to the court and the court clothes, as though something is closed off again.

In this connection, it's worth thinking of some of the other experiences Rosalind has had in the forest. I have already mentioned my acting like a 'man' with Silvius and Phebe. I think I treated that whole episode as something separate, not as playing the game that was going on in the scenes with Orlando. Early in the run I used to find it hard to knit it all in, but later I decided that I should really be knitting two separate scarves. With Orlando always on my mind I was finding it very difficult to be with these two other people and be doing something outrageous but that seemed to be actually quite unconnected. Then we discovered this quite different personality, a 'chappish' character who is more obviously the result of her trying to play a man, and not doing it very well. When I played Celia, I remember feeling confused and not really knowing what to do in this scene (Act Three, Scene Five) – as an actress as well as the character. The transition into the next scene – when they meet Jaques – is difficult, too. At Stratford when we started the run Celia and I used to come on in hysterics, two young girls who had just had a very funny experience. They met Jaques, who wanted to talk about melancholia, but Rosalind could hardly speak she was laughing so much. We seemed to 'find it' one day in rehearsals, but it never worked again. We played it that way to the first audiences but they didn't know what was going on.

As Rosalind I was very interested in Jaques – for example, when he was leaving the stage after the deer song we would stop and look at each other as I came on. I felt Rosalind had a strong sense of melancholy in her, which is why she clued into all these things she hadn't experienced but knew instinctively. This is why Jaques intrigues her, and he is a man who will talk to her seriously. He doesn't much like women, but she has the advantage that he positively wants to chat with Ganymede. He is also interesting to her because despite spending time in the forest he hasn't changed in personality or even (in the RSC production) in appearance. At the end of the play, when he addresses all the couples, it is in fact only the men he speaks to – and I always used to think that he didn't look at me now that I was a girl again. The conversation at the beginning of Act Four is cut short when Orlando comes in but the speech she makes as Jaques goes off is very particular. We played it so that she spoke quite appealingly to him as he stalked off. It was like when you're talking to someone who is a bit sad, and then someone you're mad for phones and says 'You've got to come out *now* and meet me round the corner'. You realize you've broken off something that was important to the other person. So my Rosalind tried to say helpful things to him, and tried to make it all right. She's interested and glad to have spoken to him, and he's been very intimate with her and started to talk about his sadness. Jaques, on his side, has recognized someone who understands. When she says 'and to travel for it too!' (IV.i.26) she is realizing that she too has done just that. It's a reflective moment for them both. In the final scene of the RSC production, Jaques left the stage through the door at the very back, and the lights changed. As he shut the door he closed off the strong white light that flooded out of it and the stage lighting switched back to its previous state. We wanted a *frisson*, taking us back to the play's beginning, and to the idea of the theatre breaking up and revealing the forest. And this was part of Jaques's being the man who has never really surrendered to the forest. As the lights flickered we took the audience in directly, with the notion that we had all shared the transition of the theatre-cum-court to Arden – whatever the magic of 'Arden' might be to each individual.

I see Hymen's appearance as the ultimate moment of magic in the forest, when all the games and pretending and the sense of the forest holding something special marry together in an occasion which is 'real' but at the same time on a level of *un*reality. Human beings are no longer in charge of the situation, which has been taken over by Hymen. As Rosalind I felt this was so when I 'conjured' in Act Five, Scene Two, but unconsciously. I couldn't have told Orlando exactly what was going to happen, which in the Stratford production was the arrival from the back of the stage of a figure out of William Blake, a strong man in a green costume with an angel perched on his back, leading two children by the hand. It happens because of faith, belief, magic. Rosalind didn't think when she went rushing off saying she will 'make these doubts all even' (V.iv.25) that she was going to get Hymen ready for his entrance. In Geraldine McEwan's production, on the other hand, Hymen was an old man from the forest in a rustic cart and although we aimed for an element of magic and wonder there wasn't a 'real' god there among us. In the Stratford version it was the end of human control, as though something else had taken over. Different kinds of love had been growing and being nurtured – or smashed about – and that in itself amounted to some sort of conjuring. I didn't really want to know where Hymen had come from, but I was very glad he had come. Interestingly enough, being Celia in this scene, with no lines to work on, wasn't so very frustrating. In a way, I could think, Rosalind and I were close again because now Celia has fallen in love with Oliver and that had come at the moment when our friendship was a bit strained. We used to look at each other when Jaques de Boys came in, using that moment to get a sense of the bond between us.

In the epilogue as we played it in the RSC production it looked at first as though Orlando was going to speak to the audience, but he dried after making a strangled sound and I came forward to take over. I liked that because it made you remember him at the beginning of the play, unable to put his feelings about Rosalind into words. I liked the fact that here you saw a bit of the being 'together' – and Mrs helping Mr in a rather 'social' situation! I played it as though I was making it up as I went along, but when I got to 'My way is to conjure you' (v.iv.205) it somehow changed and reminded us of the magic we'd seen. I would have a lot of hope for their love, because of everything they've been able to discover. They understand now that love isn't all romance, and that you have to work at it every single day.

Did it, then, make any difference that I had played Celia before coming to Rosalind? Certainly I felt more familiar with the play. It was good to feel aware of Celia at the times when, without having seen things earlier through her eyes, I should have wondered what was happening. In rehearsal when you play Celia you're a reactor most of the time, and until as a team you have all found what is being related to, the actress playing Celia can feel really at sea. I remembered how it felt, and how difficult it was for Celia to watch those scenes in the forest between Rosalind and Orlando. But after the first few days you know that you're doing a different play. There are so many paths that you could go down – as though it's a landscape, or that you're on the same mountain as before, but on a different path with a completely different view. Occasionally you come across a pebble, and think 'I've seen that stone somewhere before.' And sometimes when I was playing Rosalind I would hear a single line or recognize an intonation, and think that there are some things that don't change so very much from production to production, like a drumbeat – a rhythm that's always there.

# King John

## NICHOLAS WOODESON

NICHOLAS WOODESON played the title role in Deborah Warner's production of *King John* at The Other Place in 1988 and the following year in
the Pit Theatre at the Barbican. Earlier Shakespeare roles for the RSC had
been the Dauphin in *Henry V* in 1984–85 and, in 1986–87, Malcolm in
*Macbeth* and Puck in *A Midsummer Night's Dream*; for other companies he
had appeared as Benvolio in *Romeo and Juliet* and Lucentio in *The Taming
of the Shrew*. Other roles had included Givola in *Arturo Ui* for Bristol Old
Vic, Alceste in *The Misanthrope* and Straker in *Man and Superman* in the
USA, and (for the RSC) Bouller/Eichmann in *Good*, Adrian Woolf in *The
Desert Air*, Joe Shawcross in *The Party*, and Frapper in *Red Noses*. More
recently he has appeared in the West End in *The Homecoming*, directed by
Sir Peter Hall, in *The Art of Success* in New York, at the Royal Court in
*Berlin Bertie*, and at the National in *At Our Table*. A wide range of
television work includes *The Hound of the Baskervilles*, *My Kingdom for a
Horse*, and *Blackeyes*.

*King John* and The Other Place were, in retrospect made for each other.
There are two qualities which The Other Place* has in common with the
Elizabethan theatre, qualities which were poignantly illustrated in the
partially excavated remains of the Rose Theatre in Southwark. The first is
intimacy: the plan uncovered resembled nothing so much as a large 'pub'.
Inside, a lot of human beings packed tightly, standing in the pit which
sloped gently towards a stage on a level with the groundlings' eyes, or in
galleries looking down on to the action, watched dramas performed with
apparently minimal sets and props. As an architectural wonder, the building itself probably compared pretty poorly with Hampton Court, let alone

---

* Nicholas Woodeson's essay refers throughout to the original Other Place in Stratford-upon-
  Avon, formerly a storage hut, and converted into a studio theatre in the early 1970s. It was
  demolished in 1990 because of fire regulations. A new, purpose-built studio theatre, of similar
  dimensions and ambience, opened at the same site, and with the same name, in 1991 (*Editors*).

Epidaurus. It was altered at one stage to accommodate an expansion of business, the structure of brick and timber and what-have-you 'stretched', as it were. Outside in the streets were open sewers; inside, the stench must have been unimaginable to an audience today at, say, The Other Place. Elizabethan England was backward, crude by comparison with the rest of Europe. Yet on the stage was being forged a new language, of enormous power and sophistication, embracing the sacred and the secular, the sophisticated and the primitive. This is the second quality: in this rather democratic institution in an otherwise undemocratic political system, citizens from all walks of life attended dramas in which refinement of sensibility and sensitivity are juxtaposed with crudity. Free of the massive production techniques of later theatre, yet able to call upon simple and telling effects, this theatre is free to 'get on with the play': simple materials, profound ideas.

'The most creative tin hut in theatrical history', as Michael Billington once described The Other Place, began its career as a public theatre in the early seventies. One of its inspirational originators, Buzz Goodbody, directed a version of *King John* for the RSC's Theatregoround, itself started by Terry Hands, until recently the Company's Artistic Director. This version was a combination of Shakespeare's script and another play, *The Troublesome Reign of King John*. 'Scholars disagree', as they say, about which play was written first. This Theatregoround production ended up unhappily on the main stage at Stratford, for which it was not originally designed. Deborah Warner's 1988 production used Shakespeare's text only, complete and uncut, and gave it a very congenial home in The Other Place. The design, style and content of the show developed in response to the theatre space as well as to the script, so it really became 'King-John-At-The-Other-Place'.

Between us (that is Deborah, Sue Blane the designer, and the actors) we tried to give the script a visual and stylistic context, a 'home'. *King John* is as much a play about contemporary Elizabethan society as a story of the medieval king. It's packed with anachronisms and contemporary references, and it uses, not history, but what the audience understood to be the history of the time. Shakespeare's English histories have about the same relationship to historical fact as do Hollywood movies; the past is fodder for the present. A production today has to incorporate these two pasts – the subject's and the writer's – into the present. So, the notion that a history play be presented in 'period' costume begs a question – which period? The Other Place is without the technical and scenic resources of the main stage

88

NICHOLAS WOODESON: *King John*

in Stratford, so it gave us a chance to do the play by taking a similar attitude to costumes and props as the script takes to history. Its setting is the earliest of all Shakespeare's English History Plays, separated from the great cycle between the two 'Richards'. The play itself begins with England as a 'possession' among many and ends with 'England' the state. By contrast with *Richard II*, it begins bluntly, and, unlike Richard, who imagines he can abdicate and who is murdered for this error, John knows that he cannot resign; kings die on the job. The syntax of the text is both elaborate and unwieldly, as though of an age still forming itself. Sue's design, those ladders, the greatcoats, the anachronisms of dress, were also a response to this problem of 'period' as much as to The Other Place.

For me, it's the director's job to tell the audience what kind of world they're watching, to show them that it resembles their own. Our society today still shares certain common cultural assumptions, but the meaning of concepts like 'beautiful', 'ugly', 'good taste', 'noble', 'base', 'right', 'wrong' and so on, how they are appropriately manifested and displayed, is not sure. The director has to decide how these concepts are presented in the production. This isn't to burden the script with a 'concept', but to search for the meaning of the script, the author's intentions and their implications for us. For example, do lovers kiss or do they maintain a distance? Do kings wear pageant costumes, or working clothes, or both? And so on. Get this world clear and the actor is free to live in it. I can see no way that this role can really be dispensed with, but it's an artistic role, not an economic one. The debate about the proper value of directors, actors, writers, designers, technicians and so on, will run and run. It's not really a debate, but a power-struggle, in which to be articulate is to be well-armed – an appropriate enough starting-point for a role in a play about a power-struggle which begins as a debate.

Not that John seemed articulate when I first read the play, however. I didn't know it at all and tried just to let my impressions be formed by the script. I didn't read up on past performances, not initially anyway. Perhaps it would have been better if I had. I might have saved some time and taken some short cuts. John seemed opaque, silent in situations which cried out for vengeance, a crude villain with an inconvenient guilty conscience, a sort of second-rate Macbeth or Richard III. He seemed to lack self-promotion, the textual resources to reveal himself to the audience. Most damagingly, he had no soliloquies. How could the audience feel inclined to participate in his story? He was alone for only two brief moments and what he had to say there hardly qualified as passages of blazing eloquence. 'My mother

14   Nicholas Woodeson as King John

dead' is all he says on the first occasion, in Act Four, Scene Two. The preceding action has shown him on the receiving end of unrelenting bad news. Sixty lines earlier he had been told of his mother's death. This phrase is all he utters in his moment of solitude. The next action is the entrance of Hubert, with more bad news, and his mother's death is never mentioned again.

Looking for a way into the character, I found myself starting at this sequence in the script. It dawned on me that Hubert's entrance was interruptive, and that what was occurring was displacement. The ensuing tirade against Hubert is fully understandable and realizable in its own terms; you don't have to search for 'subtext'. But the impression was of a man given no time to grieve; experiencing loss, sorrow, regret, loneliness, but unable to express them. What is unspoken is expressed indirectly, or remains unexpressed, therefore dangerously unresolved. Perhaps this wasn't an isolated incident but a clue to how he functioned.

Actors work differently, sometimes never varying their approach and sometimes altering it role by role. Some have such physical confidence, such an enjoyment of their own presence, that they work best 'being themselves', allowing the part to come to them. Some have to find a 'character' or a physical characteristic, a voice, a walk, as a way to the role. I've certainly done that often enough. Mostly I think I need a sense of context, of the world of the play and of 'who he is', emotionally. Ralph Richardson's description of acting as a 'controlled dream' is the best I know. It's a strange and probably self-deluding paradox to use one's self and then pretend to be someone else, but I'm usually immediately bored when I try to 'be myself' at the start of rehearsals. I try to use the script and myself to 'dream up' other people, not have an audience pay good money to watch me 'dream up' myself.

With John, there were countless possible physical characterizations, but none of them would really seem any more justified than the other, I felt, if they weren't inescapably suggested by elements in the script. I wasn't interested in 'demystifying' Shakespeare's kings but in discovering the inside of this one, how he was different from the others. If I could sense a little of how he functioned, how he felt, then that emotional cast of mind would create its own appropriate physical characterization.

So what does his mother mean to him? Significantly, all the female characters 'disappear' at the midpoint in the action. Without them, the masculine world is rigid, the 'iron age' Arthur refers to, like pig-iron, strong but liable to snap. Not one character in the second half of the drama gains his objective. Blunder and bungle become the order of the day. His mother is his imagination, not just a crucial psychological influence. John has a son, but no wife, just a mother. To me, this implied a failed marriage, perhaps, hinted at a man unable to make emotional connections, an isolate, with an estranged wife no match for the power of the Queen Mother. She makes the imaginative decisions for him, persuading the Bastard to give up his title and join the court, thus gaining an ally and losing a potential adversary in the younger Faulconbridge. She sees the advantage in Blanche marrying the Dauphin, how it will secure him politically. And she forms his political and personal philosophy: 'Our strong possession and our right for us' (I.i.39), he says, invoking equally might *and* right. She retorts: 'Your strong possession much more than your right', impressing upon him that possession is nine-tenths of the law. She's not saying he has no right; only that right is a long way second to might.

At some stage, I did some historical research. What kind of man was the real John? How did he dovetail with Shakespeare's? The younger son of a large, talented and violent family, nicknamed 'Lackland' by his own father because there were no lands left over to give John as an inheritance, a volatile and foolish young man who learned through humiliating experience to become a resourceful soldier and conscientious ruler. He fluctuated between periods of great energy and decision, and total vacillation and insecurity. He was the last king to combine successfully all the functions of government, legislative, executive and judicial, in his own person – hence his correct judgement on the case of the Bastard Faulconbridge's claim to the lands of his legal father. He travelled endlessly, a nomad throughout his own territories, in war and peace. Eleanor of Aquitaine, his mother, was a uniquely talented woman who bore John late in life. Geoffrey, his older brother, and father of Arthur, was an untrustworthy and charming politician; Richard, the next brother in age to him, was a brilliant and feared soldier who left a near-bankrupt kingdom to John. Father, sons, all of them, had a violent temper.

> JOHN: France, I am burned up with inflaming wrath –
> A rage whose heat hath this condition,
> That nothing can allay, nothing but blood,
> The blood, and dearest-valued blood, of France.
> PHILIP: Thy rage shall burn thee up, and thou shalt turn
> To ashes, ere our blood shall quench that fire.
> Look to thyself, thou art in jeopardy! (III.i.340–6)

This last line, inflected strictly, reads 'Look *to* thy*self*, thou *art* in jeopardy', the implication being, not just 'watch it', but 'look into yourself; you're in great danger from your own self'.

The interchange between John and Philip comes at a crucial moment, after Pandulph has excommunicated John, virtually condemned him to death, and Philip has repudiated his alliance with John. The ensuing fighting is violent, uncontrolled. In the text, 'heat' and 'wrath' intertwine, and the play has this sensation running through it of heat, as rage, fear, fever, conscience, death. What is remarkable is that this historical bio-graphical element, the predisposition to 'wrath', is the predominant factor in John's psychology; it's cited again and again, but axiomatically. It's never overtly spelled out, as, 'John-has-a-very-bad-temper-which-he-inherited-from-his-father'; it's simply a given. Increasingly I felt the clues to his personality really were there, in the script, and intentionally so, on the writer's part, and that I wasn't simply putting together a convenient, plausible characterization.

In retrospect, I approached the role of John through this image and its development as part of a sort of 'emotional blueprint' in the text, an associative pattern of key words – 'possession', 'usurper', 'wrath', 'eye', 'body', 'hot', 'crown', 'kingdom', and so on. There are two central meta-phors: the body-politic, the king's identity, is his kingdom, his possessions, and vice versa, 'l'état, c'est moi'; and the humours that dominate the body, in John's case the choleric, a predisposition to hot, ungovernable rage. A browse through Roget's Thesaurus several months after we'd opened showed me that these words key with the relationship between personal identity, the exercise of the will, religion and morality. The action of the drama moves from an external, foreign, military, political, ideological struggle, which is successfully negotiated by John, to an internal, domestic, civil, personal, physical and moral turmoil, which destroys him. The structure of the language, the verse, is formal, almost pedantically so, in the first part of the play and then breaks down, as though under irresistible pressure, into fragments of action-dialogue, personal revelation, in which there are still passages of formality; reason and order fighting against emotion and chaos. Through the external physical drama, an internal psychological struggle is revealed.

Consider, for example, the leitmotif of 'eye' in the play – though its first appearance in the script is not in the text itelf. There's a painting by Holbein, *The Ambassadors*, which has as its most unusual and famous feature a long obscure smudge in the bottom foreground. If the painting is tilted, translated and rotated to the appropriate angle, there is revealed to our point of view the unmistakable image of a skull. From John's point of view, and I mean literally from his point of view, two extraordinary sights appear in the first two scenes. About fifty lines into the play, two men come on stage. One of them, looking right back at him, is the spitting image of his older brother, Richard I, as a young man. We know he is because we're subsequently told he is:

> Mine eye hath well examinèd his parts
> And finds them perfect Richard. (1.i.80–90)

In the second scene, Philip of France pushes forward a young boy into John's eyeline. He, looking right back at John, is the spitting image of Geoffrey, another older brother, as a young boy. We know he is because we're told so:

> Look here upon thy brother Geoffrey's face.
> These eyes, these brows, were moulded out of his;
> This little abstract doth contain that large
> Which died in Geoffrey; and the hand of time
> Shall draw this brief into as large a volume. (II.i.99–103)

We staged this moment to point up the visual shock, Arthur pushed to centre stage, the sight of the boy, the uncanny resemblance pressing John back, rendering him speechless, the initiative passing to Philip.

It's from these two visual connections that the imagery of 'eye' springs in the text. For me, it raises some wonderful questions. What does John feel about his brothers? What *did* he feel about them then, at the ages that the Bastard Faulconbridge in Scene One and Arthur in Scene Two are now? In the first instance John was the same age as the young Faulconbridge, so cheerfully bullied in front of John, and I felt that John must see his brother Geoffrey as a boy, looking back at him out of Arthur's face, and remember himself as a child.

Incidentally, the Bastard's sense of identity and John's are direct opposites. 'I am I, howe'er I was begot' (1.i.175) is Faulconbridge's credo. John's sense of identity is determined by what he possesses. The illegitimate son of Richard I is the legitimate heir to Faulconbridge's lands. The text in this first scene crackles with 'brother', 'mother', 'father', and surely the clues are there to what John is, how he sees himself. John and the Bastard slowly change places in the drama. Subsequently the Bastard becomes his uncle's 'uncle', becoming his protector, his conscience, his support as he matures, and John, bereft of his 'possessions', dispossessed of self-possession, crumbles.

'Heart', 'eye' and the body and its parts all come together in John's two scenes with Hubert. Until relatively late in rehearsals, I played both these scenes with a strong element of calculation. They seemed plausible enough this way, but flat. The emotional identification I had initially made with 'my mother dead', for example, was missing. I think it was bound to be so long as I 'played' calculation. Without an emotional identification, without playing the part from the character's point of view, literally and metaphorically, it borders on satire; one's emotional identification is not *with* the character, but rather with the character's enemies. This emotional identification is not the same as 'playing for sympathy', which is playing for calculatedly sentimental effect. Take, for example, a character not from Shakespeare at all, like Stephen Sondheim's Sweeney Todd. Play for sympathy and he collapses into a wet noodle of self-pity. Play with emotional identification, from the character's point of view, and you have a figure out of revenge tragedy, sad and terrifying.

I stumbled on a review of Kean as King John which spoke of him as being particularly good in the scenes with Hubert and I realized I was way off. I tried playing the first scene with Hubert (III.iii.19ff.) as though there was no calculated plan to kill Arthur, and tried to let the speech unfold – and it was a revelation. Not of my acting, I hasten to add, but of the astonishing subtlety of Shakespeare's writing. Suddenly, after about an hour to an hour and a half of playing time, in which this character's intention seemed always to *hide* his feelings, during which he has been subjected to visual scrutiny, psychological and visual shocks, vilification, excommunication, a sentence of death, the near-loss of his mother, there flows out the most eloquent speech of child-like yearning, for friendship, connection, and illicit and murderous desire.

Deborah staged an incident with Arthur which helped illustrate the emotional stakes. Arthur alone with John's men around him, face to face with John, bemoans his fate: 'O, this will make my mother die with grief!' (III.iii.5). Deborah had me try to jolly Arthur out of his depression, trying to be reassuring, tickling him – with genuinely good intentions but clumsily, awkwardly. Arthur, frustrated, takes John's hand and bites it, hard. John, stunned, strikes the boy down before he realizes what he's doing. Arthur isn't hurt, but everyone is shocked. John's subsequent lines to the Bastard are coloured with rage and embarrassment, as he instructs him to fleece the church, as though Pandulph were personally responsible for his present humiliation. As the Bastard leaves and Eleanor goes to comfort the boy, John finds himself alone and calls out to Hubert: 'Come

15 King John with Hubert (Robert Demeger): 'Death ... My lord ... a grave ...' (III.ii.66)

hither, Hubert.' The ensuing passage between the two of us started on stage level and ended on the upper gallery. I couldn't get away from the sight of Arthur's eyes looking back at me, as I got to

> Or if that thou couldst see me without eyes,
> Hear me without thine ears ...                    (line 49)

And it's no coincidence that the attempt to murder Arthur centres on blinding him, taking away the windows of the soul, the sources of accusation:

> The light of the body is the eye; if therefore thine eye be single, the whole body shall be full of light. But if thine eye be evil, thy whole body shall be full of darkness.
> (Matthew, 7:22)

John's case exactly. Pandulph's *fatwa*, his excommunication and sentence of death, function like a mental and moral assassination. The father-figure punishes the son in religious, psychological, literal terms. Cast out as a sinner, John commits sin. The second part of the trial, the criminal one, begins here.

As I worked on the language, not just on digging up the psychology, but actually speaking it, I tried strictly to observe the five stresses to a line of the rhythm, as

> Or *if* that *thou* couldst *see* me *with*out *eyes*.

The stressed '*if*' and '*thou*' are obviously evocative sounds and their emphasis reveals the meaning of the thought and intention, but even a nod in the direction of stressing the '*with*' of 'without' releases the breath to give 'eyes' a fuller sound than if you stressed thus: '*see* me with*out eyes*'.

In the second scene with Hubert, the yearning of the first scene is matched by remorse, self-disgust, a sort of moral backsliding, like Adam's in the Garden of Eden: 'I wouldn't have done it if it hadn't been for you, therefore it's really your fault.' From this point the imagery of the body takes over:

> Nay, in the body of this fleshly land,
> This *king*dom, *this* con*fine* of *blood* and *breath*,
> Hostility and civil tumult reigns
> Between my conscience and my cousin's death. (IV.ii.245–8)

Again, the stress points to the meaning: 'This kingdom *here*, my body.'

At other moments, too, the correct stress revealed an unexpected meaning: 'There *is* no sure foundation set on blood' (IV.ii.104), at the moment when his nobles walk out on him. It's as though in reply to someone – his mother: 'The only sure foundation for power is set on blood, my son'; 'No, it *isn't*.' A few lines later, he'll discover she's dead.

We tend to redistribute the stresses, in the manner of the sprung rhythm of Gerard Manley Hopkins, and miss out. The great strength of English, that it can stress percussively, like Anglo-Saxon, or through length of vowel, like Latin, means we can just about always observe the five even stresses in a line without its seeming odd. The ideal today, I think, is that observed strictly as verse, the verse needs to be *phrased* conversationally, sounding as though it's being made up.

At the end, John's language is unexpectedly poetic. I tried to play these lines at first as though all energy had gone, all passion spent, and the botulism really was in the final stages of paralysing the breath. It didn't work; it couldn't be heard. I managed eventually to work it out that the will-power, the outer aggression, has let go, and the inner man, a little child-like, is released in the wonderful invocation to the natural elements of his kingdom, the rivers, woods, the icy water, to come and soothe the agony of his body, the image of the body-politic transformed:

And none of you will bid the winter come
To thrust his icy fingers in my maw,
Nor let my kingdom's rivers take their course
Through my burned bosom, nor entreat the north
To make his bleak winds kiss my parchèd lips
And comfort me with cold.                                    (v.vii.36–41)

Nobody who really believed he had no right to wear the crown would talk about his kingdom like this, would he?

John emerged in my conception as a sort of adult-child, something of the personality found in the children of violent or alcoholic parents, irresponsible and over-responsible at the same time, not entirely certain what constitutes normal behaviour. He became physically sloppy, his shoulders hunched permanently, as if expecting attack; he took his status absolutely for granted, like a tin-pot tsar, not concerned about 'looking regal'. At the same time he cared for the law as he understood it and cared for his own, his mother, his nephew, his possessions as he had been taught by his parents and by the example of his brothers. In the siege before Angiers, he carried his crown on a chain attached to a belt around his waist, the image of the nomadic monarch coinciding with the inner feeling of insecurity.

I became increasingly relieved that *King John* was being performed in The Other Place. The main rule of thumb is that the action is carried by the speaker, and the main stage's size and technical challenge often stress this textual emphasis to the exclusion of any contextual awareness. In the studio space I felt that the whole script, the situation, the place, the action, the entrances and exits of characters, the listeners, the relationships between people, and not just the text and the speaker, had a stronger chance of being realized. It could have been a production based on the 'close-up' intimacy of the Rose.

# Henry VI

## RALPH FIENNES

RALPH FIENNES played Henry VI in Adrian Noble's production of the adaptation of the three parts of *Henry VI*, with *Richard III*, titled *The Plantagenets*, at the Royal Shakespeare Theatre in 1988 and at the Barbican the following year. In the same season, his first with the RSC, he played Claudio in *Much Ado About Nothing* and the Dauphin in *King John*, and added to these at the Barbican Bert Jefferson in *The Man Who Came to Dinner* and Gant in *Playing with Trains*. Earlier Shakespeare roles were Lysander in *A Midsummer Night's Dream* and Romeo for the Regent's Park Open Air Theatre, and Theseus/Oberon in *A Midsummer Night's Dream* for the New Shakespeare Company's European Tour. Other theatre work has included the son in *Six Characters in Search of an Author*, Arkady in *Fathers and Sons*, and Lisha Ball in *Ting Tang Mine*, all at the National Theatre. In the 1990–91 Stratford and Barbican seasons he returned to the RSC to play Troilus, Berowne in *Love's Labour's Lost*, and Edmund in *King Lear*. Recent film roles have been as Heathcliff in *Wuthering Heights* and T. E. Lawrence in *A Dangerous Man: Lawrence after Arabia*.

What did I think when I was first offered the part of Henry VI? I was, of course, very excited. I didn't know the plays well and I didn't really know the part itself at all. I had only ever seen it on television when the BBC did the full cycle; I had enjoyed the *Henry VI* plays possibly more than any of the rest, mainly because of the directness and simplicity of the presentation. So my impression of Henry was mainly of Peter Benson's performance – a gentle, thin, stooped figure with his 'molehill' speech particularly memorable. My main recollection of the part was of this pathetic figure, lovable but frustrating because, although he was clearly a good man, he was completely unable to control the forces of ambition and dissent around him. I remembered it as a beautiful performance and a very vivid one.

I met Adrian Noble and auditioned for the part of Henry VI and soon after found myself coming to Stratford to play Henry, Claudio in *Much*

*Ado About Nothing*, and the Dauphin in *King John*. I read the *Henry VI* trilogy and was thrilled by what I read – but also slightly disappointed because I knew that what I was going to be part of would be an edited version of the trilogy, in which a third of the plays would have to go. Adrian wished to do *Richard III* as well and he wanted it to be possible to perform the complete drama, from *Henry VI, Part 1* to the end of *Richard III* in one day. So the three *Henry VI* plays had to be edited to make two plays with *Richard III* to complete the trilogy. This was exactly the arrangement Peter Hall and John Barton had created in 1963 for their hugely successful *Wars of the Roses*.

I knew when I read these three wonderful plays, and received the first images and thoughts about Henry, that I would have to lose about a third of the part, but I had to wait from December to May before rehearsals started. By that time the company knew each other quite well, and we knew that our version of these plays was going to be adapted by Charles Wood, whose work I was not terribly familiar with. I had seen *Tumbledown*, a controversial television film about the Falklands, which was very good indeed, but unfortunately I thought (as did many of the actors) that his adaptation of the *Henry VI* trilogy was disappointing, not because the ideas for staging it were not good, but because the wonderfully rich, strong and sophisticated writing of the young Shakespeare had been cut and slashed about and rearranged to such an extent that when you read the lines of the characters aloud, without the conceptualized stage directions, you didn't understand what was going on. There were many good ideas for staging the plays, but, frankly, I feel that such ideas come better from the actors. Even if they fail to find something original and exciting, what they do find will at least belong to them, with the result that they will properly inhabit it knowing it to be theirs. I think Adrian Noble saw the problem at once, so the first part of the rehearsals became a process of realigning the script, of putting lines back in, with Adrian himself taking over the editing of the plays. We ended, therefore, with a shortened version of the *Henry VI* trilogy which, by and large, was acceptable to everyone. This process, although it was very frustrating, was also enriching because Adrian was extremely good at using what the actors had to offer and there were many good discussions about what the scenes meant and about what lines should be restored and why. This was often a strain because you always wanted more lines than you were allowed, but once you had swallowed the pill, as it were, good things started to happen and rehearsals became rather inspiring.

Our production of *The Plantagenets*, then, offered a condensed version of the *Henry VI* trilogy in two plays which we called *Henry VI* and *The Rise of Edward IV*, followed by *Richard III*. There are clearly advantages to be gained from cutting the text so that the narrative is sharpened: extraneous and superfluous episodes are removed, characters streamlined, and everything is generally made 'easier to understand' and 'more accessible'. The story then races along with the certainty of a well-aimed arrow and there is no time left for the audience to disengage and moan about who is Richard Neville and who is the Earl of Warwick. The project required three three-hour plays and one simply had to accept the constraints that this imposed. But I suppose I never did quite get over my first excited memories of reading *Henry VI* in its entirety. The enormity and scope of Shakespeare's perception of the condition of England had been quite staggering. In the full texts the spectator is taken from England to France and back again; witnesses the angry political dissension between Duke Humphrey and the Bishop of Winchester; watches the manic patriotic waging of warfare in which the minutiae of personal relationships between different soldiers are established and the scope of their opinions is carefully drawn; sees the King's coronation in France; the attempts of the Duchess of Auvergne to capture Lord Talbot; the impressive rhetoric with which Suffolk persuades Henry VI that Margaret of Anjou is by far the best choice of woman to be his Queen. There is vast breadth and detail in the *Henry VI* plays which I believe is intrinsic to their real identity. In giving them a more tightly knit, coherent, and 'complete' structure something of their nature is inevitably lost. Many of the works with which Shakespeare would have been acquainted – the Bible, Malory's *Morte d'Arthur*, Boccaccio's *Decameron* – have a digressive structure, a narrative that can go where it wants. The writers of these works do not concern themselves with a taut, well-woven, well-balanced narrative; they compose their stories from many and various events; they bring in different characters and with them create new, surprising situations, not always directly concerned with the main story they are apparently telling. Many episodes within the 'greater narrative' have an instructive or allegorical value. The parables of Christ's teaching take on a life of their own whilst at the time being part of the Gospel story. In the *Morte d'Arthur*, Malory embellishes Arthur's personal story with many separate tales involving the different knights of the Round Table; courage, faith, and 'gentilesse' are important qualities guiding the narrative. The *Henry VI* trilogy is, by comparison, an extremely direct piece of story-telling: the central focus is always the

English crown. Yet there are moments when the narrative shifts the focus firmly onto the people of England in scenes and episodes that seem extraneous, but which are in fact instrumental in guiding our perception of the play's story. The Jack Cade scenes are brilliant in this respect. They parody the ghastly political intrigues of the English court in the form of Cade's crude, aggressive, but dangerously intuitive despotism and expose the mercenary, opportunist, and ambitious attitudes of both sides. Constantly, throughout the three parts of *Henry VI* and *Richard III*, Shakespeare gives the ordinary people a voice, a voice that seems always to be clamouring for justice from the King. It is either exploited, or stifled, never properly heeded. If full measure is not given to the many scenes involving the citizens of England the balance of the plays may be damaged. We must hear the voice of ordinary people whenever the writer intends us to in order to understand the context and landscape in which Gloucester, Suffolk, York, Winchester, Warwick, Clifford, Margaret, Buckingham, Exeter and Henry are living. Our production obviously created a vigorous narrative, but I am not sure whether the drastic abbreviation that practical circumstances forced on us was quite able to preserve the sense of panorama, the vision of the whole, inherent in the rich detail, the dozens of small parts, and small scenes, of the full text.

Half way through the rehearsal period, and after all the discussion of the text and of the cutting and reinstating of lines, Bob Crowley showed us the design, which was stunning. The company was thrilled by what Bob had created because it had been conceived from what the actors were doing in the rehearsal room. From the early mood of the rehearsals, which was one of frustration and a sense of being in something which didn't have any coherent shape, we found that the plays were attaining a sense of identity and with it the confidence of the company grew. By the time of the first previews, we were obviously anxious to know how the work would be received. I think initial reactions were mixed. It was not until we saw the plays in sequence that we really knew what shape and form the narrative had. It is a peculiar thing being in a play at its first performances: you are continually trying to sense what the audience is actually receiving. Slowly you realize more clearly what it is you are trying to do and with that develop the antennae to gauge (and, slowly, to manipulate) the audience's responses.

*Henry VI* seems to me a wonderful creation. No major character exists in a vacuum, but is defined by the people around him. Henry is unique in the way he acts and thinks, for there is virtually no one else in the plays advocating non-violence and compassion. The trilogy is peopled with representatives of the nobility: Warwick, York, Gloucester, the Bishop of Winchester, Suffolk, Exeter. Beneath them are the people of England – Jack Cade's mob, the servants of Gloucester and Winchester, the soldiers who make up Talbot's army. Constantly through the plays the people of England and of London emerge, giving the trilogy a broad social context. The main protagonists are the nobles and, of course, the Kings. The three Kings of the sequence are very strongly contrasted. Henry is different because he has inherited a kingdom that has achieved glory and power through the conquests and military victories of his father. There is a feeling of huge loss at the beginning of the sequence: one is aware that here is a young king who has inherited an empire and who is expected to follow in the footsteps of his father – an awesome act to follow. His father died when he was nine months old and he has been primed and trained for kingship ever since. The first time Henry opens his mouth one knows that something has already gone wrong: he is surrounded by dissent, by the opposing factions of Gloucester and Winchester (who are quickly to be superseded by the parties of York and Lancaster). He asks his uncle, Humphrey, Duke of Gloucester and great-uncle, the Bishop of Winchester, to 'join your hearts in love and amity' (*Part One*, III.i.68). Immediately, one is uncertain where to place him. What I became acutely aware of was the individuality of Henry.

Most characters share a common view of kingship: the king is to rule firmly, from a strong secular base; the spirituality of the king comes second to his material well-being, and his need to sustain military power, financial power, economic power. It is easy to forget that our perception of the king as a political leader overshadows our perception of him as a spiritual leader, that in Shakespeare's time the monarch would have been thought of very significantly as a spiritual leader, following the settlement of 1559, when Elizabeth was firmly instituted as supreme head of the Church of England. And the preceding Catholic kings would certainly have been seen as spiritual leaders, too. What I am trying to say is that here is a young king speaking for the first time with his highly individual voice and asking for clemency and understanding, and love between people. The tone of what he says is heightened by the strongly political and secular nature of the people around him, but there is nothing in what he says that is in any way contradictory to what a king should be about. On the contrary, there is in fact perfect harmony between what he aims to do and the position he is in: he is the anointed Deputy of God on earth.

In approaching and rehearsing the part of Henry, I knew with some certainty that I didn't want him to appear as a weak, dithering fool. There were clearly moments of weakness, of panic and indecision, but I felt that his commitment to what he believed, to his Christian faith, was deep and passionate, and that his whole dilemma was that he could not find a way to assert his rule through purely Christian values. The area an actor has to tackle in playing the role of Henry VI is *faith*. One simply cannot take on the part unless one tries to take on board his Christianity. I don't mean that the actor has to be religious – but he does have to absorb the importance of Henry's beliefs. I do not believe Henry is a blinkered, pious weakling: if I had judged him like that I could not have played him. He may appear to be sinking in his own piety, but from *his* point of view he is seeking to find a way of ruling England, as the anointed Deputy of God, through a firm commitment to Christian values and Christian morality. At times this approach leads Henry into vengeful, 'Old Testament' actions; at others he follows an approach of forgiveness, tolerance, and pacifism.

Henry constantly makes us conscious of his own continuous awareness of the Almighty. He talks to God frequently and speaks to people as if he is in God's presence, as if he knows that God is watching him, guiding him, and supporting him. I cannot be specific about what Shakespeare might be implying about the precise doctrinal nature of Henry's religion. We know through the machinations of Cardinal Beaufort that the Pope is somewhere in the background, but Henry never refers to the Pope, though nothing he says about his own faith suggests that Shakespeare meant the England of Henry VI to be anything other than firmly Catholic (as, of course, it was historically). Certainly I felt there was no need to complicate the narrative by questioning the validity of Henry's beliefs and it is clear, I think, that his faith transcends differences of dogma and doctrine. He is truly Christian, placing himself at God's disposal, aware of his weaknesses and failings, continually seeking a chance to heal and bring together the dissenting parties of York and Lancaster. His belief that he *can* do this is total – he recognizes his failures and the destruction his reign has caused, but he never loses hope.

In attempting to realize the nature of Henry VI, I was desperate that his faith should not seem too ethereal. His religion and his commitment to it, I felt, had to be a hard, concrete reality. The words he speaks just after the death of Winchester – 'Let us all to meditation' – had to mean a firm command to focus mind, body, and spirit on the benevolence and eternal forgiveness and love of God as a means towards reconciliation and under-

16   Ralph Fiennes as Henry VI with Queen Margaret (Pennie Downie) at
the end of *Henry VI* (the first part of *The Plantagenets*)

standing between himself and Margaret. Sometimes in performance these words got a nervous, almost cynical, laugh from the audience which I felt indicated that I had failed to make Henry's faith believable. That may be over-anxious, and it may seem that I am dwelling too much on Henry's religious beliefs, but I believe strongly that Shakespeare meant them to be central to his character.

All this, however, does not mean that Henry is a saint. Where Shakespeare's genius makes itself so apparent is in the very weakness and fallibility of Henry. He is altogether human: he is not physically brave; he changes his mind; he rashly decides to marry Margaret against the advice of Humphrey Duke of Gloucester; he does not intervene to save Gloucester during his impeachment; he agrees to 'entail' the crown to York and his heirs, thus disinheriting his only son. If one were to judge Henry VI (Shakespeare's Henry VI) on his political astuteness, foresight, and courage he would come off very poorly. But as the actor playing Henry, the person trying to get under his skin, it seemed to me that his intentions were utterly honourable. In fact at its simplest, one could say that Henry sincerely tries to rule through Christ's teaching of love, forgiveness, and understanding. Being human he fails and deludes himself. He thinks because he has tried to conduct his reign on principles of pity, mercy, and mildness, that he has deserved complete and wholehearted support. I felt throughout that one of the main challenges of acting the part was to try to make Henry immediate, to root his beliefs as much as possible in the present, to make him human.

Different people have different reactions to the figure they see on stage. Some simply label him 'wimpish' and wonder why he lacks the guts to stand up for himself, to tell York and Suffolk where to get off. Others regard him as being well ahead of his time: 'If only they would all listen to him, he's the only one speaking any sense.' It is good that reactions to Henry are so diverse. Shakespeare is always showing us a variety of facets of his characters; we are made aware of their ideals, their dreams, their fears, their loves, their selfishness, their generosity. In this respect the so-called 'early histories' are no exception. I read some critical appraisal of the *Henry VI* trilogy whilst rehearsing the part and came across many claims that Shakespeare's characters in these plays are 'undeveloped', lacking the 'complexity' of his later work. I could not disagree more. In fact I would argue that the characters of *Henry VI* are frequently almost too complex for the simple chronicle narrative that contains them. It is almost as if the young Shakespeare had decided on the story he wanted to tell, but then found he was creating characters whose complexity could not be contained within the plan he had outlined for them. Indeed, nearly all of Shakespeare's characters have a rather Pirandellian life of their own outside their respective plays. Certainly when I'm rehearsing, my imagination has to embrace the character's life outside the play. What was Henry's childhood like? The routine of his daily life? And, particularly in Henry's case, what about his *inner* life? What is he thinking and what is he observing, or, rather, what does he think about what he observes?

Henry seemed to me, then, to be a highly perceptive person. He watches and listens a great deal, always anxious to hear both sides of the argument. I felt that from Henry's point of view the ambition and resentment surrounding him were more akin to the behaviour of aggressive children. His perception of life – of earthly life and spiritual life – is, I believe, more profound than theirs. He senses that he can't enforce a strong tyrannous or authoritarian regime without in some way causing more suffering. If a king decides to live by Christ's teaching (or the teaching of any great spiritual leader) he cannot follow a path of understanding, forgiveness, and love. Henry knows that his life on earth is transitory; he sees events and people from this point of view, and it makes him an appalling political leader. As soon as he perceives York's ambition, or even Margaret's infidelity, in the context of God's omnipotence, God's will, and God's love, then their political importance and urgency is lessened, enormously. The chief problem with Henry is that he is totally *human* and there are moments when it is appalling for him to recognize that he has entailed his crown to York and disinherited his only son Edward. Constantly, I sensed while rehearsing the part that Henry is truly tragic because he is trying to follow the path of deep spiritual commitment but is continually brought face to face with his own human fallibility.

In our first play *Henry VI*, events reached their peak with the death of Gloucester and Suffolk's banishment. Henry is unable to stop Gloucester's arrest. He simply does nothing until Gloucester has been removed from the room and then in a speech of bewilderment and grief 'wails' his loss. This moment must be one which any actor playing Henry must question very deeply. Why? Why does Henry do *nothing*? He clearly states his belief in Gloucester's innocence, but yet does nothing to stop his arrest though he certainly has the power to do so. Is he terrified by the violent accusations against Gloucester? Is he physically afraid of the power of York and Suffolk? Does he think they might be right in their accusations? I could only feel that Henry's is the reaction of a man who is distraught with his own lack of experience, lack of equipment, lack of political initiative, of someone who has always had the answers provided for him by Gloucester, and now Gloucester has been taken away from him he has no crutch upon which to lean and so in that crucial moment he can only react emotionally. I think if one were to ask Henry 'Why did you do that? Why did you allow that to happen?' he might answer, 'I don't know; I was so appalled by what I saw happening around me, that I completely lost all sense of my own authority.'

From the arrest of Gloucester and his execution I sensed that there was in Henry a sudden realization of his own rightness, or self-righteousness. He had lost Gloucester, he had allowed something awful to happen, and he therefore suddenly saw things in a clearer light. He saw that Suffolk was a traitor; he saw the way Suffolk was manipulating him; he saw, in fact, the reality of Margaret's behaviour – that she was Suffolk's lover. There is no moment in the text where Henry expresses any knowledge of Margaret's infidelity, but I had a strong sense that he knows, as the play progresses, that he is not satisfying Margaret as a husband – not just physically, but in many other ways too. There is a peculiar vacuum between them which I think Penny Downie (who played Margaret in our production) and I came to understand. At the end of *Henry VI* (the first play in our *Plantagenets* trilogy) I felt that Henry was starkly aware of his position as king and that he was unworthy to inhabit it, but that he could also see very clearly what was happening among those around him. Up until then he had thought they were behaving like misguided children, and that he could persuade them to come to understand and love each other. Then, suddenly, he perceives how dark the situation really is. The play ends with the death of Winchester, failing conspicuously to make any sign of reconciliation with God, and with Margaret's entrance carrying Suffolk's head, grieving his death. At this point Henry is thrown firmly into the arms of his faith as the only thing that will give him strength.

At the beginning of our second play *The Rise of Edward IV* (IV.iv of *2 Henry VI*) Henry is seen to be crucially indecisive, not knowing how to handle the rebellion led by Jack Cade. He says:

> I'll send some holy bishop to entreat;
> For God forbid so many simple souls
> Should perish by the sword! And I myself
> . . .
> Will parley with Jack Cade their general. (IV.iv.9–13)

For a minute he thinks 'I'll go forward and talk to them; instead of fighting Jack Cade I'll negotiate peacefully.' But by the end of the scene he bottles out. He leaves with the Queen for Kenilworth Castle. It is in this scene that Henry and Margaret exchange virtually the only words that reflect their attitude to each other. Henry says:

> How now, madam?
> Still lamenting and mourning for Suffolk's death?
> I fear me, love, if that I had been dead,
> Thou wouldst not have mourned so much for me. (lines 21–4)

She replies:

> No, my love; I should not mourn, but die for thee. (line 25)

Henry has no response to this. I could only think that he is shocked and totally surprised by her answer, probably not clear exactly what she means. I do not think it matters that it is not clear to him. To me it seemed that she is saying 'I'll die for a king; I'll die to keep the blood of Lancaster on the throne.' What she is not saying, clearly, is that she loves him, although Penny Downie and I both decided there was a kind of stillborn love somewhere between them. In a funny way the incompatibility of Henry and Margaret is a continual stimulus to the two actors playing them (though Penny may not altogether agree). Their relationship is an enigma: Shakespeare never develops their attitudes to each other, although one detects Henry's love for her and her resentment and frustration with him. It is a marriage that never grows.

At Kenilworth Henry opens his heart to the audience:

> Was ever king that joyed an earthly throne,
> And could command no more content than I?
> No sooner was I crept out of my cradle
> But I was made a king at nine months old;
> Was never subject longed to be a king
> As I do long and wish to be a subject. (IV.ix.1–6)

Those six lines are an eye-opener into the way Henry is thinking. He knows he is failing. He has been a king since he was a baby and loathes the position. There is here a kind of paradox: here is this man groomed for kingship from the age of nine months and none of it has worked. He cannot govern his kingdom; the Cade rebellion is raging and he has made no real attempt to control it. And yet there is a huge awareness of his own belief in his position. All the time as I played the part I had a sense of the ambiguity of someone who would rather be a priest, who would rather be living in a monastery, but who also *knows* he is the king, who knows he is the son of Henry V, who knows he should be ruling England and at the same time doesn't want to. And even as he knows he should be ruling the country he is also profoundly aware that his dynastic claim is weak.

The most famous and most revealing moment for Henry is the soliloquy he has on the molehill at the Battle of Towton. He imagines himself living the life of a shepherd and how he could order that life peacefully until his death. In essence it is a very simple speech and what Henry is envisaging is itself very simple. It is common to most people that at some point the pressures of life will make them want to find an alternative which is simple, peaceful, and without anxiety. In this case, however, it is the King of England who is sitting on a molehill wishing away his authority and responsibilities. He is not aware when he starts the speech that his imagination will lead him to contemplate the regular, ordered life of a shepherd, minute by minute, hour by hour. So each line is a new thought – or rather a thought developed. It is a very rhythmic speech, regularly stressed, and I think one has to trust the rhythm and let it take you, without being seduced by its lyricism and without losing spontaneity.

There is, indeed, a particularly lyrical quality to Henry and at one point I was told by someone whose advice is gold-dust that I was 'singing' the part and, although I wasn't overjoyed to be told that, I knew he was right and that I had developed a delivery which was, at its worst, the 'sound' of someone speaking poetry. That is obviously a danger with any verse play, particularly when the verse is regular and of a lyrical quality. In later Shakespeare, the verse is much more erratic in the way the sense of the line fits (and at times does not fit) the rhythm, and you have to deal with unexpected emphases on words. In the *Henry VI* plays the sense follows the iambic stress almost without fail.

During the second half of *Edward IV* Henry is on the descent, to his death. He is no longer king, but his perception is greater because of what he has endured. He has lost his kingdom, the respect of his wife, and the respect of his son. He is a wanderer. Two keepers discover him on the borders of England and Scotland and arrest him. This scene shows rather ironically the two sides to Henry's nature: he describes to the keepers how his crown is not a visual one but a metaphorical one, for he wears in his heart the crown of contentment. But once they arrest him, declaring themselves sworn subject to the new King Edward IV, he immediately reminds them that they have sworn allegiance to him and that their oaths of allegiance have been broken. The scene shows once again the ambiguity of Henry, on the one hand a man finding great contentment in having lost his crown, but on the other asserting, the moment he is challenged, his

17 Henry VI in *Edward IV* (the second part of *The Plantagenets*)

belief in himself as king. It is not the wanton assertion of 'I am king and therefore superior to you'; it is the belief that he has been put on this earth by God to lead his people spiritually.

Henry's penultimate scene, which we labelled 'Richmond prophecy', is rich in indicating Henry's complex, albeit naive, attitude to his predicament. Henry has been briefly placed back on the throne; he is really Warwick's puppet and opts out of any responsibility by making Warwick 'Lord Protector'. He has, I think, a very ironic view of what has happened to him (he almost laughs at himself being used as a puppet) and is ambivalent in his gratitude to Warwick for giving him his 'freedom'. Later in the scene they hear that Edward has escaped from Holland and is back in England leading an army against Warwick; Henry, left on his own with the Duke of Exeter, asks him:

> Cousin of Exeter, what thinks your lordship?
> Methinks the power that Edward hath in field
> Should not be able to encounter mine.　(*Part Three*, IV.viii.34–6)

To which Exeter replies: 'The doubt is that he will seduce the rest' and in reply to Exeter's very pessimistic but totally realistic assessment, Henry, apparently surprised, justifies his whole reign, completely perplexed as to why anyone should wish to see him deposed:

> That's not my fear. My meed hath got me fame;
> I have not stopped mine ears to their demands.
> 　　　. . .
> My pity hath been balm to heal their wounds,
> My mildness hath allayed their swelling griefs,
> My mercy dried their water-flowing tears.
> I have not been desirous of their wealth,
> 　　　. . .
> Nor forward of revenge, though they much erred.
> Then why should they love Edward more than me?
> No, Exeter, these graces challenge grace;
> And when the lion fawns upon the lamb,
> The lamb will never cease to follow him.　(lines 38–50)

This speech, is, I believe, a beautiful, sad, hopelessly misconceived, but honest statement of Henry's view of himself. None of the qualities he gives himself (pity, mildness, mercy) have shown themselves to be at all effective in inspiring the allegiance of his people, but Henry cannot see this, or rather will not believe it. He believes that 'when the lion fawns upon the lamb, / The lamb will never cease to follow him.' For him it is as much a matter of faith as of political leadership.

Henry's death in the Tower of London is a wonderfully written scene. It is the meeting of Good and Evil, and has strong archetypal resonances: the Good Angel and the Bad Angel; Cain and Abel; Arthur and Mordred. Anton Lesser, playing Richard, and I agreed that there was a powerful understanding between Henry and Richard, an understanding deriving paradoxically from their utterly opposed sets of values. Because of this they can talk to each other quite easily. There is the possibility of an almost conversational start to the scene which builds into Henry's frightening prophecy and condemnation of Richard. It is as if Henry is taken over by a peculiar power: he knows he is going to die and is given the gift of prophecy which allows him to make a terrible judgement on Richard.

What was wonderful about playing the *Henry VI* trilogy was the nature of the journey the characters make. I think everyone who was in the production had a sense of the hugeness of this journey, from the opening scene over the catafalque of Henry V through to the death of Richard III – a wonderful narrative path to go on. I read a bit about the 'real', the 'historical' Henry VI, and I found some historians' assessments of him to coincide very much with Shakespeare's plays, not so much in terms of dates and accuracy of events, but in essence, as it were. The character they described fitted very much with the character I found myself playing: someone obstinate, certain of their faith, wishing to appease people through granting favours, talking them into loyalty, into peaceful ways of conducting their affairs, but, on finding himself crossed, as Henry is by Suffolk, passionately decisive, however unwise the actual decisions may be.

Actors are often wary of putting into print their emotional response to a part; it is something quite private that manifests itself in rehearsal and performance and is not easily articulated. With Shakespeare especially the actor is party to something essentially profound, which, whatever the production does to the play, almost always comes through in some form to the audience. I felt this particularly strongly being part of *The Plantagenets* and especially in playing Henry VI. Occasionally the actor will realize that he must stop getting in his own way, that he must not attempt to achieve the part for himself, and in so doing he will allow the peculiar power of Shakespeare to speak for itself. That is probably a lifetime's journey, but my own awareness of the *possibilities* of Shakespeare, however unachieved, has grown through the experience of playing Henry VI. Shakespeare seems to make infinite demands on actors. Always a scene or speech yields more than is at first apparent. There is no 'right way'. But the possibilities are endless.

# Queen Margaret in
# Henry VI and Richard III

### PENNY DOWNIE

PENNY DOWNIE played Queen Margaret in Adrian Noble's production of the adaptation of the three parts of *Henry VI*, with *Richard III*, titled *The Plantagenets*, at the Royal Shakespeare Theatre in 1988 and at the Barbican the following year. Earlier Shakespeare roles for the RSC had been Hippolyta/Titania in *A Midsummer Night's Dream* and Lady Capulet in *Romeo and Juliet* on the regional tour in 1983 (Stratford 1984), Lady Anne in *Richard III* (1984–5), Lady Macduff in *Macbeth* and the doubling of Hermione and Perdita in *The Winter's Tale* in 1986–87. Other work for the company has included Peggy Smith in *Today*, Agnes in *Dreamplay*, Anne in *The Castle*, and Sarah Sprackling in *The Art of Success*. A wide range of theatre work in Australia included Elise in *The Miser*, Bianca in *The Taming of the Shrew*, and Rose in *The Shoemaker's Holiday*. More recently she has appeared in *Death and the Maiden* and *Berlin Bertie* at the Royal Court and *Scenes from a Marriage* in the West End. Television work has included appearances in *Inspector Morse*, *Minder*, and *A Taste for Death* and films include *Lionheart*, *Wetherby*, and *Cross Talk*.

Queen Margaret was the biggest Shakespearian role I had ever played – the biggest in emotional range and intensity, in spiritual dimension, in the length of the journey from youth to age taken by the character. I suspect it may well be one of the biggest parts in English drama. It became for me very much a single character over three plays, even though the three *Henry VI* plays, which were reduced to two, were written rather earlier than *Richard III*. There are differences, of course; the earlier trilogy seems very straightforward, very emblematic, with little of the psychological warfare within characters' minds which one finds in *Richard III*. Even so, in playing Queen Margaret there remains a powerful sense of a single character's life discovered as one travels over a young man's writing career.

I had little warning of being cast for the role, about two weeks at the most. I had been in *Richard III* before, in Bill Alexander's production, playing Lady Anne, and used often to wonder, listening to Queen Margaret's curses, how audiences could hope to know the names of all the people she goes on about. I made a pact with myself to try to make even those audiences who were there only for *Richard III* understand, to try to bring on the history of the Wars of the Roses with me. I remember that clearly as an early objective, but before rehearsals began I had hardly read through the plays, and though I knew the famous molehill speech, and was aware of the high reputation of the part, I did very much begin at the beginning as far as *Henry VI* was concerned.

I knew, of course, that my two Stratford predecessors in the role had been Helen Mirren (in 1977) and Dame Peggy Ashcroft (in 1963–64). Dame Peggy had been in her late fifties when she played Margaret, but was utterly convincing as a young girl at the beginning of the part and had then gone through an amazing ageing process. I talked a little to John Barton at the beginning and looked at some passages of the video of the 1964 version. We also occasionally consulted the Barton adaptation (*The Wars of the Roses*) as we prepared our version, but as he had done a good deal of rewriting as well as cutting, it was not often relevant to our particular needs. As our preparation time went on I found myself increasingly alone with the part, discovering many things between me and the page, and that I really enjoyed.

The main reaction to my news of having taken the part was always 'O, mad Margaret. You're playing mad Margaret, are you?' I'd recently played Sarah Sprackling in *The Art of Success* and so had some experience of playing a mad character, but it quickly became clear that to call Margaret simply mad is a crude reduction of her complexity: the same woman who cradles the head of her lover is capable of the atrocity and depravity of that molehill speech. She is altogether so original that labels are unhelpful.

An early idea that developed and remained was that of her foreignness. As an Australian living in England I think I have a notion of what it is to feel that one doesn't quite fit. Early conversations with Adrian Noble supported this idea, since he was very keen to present the sense of English xenophobia in the production. Poring over the text after I'd formally accepted the part increased this sense of her foreignness, her originality, her not-quite-belonging (in England, and later, when she returns there, in France too). She's out of place, and also out of time, particularly in *Richard III*. She's like that from her first entrance: she doesn't fit, and she never fits.

My most obvious response to this sense of her as an outsider was to give her a trace of a foreign accent. I knew that Dame Peggy had played it with intrusive French r's and I toyed around with that but finished up with my own version, not nationally specific, but I hope consistent (though dwindling as the trilogy progresses, since she has by then been longer in England) and marking her off as alien. I visited France early in the preparation period and enjoyed watching that French sense of superiority in action. I remember asking directions of a man in my very bad French. 'Do you speak English?' he asked: 'perhaps we should try that then'. It isn't arrogance in any aggressive sense, it's an *hauteur* that comes from a natural acceptance of the belief that they are the *most* elegant, the *most* stylish people in the world. And that is there, it seemed to me, in Margaret's speeches, and the English hate her for it, hate her for being an alien, and especially for being a Frenchwoman. Many of her speeches, I felt, represent instinctive and immediate reactions coming from this sense of confident superiority.

As well as accent I worked hard also during rehearsals on my voice register. I wanted to be able to stress Margaret's emotional changes not just physically but with a vocal range that would move from the colours of youth to age, offering in the very sounds of the voice a reflection of the meanings of the verse. I did a great deal of work throughout the rehearsal period with Andrew Wade, the RSC voice teacher, and found, I think, vocal notes I had never used before, even though, to begin with, they were perhaps a little stiff and self-conscious.

The rehearsal period was an extraordinary one for the RSC with eighteen weeks to prepare three plays rather than the usual six weeks to prepare one. It meant that designs for set and costume could emerge organically from the rehearsal process instead of being, as is normal, preordained. It was a period of desperately hard work, often tiring, sometimes despairing, sometimes exhilarating. Above all it was a profoundly collaborative process, full of people's good will and excellence in a way that plays should be but often aren't. Many of the company were known to me before we started – indeed, I realized I had been in England for as long as I have when I walked into the rehearsal room on the first day and I knew half the people in it. I have particularly vivid memories of doing pike drill in the Bancroft Gardens in front of the theatre with forty other actors carrying pikes, and Malcolm Ranson, the fight director, trying to explore the notion of how you could make an image for a battle without going in for the standard battle scenes. The women in the cast were particularly impressive in this work, doing as much fighting as the men, as much forming part of either (or both) of the armies, though often without the reward of small, speaking roles that the men had. Their willingness to make do with just being 'the war' was a register of the commitment and good will that the company showed through the rehearsal (and performance) of the production.

The text came to us little by little, with Adrian and his assistant Stephen Raine often working late into the night after rehearsals, cutting, arranging, and restoring. Actors demanding lines back were always reminded of the 'three evenings of three hours' project we were embarked on, but there were occasions when it had to be agreed that the coherence of the narrative or of a character meant that cut lines must be restored. There were some heated debates and at times some aggrieved actors, but the enterprise demanded an act of faith and the occasions when we would all get very excited about what we could see beginning to emerge in the rehearsal room gradually came to outweigh the problems. We workshopped various aspects of war, then started on *Henry VI* and rehearsed that for about four weeks, moving on to *Edward IV* for the same length of time, then back to *Henry VI*, then to *Richard III*. Scenes worked on the day before would come back the next morning with textual revisions worked out overnight by Adrian and Stephen, sometimes to a universal groan, sometimes to great excitement. The energy in the rehearsal room was huge, and as we worked Malcolm Ranson was coming up all the time for fight calls. Returning to *Henry VI* after *Edward IV* made it seem more simplistic than *Edward IV*, and moving from play to play meant that I and many others were having to make huge emotional jumps all the time, and great age adjustments too. When we went back to scenes we'd worked on we would find that something had been lost from what had seemed solid, that the ground had shifted. But one had to allow it to be fluid and that, again, was an act of faith.

All through this time the designer Bob Crowley was sitting watching rehearsals and for the first ten weeks we didn't see a design, though all through that period we were exploring visual images in our work. Bob sat there taking it all in, discussing ideas with Adrian after rehearsals; many dinners at the Dirty Duck later we had a design which had (for once in the RSC) grown naturally out of the actors' rehearsal work. Everybody was greatly excited by it: a solution to our needs derived from much hard work which nevertheless seemed so simple. Costumes, too, evolved directly from the work we were doing. Bob Crowley came to me one day early in the rehearsal period and asked me, as he asked everyone in the cast, what I thought about Margaret's appearance. I remember saying that I didn't know exactly what I should look like, but that I thought Margaret should be sinewy, sexy, a great body under very simple frocks. I felt sure that the statement of all her clothes should be very, very simple, but that the whole sexuality of the writing of the role of Margaret should be reflected in her dresses. A couple of weeks into rehearsal, we had a long weekend break and I paid my visit to Paris and looked at the statues in the Luxembourg Gardens. And among them was this woman in an enormous tall hat, hugging a little boy to her chest and pointing a finger as if laying down the law. I looked and saw to my amazement that it was 'Marguerite d'Anjou'. Then at the Musée de Cluny I went and gazed on all those wonderful tapestries, the lady and the unicorn and the rest, and bought a book which I took back to Bob and we fell in love with one of the designs, a small female figure in cascading gold material. 'If only I could find that sort of material' (we hadn't yet seen the designs, but the French were clearly going to be in gold – armour, horse cloths, etc.), and a little while later I walked into the wardrobe department and they had found this amazing golden material and Bob had designed a very simple medieval dress, in a very flattering form. For my first appearance in France we had this idea of Margaret's youth, her real youthfulness, providing a complete contrast to all the warfare and bloodshed, so for that scene Bob chose a very pale olive green. After being a bleached blonde for some years, I had decided for this role to be chestnut red and short-haired; the feeling of liberation allowed me to do a lot of 'head acting' in rehearsals, later incorporated into the performance and forming an element in the presentation of that French *hauteur* which I was instinctively seeking. I was determined not to wear wigs for the part but hair extensions and the chestnut and olive green made a powerful visual statement for the first entrance. For later scenes Bob designed an exquisite black dress, still with a splendidly French sense of style, beautiful, simple, elegant, walled right up under the chin. For the war costumes there were no extension hair-pieces, so that it looked as if she had just grabbed her long elegant tresses and scissored them through to fit her head into the camail that now encased her, a further extension of the walling-up process. The shortness of her hair, when it reappeared during her faint at Tewkesbury, crown and camail falling off as she lay in agonized grief at the death of her son, revealed the head of an exhausted and plain old woman. Even through her hair, then, Margaret's spiritual journey can be charted; the production's thoroughness brought home to me the importance of acting with every sense you have – and also, of course, the joy of working with someone as talented as Bob Crowley and the RSC wardrobe department. Costumes are more than clothes to wear; they can and should be part of the creation of the character.

As the rehearsal period was drawing to its close we were jumping from a day on *Henry VI*, to a day on *Edward IV*, to a day on *Richard III*. For the final run-through of the plays the concentration in the rehearsal room was extraordinary, actors sometimes in tears as they watched, so profound was the involvement. The technical rehearsals when we reached the stage were long, much longer than most technicals, and terribly laborious. The set appeared deceptively simple, but there was an enormous amount under and over the stage, with hydraulics, and flying, and what not. Technical problems, sadly, meant that we had to cancel the first preview, which was a great disappointment, but since we had three plays to present in preview it was the right decision, or all the work could have been upset. Our first audience for *Henry VI* seemed to have a reasonably good time, but slowly it all began to take off and by the time we were previewing *Edward IV* there was an extraordinary buzz, with people stopping us in the street to say they'd never had such a good time in the theatre. We did one press day of all three plays of the trilogy, reeling (from exhaustion and from excitement) after a week of nine performances and a new dress rehearsal of *Henry VI* because we hadn't done it for three weeks. That somehow encapsulates the spirit of the venture. Some people talked of the cycle as an Elizabethan 'soap opera', but that seems to me to be rubbish. As we opened them to the press I felt we were presenting one of the most profound human sagas that have ever been written for the theatre and that, in spite of early doubts about cutting, and loss of some of the poetry, and of worries about getting from beat to beat in our abbreviated text, what we were finally showing vindicated and validated the choices we had made.

To describe Margaret of Anjou's journey through the plays is to describe a journey from extreme youth to extreme old age. Historically I think she was fifteen when she married Henry and fifty-three when she died, but the plays seem to deal in broader concepts than this. We set out initially to present 'youth', 'mother-figure', and 'aged revenger', with the idea of ageing fifteen years in the gaps. But I realized early on that there was a spiritual ageing that went on within as well as between the plays, and that this had to be shown physically too. So we couldn't simply show, say, seventeenish, thirty-fiveish, and then as old as I could manage; a somewhat more complex route became desirable.

Margaret's first appearance is close to the end of *Henry VI Part One*, though it was rather less than half way through our first play. It is not an easy scene. You can play false naive to some extent, because the asides to the audience give you the two levels. You are, however, as a character, encountering the audience for the first time just at the moment that you first meet the man who is to be the great passion of your life. I didn't want to come on playing the whole character in the first scene; there is a long way to take the audience from this opening moment and you must leave yourself somewhere to go. 'You only have to make them feel that this is someone who might be fun to be with' was Adrian's very helpful advice. And also, of course, there is a very real sense in which she's unformed, a person yet to be shaped by the experiences that await her. In this first appearance what I wanted to suggest was simply her Frenchness and her directness, her way of saying what first comes into her head and only afterwards (even if, often, immediately afterwards) realizing the effect it has had. So, basically, I came on with virtually nothing, having tried to clear my head of all the work on later scenes. The original stage direction is 'Enter Suffolk with Margaret in his hand', but we had altered the order of scenes here, moving Margaret's first entrance to follow rather than precede the death of Joan of Arc. Our intention was to show Margaret in a sense taking over where Joan left off, a new Frenchwoman to be a scourge to the English. With Joan of Arc at the stake and dead bodies on the stage, I came on covered in a brown cloak, hungry, a scavenger on the battlefield, like a sewer rat sniffing for the remnants of the picnic that York and Warwick had been eating while Joan was burning. That idea of being hungry, suggested by Adrian, gave me a vivid visual image to present for this first entrance, and one that is entirely compatible with what we hear of her father: he may be the King of Naples and Jerusalem, but he has no bread. The idea was of the siege of Berlin, of the casualties of war, of a battlefield from which everyone has run away, and she has been hiding in a cellar somewhere, but she still has the will to scavenge, to stay alive. The cloak, completely hiding my clothes as I rummaged, rat-like, around the food was then pulled off by Suffolk – and, *voilà*, the fairy-tale transformation, the pale olive dress, the long chestnut hair, the princess alone with her captor. That sense of captor and captive was important for all of us – Adrian, Oliver Cotton playing Suffolk, and me: there must be the threat of rape here, there must be danger; behind all the questions, asides, jokes, there must be the possibility that all this could go horribly wrong. 'What ransom must I pay before I pass?' she asks, and given her family's financial status, there must be the suggestion that her sexuality is all she has to trade for her freedom. She is very young, but she also seems here to be experienced. What sort of verbal bluff is she playing as she seems so poised? Is she as completely in control as her ability to offer asides to the audience seems to suggest, or are the asides part of her anxiety; and where do the asides begin and end and the dialogue between them return? Margaret doesn't get another aside until the scene with King Louis and the Lady Bona late in *Edward IV*, so it was vital to get the relationship right. Simultaneously one has to suggest her fear of being assaulted, her puzzlement that the man seems to be talking to himself, and her absolute delight, even exhilaration, in the battle of wits, the word game – a mixture of naive and knowing. Here she is, at her first entrance, a spoiled and beautiful French girl, with no money. It is a remarkable scene.

It is also the scene that establishes Margaret's relationship with Suffolk. It is a relationship based, I believe, on delight in each other's ideas, expressed through verbal dexterity. In their parting, for example, there is the need to keep trying to define in words what each of them feels that almost amounts to an obsession. They keep coming back to it:

> Give me thy hand
> That I may dew it with my mournful tears.
> . . .
> Go speak not to me; even now be gone.
> O, go not yet.
> . . .
> Loather a hundred times to part than die.
> . . .
> And take my heart with thee.
>
> (*Henry VI, Part Two*, III.ii.339–408)

We see the relationship establishing itself at the scene of her first arrival in England. She has had her honeymoon, as it were, at Tours, with Suffolk wooing her for the king, and then she arrives and the fairy-tale ends. There is disappointment, real disappointment, here and Suffolk perceives it immediately. Later, when she expresses her hatred of the Duchess of Gloucester ('Not all these lords do vex me half so much / As that proud dame, the Lord Protector's wife' (*Part Two*, I.iii.73–4)), he immediately reassures her: don't worry about it 'Myself have limed a bush for her' (line 86). They think together; hardly has one of them spoken than the other comes in, immediately on the same wavelength. That's the sort of relationship it is: so it begins in the first meeting, so it ends in the verbal inventiveness of their parting.

Margaret's relationship with Henry could scarcely be more different.

She arrives in England to meet her husband in front of the full court. Her disappointment is expressed later to Suffolk – 'I thought King Henry had resembled thee ... But all his mind is bent to holiness' (1.iii.51–3) – but in the scene itself she is largely silent, since it is hardly her place to speak. Henry's talk is all of thankfulness to God for bringing him this glorious creation, this vision. She has just one extraordinary speech that seems to mark the beginning of her political brain. It is a very carefully judged, convoluted, and politically astute speech:

> Great King of England and my gracious lord,
> The mutual conference that my mind hath had
> By day, by night, waking and in my dreams,
> In courtly company or at my beads,
> With you, mine alderliefest sovereign,
> Makes me the bolder to salute my King
> With ruder terms, such as my wit affords,
> And overjoy of heart doth minister. (1.i.24–31)

She's straight in there, in front of all the court, with this very erotic speech, making her mark above all, obviously, on Henry. It's politically very shrewd, of course, not to be upstaged by the hostility of the English court. It's the beginning of her ability to use political language effectively, a point from which she grows to genuine statesmanship. Henry is very aware of the feeling towards her in the court, but he has made his choice and he believes it to be from God. So in this very first meeting we see her acting politically while he follows his own spiritual and religious path.

Then comes the scene with Suffolk, when she expresses her sense of disappointment and sizes up the whole court with great accuracy. At the end of that scene we chose to make it clear that Margaret and Suffolk are lovers. When it began we deliberately left unclear, but here the audience was left in no doubt that it had happened. Suffolk had kissed her at the end of the scene of their first meeting, pretending he takes the kiss for Henry. Her riposte is brilliant:

> That for thyself. I will not so presume
> To send such peevish tokens to a King.
>
> (*Part One*, v.iii.185–6)

Her meaning is clear, but wittily elusive. She's experienced, but not experienced sexually. But I wanted to make it clear, in that later scene as she reveals her disappointment with Henry, that she really does desire Suffolk, that her feelings for him are overwhelming. At the same time she is expressing her utter frustration with Henry, for his political inadequacy and for his caring only about his own holiness. 'I thought King Henry had resembled thee': she goes on about it, obsessively, for she has an obsessive, jealous, destructive, capricious nature. At this point it is by no means fully formed; the experiences through which she is to pass will form it.

The great difficulty of presenting the relationship between Margaret and Henry is that they have so little to say to each other. You just have to play it and see where you get to on the stage. Ralph Fiennes (playing Henry VI) and I used to feel great frustration during the rehearsal period, and then one day Ralph pointed out that perhaps the frustration *we* were feeling was the frustration they felt with each other, because they never seem to meet. Henry is a man who always speaks out too late, or at the wrong time. Margaret is a woman who always speaks out, at precisely the right time, and seems to get away with it. So the relationship has a curious dynamic. I believe absolutely in her sense of honour, and part of that honour is in her faithfulness to her marriage. If Suffolk said 'let's run away together' she would refuse. She is married to the King of England and wants to be queen. She wants Suffolk as well, of course – very much like a medieval love triangle. Suffolk believes, once their affair is established, that vicariously through her he is running the kingdom, but it soon emerges, when he is banished, who is actually in charge. There's a sense in which contact with her is destructive, and we see that in what happens to Suffolk.

There's a moment that we chose to heighten in the falconry scene. She has already begun the liaison with Suffolk but here you see her very much at ease with Henry:

> Believe me, lords, for flying at the brook,
> I saw not better sport these seven years' day. (*Part Two*, II.i.1–2)

She is fantastic at falconing and Henry loves it as well, so we wanted to show her as someone who is great fun to be with. Margaret here is physically very happy. Then at the end of the scene, after the exposure and flight of Simpcox, Henry reflects on the event: 'O God, seest thou this, and bearest so long?' while she remarks simply 'It made me laugh to see the villain run' (lines 150–1). We made here a moment simply to look at each other, to show how impossibly far apart they are, and that there's no hope of a bridge. He thinks that way, she thinks this way; the moment is a telling one.

A vital turning-point in the relationship and in Margaret's exercise of her power comes in the next scene when she and Suffolk decide to get rid of Gloucester. From the first, from his reading out of the terms of the marriage settlement, Gloucester has been against her. Her resentment of him is seething:

> Am I a Queen in title and in style,
> And must be made a subject to a duke? *(Part Two,* I.iii.46–7)

She also hates Gloucester's wife, fiercely; it's as though she goes for people's ankles. Suffolk starts the attack on Gloucester in that little group scene of the choosing of a Regent for France. Suffolk defies Gloucester's wishes and Margaret chimes in with an explanation: 'Because the King, forsooth, will have it so' *(Part Two,* I.iii.113), and everybody just goes – 'What?' She wins, and all of a sudden she realizes her power. Henry, of course, says nothing, and she begins to sense her political muscle. Then, like a pack of dogs, Winchester, Suffolk, Somerset, Margaret, begin to invent their trumped-up charges against Gloucester. He is a force to be reckoned with – that was clear in the falconing scene – and he is also, from her point of view, a threat. So, as well as being spiteful and vindictive and jealous and obsessive in wanting Gloucester out of the way, she is also responding to the fact that her own position is precarious, with Henry so uninterested in power-play. But when he's got caged animals for a parliament, as we see he has, somebody's got to be interested in power-play and if he isn't she must be. And of course the relationship with Suffolk is always based on their belief that 'we can fix this'. So that when, at the end of the falconing scene, the news comes that the Duchess of Gloucester is involved in witchcraft, Margaret really relishes the moment. Suffolk was actually trying to fabricate the charges, but they turn out to be real – that's one of the splendid ironies in the writing. And one thing Henry will never countenance is witches – Antichrist, evil, all that he abhors – so the news produces a moment of real decision: 'Henry will to himself / Protector be' (II.iii.23–4). Because Henry will never in fact do anything but address himself to God there seems at this moment to be a power-vacuum, but Margaret sweeps across with the decisive words:

> Why, now is Henry King and Margaret Queen.
> . . .
> This staff of honour raught, there let it stand
> Where it best fits to be, in Henry's hand. (II.i.39–44)

'Just in case any of you lot might think you might be going to be next!' She's straight in, and we tried to stage it as a real turning-point. This is the beginning of her 'she-wolf' personality: 'Pick up that staff, Henry', she seems to say. 'Right, now it's you and me babe.' The whole idea that

Suffolk is behind her gives her complete confidence, and in the next scene you see her political brain really beginning to work as she moves in for the kill. 'Can you not see? Or will you not observe ...' (III.i.4). And nobody will say anything, so she prods and probes and takes over the running of the parliament scene. 'My lord of Suffolk, Buckingham, and York, / Reprove my allegation if you can', she challenges them (lines 39–40) and so they all begin to trump up charges. Then in comes Somerset with news that he has lost France and she knows York will be on the warpath because she got Somerset the job. Then, just as everyone wants to strangle Henry for his limp reply to the loss of France – 'Cold news, Lord Somerset, but God's will be done' (line 86) – in comes Gloucester and the dogs come out of the cages and Henry cannot cope. He delivers his impassioned speech and leaves: 'What, will your highness leave the parliament', she asks (line 197); and beneath it her meaning – 'I want him dead' – is clear. When he's gone she grasps the moment:

> Free lords, cold snow melts with the sun's hot beams:
> Henry my lord is cold in great affairs,
> Too full of foolish pity.                    (lines 223–5)

It is the first time she has really exercised her power, and she gets away with it.

> This Gloucester should be quickly rid the world
> To rid us from the fear we have of him.                    (lines 233–4)

It's as though she has lobbed the notion into the conversation, and held her breath to see how it works, but although they go on about finding 'some colour for his death', they all accept it. She is the sort of person that no one has ever said no to, and it happens again, even though they all hate her. 'Cold snow melts with the sun's hot beams': what exactly does it mean? It might mean (and on some nights this is what I tried to play), if we let Gloucester go, he will infect ('melt') Henry, since a very angry man just walked out of this room, so we have to kill Gloucester or he may easily turn the tables on us. Or it might mean that *we* are the sun's beams and Henry is cold, so there's no problem about our just having Gloucester killed. The meaning I chose from performance to performance depended on how Ralph and I had responded to each other in his exit speech. We next see Margaret with Gloucester dead and suddenly, in a minute or two of playing time, someone does say no to her and her world is completely shattered.

One gets the feeling that Henry has known all along about Margaret and Suffolk and has simply tolerated it; then suddenly you see a man possessed by jealousy. It's not just that Suffolk has killed Gloucester; it's everything, and in his rage and frustration he breaks down:

> Upon thy eyeballs murderous tyranny
> Sits in grim majesty to fright the world. (III.ii.49–50)

Margaret is completely shocked: 'Why do you rate my lord of Suffolk thus?' (line 56) and then speaks the most incredible emotional blackmail:

> What know I how the world may deem of me?
> . . .
> It may be judged I made the Duke away. (lines 65–7)

She is sailing extraordinarily close to the wind here: if Suffolk is for the chop, then so am I. Yet she's also challenging Henry: is this what you want, for your wife to be a killer as well? Suddenly everything has gone hopelessly wrong and she has to beg; 'O Henry, let me plead for gentle Suffolk' (lines 289). There are no holds barred now; everything is in the open. Warwick has stirred up the Commons (how else would they know that Suffolk did it?) and she can no longer brazen out her relationship with Suffolk, as we had earlier dramatized her doing when York and Warwick discover them kissing. She is now forced to beg publicly against her lover's banishment: all at once she's grown-up. She's rejected, and she begins her cursing career. It's the only way she can stay sane.

Margaret's next scene is the one we placed at the end of our first play, *Henry VI*. 'This way fall I to death', says Suffolk; 'This way for me', she replies (III.ii.412), and from that point she is alone. Margaret becomes the sum total of her experience, and this is a vital stage in her development. She is amoral, in the strict sense of the word. She is not immoral, she simply has no morality, but responds to the world she has to operate in, reacting in a sense simply as an animal to stimuli, but then politicizing her responses. Shakespeare gives her and Suffolk a parting scene of splendid poetry. An early idea of Adrian Noble's was that she might be visibly pregnant here, to prepare for her image as a mother-figure in the second play, where she is operating very much as the champion of her son's cause. But we rejected this idea on the grounds that everyone would simply conclude that it was Suffolk's child she was expecting. But the mothering idea remained. In expressing his grief at parting from her, Suffolk says that he would prefer to die in her lap 'As mild and gentle as the cradle-babe / Dying with mother's dug between its lips' (III.ii.392–3). The line was cut, but the idea returned with Margaret's entrance in her next scene, cradling

Suffolk's severed head in her arms like a baby. The moment grew rather accidentally out of the rehearsal of Winchester's death scene (III.iii). Adrian asked me to come into this scene, Suffolk's death by drowning having been cut, though in the text she does not appear, and we took a couple of lines from a later scene (IV.iv), because she needed to speak –

> Here may his head lie on my throbbing breast;
> But where's the body that I should embrace? (lines 5–6)

– but it still didn't seem to work. Ralph Fiennes then suggested that I needed to challenge them with the head, so we added a little more, and what is formally (in IV.iv) her reflection on those who murdered Suffolk became here a direct address to Henry, Warwick, and the rest of them beside Winchester's deathbed:

> Ah, barbarous villains! Hath this lovely face
> Ruled like a wandering planet over me,
> And could it not enforce them to relent,
> That were unworthy to behold the same? (IV.iv.15–18)

It became an extraordinary moment when we tried it like this, Margaret coming into the court, carrying her lover's head like a babe in arms, challenging her husband. Ultimately more lines from IV.iv were moved to this scene of Winchester's death:

> Oft have I heard that grief softens the mind,
> And makes it fearful and degenerate;
> Think therefore on revenge and cease to weep. (lines 1–3)

You think I'm going to go mad, she says, but you're wrong, I'm just going to concentrate on vengeance. That is the little pinhead of light in all the darkness of her life at this point. Then Henry says 'Close up his eyes, and draw the curtain close; / And let us all to meditation' (III.iii.32–3). These were the last words of our first play. After we had rehearsed the scene for some time the idea came that Ralph might put out his hand to me. It is, after all, a marriage between Henry and Margaret, a curious one, in many ways, of course, but though it's often difficult to find, there is a kind of love between them. He knows of her love for Suffolk; he knows that Suffolk had Gloucester killed and that she was implicated in that. But he is a man who nevertheless has the moral strength to extend his hand, whatever that may mean. At first I wasn't looking, but just before the lights went down I turned from being totally absorbed in Suffolk's head; not to look at Henry but just to be aware of his extended hand. It was not quite textually based, as nearly everything in the production was, but it seemed right, one of those rare moments when things seem to come together, and I think audiences caught that too.

The next play in our arrangement, *Edward IV*, shows the destruction of this fragile relationship, this strange but not loveless marriage, and of Margaret's response to the next stage of experience. Her first scene here, however (IV.iv of Shakespeare's *Part 2*), from which we had already taken lines for the end of our *Henry VI*, includes perhaps the most telling moment of her relationship with Henry. In the full Shakespearian text this is when she comes on with Suffolk's head, but as our second play is fifteen years later and her son is now grown up, we discarded, after some rehearsal attempts, the idea that she is still carrying round a mummified head in a handbag. I was, therefore, left 'black hole acting', showing grief but only able to hope that the audience remembers its cause. Then comes Henry's rather sharp remark and her surprising reply:

> How now, madam?
> Still lamenting and mourning for Suffolk's death?
> I fear me, love, if that I had been dead,
> Thou wouldst not have mourned so much for me.
>
> No, my love; I should not mourn, but die for thee.    (ILV.iv. 21–5)

We tried this in every conceivable way. I even rang up John Barton, who felt her reply had to be ironic. But I still had the feeling that she meant it: 'no, I wouldn't mourn for you, but I would die for you, because that's my duty, and my honour'. It took a long time to find that and feel confident with it (particularly as I was working on this scene while rehearsals were largely concentrating on the Cade rebellion) but I think it was right, and further evidence of the complexity of the marriage. We next see them together at Kenilworth, with Henry again going on about

> No sooner was I crept out of my cradle
> But I was made a King at nine months old    (IV.ix.3–4)

and we know that Henry has been going on about this forever and that for fifteen years she has brought up a son – and it was Adrian's decision to bring him on here and to show the complete family – in a sense having gone into retirement. Then comes Henry's capitulation to the Yorks and the disinheriting of his son.

The big laugh on the king's desire to escape his approaching wife's fury ('I'll steal away ... Exeter, so will I' (*Part 3*, 1.i.212)) is easy to get, but for

Margaret this is an important moment. She's been retired from politics for fifteen years, but though it's dormant she still has enormous power. She's always known he was capable of doing something like this, but now he's done it. York has many sons, but she has only one – again part of her obsession – and somehow she believes that York was responsible for Suffolk's death. Whatever the nature of her relationship with Henry, the fact is that the child is everything;

> Had I been there, which am a silly woman,
> The soldiers should have tossed me on their pikes
> Before I would have granted to that act.
> But thou preferrest thy life before thine honour;
> And, seeing thou dost, I here divorce myself
> Both from thy table, Henry, and thy bed,
> Until that act of parliament be repealed
> Whereby my son is disinherited.                    (*Part 3*, I.i.243–50)

It is a decisive moment, for whatever has been the nature of this marriage, it has somehow survived to this point, and here she ends it. I chose to take the word 'divorce' in its fullest and most absolute sense, severing the ties between two people. She stands up and says, in open court, that I, the Queen of England, here divorce you, the King of England. She begins a second career, in a sense she reinvents herself. She becomes a warrior.

Her most notorious scene as a warrior is when she captures York. This is, of course, one of the most famous scenes in the play, even in Shakespeare. Fortunately I didn't know it when I first came to it, and had no preconceptions about it. The shape of the scene is an initial question to face. Basically there are two huge speeches: why does she speak for so long and he stay silent, then why does she say nothing while he speaks for so long? David Calder (playing York) and I used to have long talks about this after rehearsals, and about the nature of the relationship between York and Margaret before this molehill scene. In the parliament scene earlier, for example, when they are all trying to destroy Gloucester, Somerset arrives with the news of the loss of France. Henry has his feeble 'God's will be done' response, but York reacts very sharply. Margaret doesn't hear his aside, but she registers his response, since it was through her that Somerset was sent to France in the first place. That was her first exercise of power and it had gone sour. She knows that York is aware of that, though for the time being they act together to topple Gloucester. Then there's the fact of York's numerous sons where she has only her Edward, and of her vague sense that York was in some way responsible for the death of Suffolk. All this stored-up frustration, bitterness, and revenge lies behind the

18   Penny Downie as Queen Margaret with the bloody handkerchief in
*Edward IV (Henry VI, Part III*, 1.iv.79)

confrontation on the battlefield, the product itself of the chaos of war. The basic rhetorical form of her speech is straightforward: she keeps asking him questions. What does she want from this man? She has walked on to the stage thinking she has everything: she has won the battle, she has him and he is about to die, and she has Rutland's blood on the handkerchief next to her bosom, wet, and red. Why Rutland? Because he is the scholar, the innocent, the good, the junior version of Henry VI, and that's now reduced to the bloody handkerchief. In York she has what she most wants, and when she says 'Hold, valiant Clifford' (1.iv.51) she is revealing her power over the situation, over the chaos and the war. She can actually decide to go beyond the norms of war, to say 'I am going to torture this man'. She shows no sympathy for York and it is difficult to feel any sympathy for her after this episode. She diminishes through the scene, as York grows, and after it she is merely a fit match for Richard. Her behaviour here is primeval, tribal, animal; she's turning herself on in this toying, teasing, cat-and-mouse treatment of him. She stands there, asking the questions. Initially in rehearsal I used to play the whole speech as if really mad, and David did a lot of weeping. Later we went back to something simpler, to just asking the questions – what *do* I want out of this man? 'Where are your mess of sons to back you now?' – to just creating the images – 'wanton Edward' 'lusty George' 'that valiant crook-back prodigy'. Where, where, what, what – so many questions.

> What! Hath thy fiery heart so parched thine entrails
> That not a tear can fall for Rutland's death?     (lines 87–8)

You aren't reacting the way I wanted you to react. React! – but he's not going to give her anything. Though he doesn't speak, it's a kind of dialogue; he knows what she wants and he isn't going to give it to her, and she doesn't quite know what it is, but she wants it to be ugly and painful. The extraordinary moment of the speech is the paper crown. From night to night it used to vary a little, depending on the position of the crown. Sometimes it was a complete improvisation since I saw it halfway through the line, sometimes it was more premeditated: 'O, I see; you don't speak unless you wear a crown.' Then, at the end, she's had enough:

> Off with the crown; and, with the crown, his head;
> And, whilst we breathe, take time to do him dead.     (lines 107–8)

At last he gives it to her, but it's not what she wanted, because in fact what is it that could satisfy her? Her speech, too, is full of questions: how could you do this? And it's the idea of her as a mother that is most powerful, and that, in spite of all her power as a warrior, gets to her. It must do so, or the death of her own son, later, at Tewkesbury, would not affect her. There are conventional within-law feminine principles being invoked in York's speech, of course – 'Women are soft, mild, pitiful' (line 141) etc. – and Margaret has, in formally 'divorcing' herself from Henry and taking on his warrior role, moved beyond these, but I found that those early attempts to play the whole scene mad and joyously, to suggest that she's done what she set out to do and that she's not being affected by what he says, made it impossible to deal with her emotions at Tewkesbury. In the end, even though she has behaved like an animal, she remains human.

There are two last brief meetings between Margaret and Henry VI, on either side of the Battle of Towton. The first is the extraordinary encounter when Margaret gloats over York's head on the gates of York, 'Doth not the object cheer your heart, my lord?' and he replies 'Ay, as the rocks cheer them that fear their wrack' (II.ii.4–5). Once again one sees the terrible gap between them. It's as if Henry thinks he can separate himself from the way the real world works. She has to go on fighting; it's her journey into hell, really. She simply says to him 'our foes are nigh / And this soft courage makes your followers faint' (lines 156–7) and changes the subject to the knighting of their son, but one senses what she really means: 'Yes, I know about your view of honour, but it's not that sort of world; there's his head, this is what I've done, and that's the way the real world works.' Henry goes off to *his* molehill scene, there is their brief parting afterwards, as they flee in opposite directions, and we never see them together again.

Margaret is next seen in France, seeking help from the King of France. It is an odd scene. In one sense she is returning home, but there is no feeling of her belonging there either. When we next see her back in England there's a feeling that she's pleased to be there; she hates them all, but she's pleased to be back. I played her older in the French scene, the gap since her last appearance useful in moving her on a step nearer the age at which we shall see her in *Richard III*. Her experiences in running the country, and in battle, have taken their toll. She comes in as a woman who has nothing more to give, nothing at all. She is deeply depressed, though still capable of pursuing her political ends by flirting with Louis. She comes empty-handed, but by the end of the scene her fortunes have been reversed and she's immediately ready to respond, to adapt to the new circumstances – 'Right! I'm on top again'.

Shakespeare keeps Margaret away from the scene in which Warwick, in token fashion, puts Henry VI back on the throne. We see her next at

Tewkesbury, at the final ruin of her cause. Her speech before the battle is extraordinarily bleak. It's a different kind of war now. Battles are no longer honourable. There's no more chivalry, no more York and Clifford pausing in mid-fight to admire each other's prowess. At Tewkesbury the chaos Margaret herself made possible in her treatment of York has come; it's the world of the York boys, where if you are down in the battle, as our scene showed, you are clubbed to death. So in her speech she doesn't try to praise her followers' valour, or encourage them. She just warns them that if they think, for a minute, it might be a good idea to run away, then forget it, the York boys aren't going to help you: 'there's no hoped-for mercy with the brothers / More than with ruthless waves' (v.iv.35–6). By her next speech she is crying. After all we've seen of her, can we trust her tears? I decided that we could, though obviously she also knows the effect they are having:

> Lords, knights, and gentlemen, what I should say
> My tears gainsay.
>      . . .
> You fight in justice; then in God's name, lords,
> Be valiant, and give signal to the fight.       (lines 73–82)

'Justice' – Margaret, after all we've seen, is now presenting herself as the champion of justice. Shakespeare has managed to make her a complete contradiction.

In the battle scene that follows we hear her speak with queenly dignity (and she *is* a queen) to Oxford:

> So part we sadly in this troublous world,
> To meet with joy in sweet Jerusalem.       (v.v.7–8)

It's a most proper thing to say. And then, in front of her eyes, her son, for whom her life has been lived, is battered and stabbed to death. He has been speaking and conducting himself like the young Henry V she thinks he is, and the York boys smash him down. She begs to die, too, and Richard would do it, but Edward stops him, embarrassed by her grief. She swoons, as she takes on the incredible pain of it: 'O Ned, sweet Ned, speak to thy mother, boy! / Canst thou not speak?' (lines 51–2). As she had in her separation from Suffolk years earlier, she finds the pinpoint of light in the darkness of grief in her ability to curse, looking directly towards her role in *Richard III*:

> But if you ever chance to have a child,
> Look in his youth to have him so cut off.       (lines 65–6)

She has to channel the pain somewhere or her brain would explode, so she seeks relief in cursing, which turns to prophesying. I felt that a physical expression of her anguish was also needed, and in rehearsal one day I embarrassed everyone by letting rip and rushing round the room like a flailing animal; other people started trying to hit some sense into me, and we kept this general idea for the performance, the 'she-wolf', as York calls her, rushing round in anguish at the loss of her offspring, begging for death, and Edward and Clarence unwilling to 'do her so much ease'. Margaret's position at the end of our play *Edward IV* resembled that at the end of our *Henry VI*, though greatly magnified: cursing her enemies she has found refuge from the anguish of separation from what she loved. Between these two moments there has been her revenge, her defeat and baiting of York, her soaking of the handkerchief in Rutland's blood. And now they've had their revenge on her and she's left, empty, waiting for death, her ability to curse the only refuge from her agony.

'Wert thou not banished on pain of death' Richards asks her on her first appearance in *Richard III*. And her reply is a challenge:

> I was; but I do find more pain in banishment
> Than death can yield me here by my abode.          (I.iii.167–8)

'So are you going to kill me? No – yellow! You had your chance, boys, I even asked for it, and you didn't do it.' So now she is somehow untouchable; they cannot lay a finger on her and they don't try. This is clear from the text, since she is allowed to rave on for so long.

We had a lot of discussion about Margaret's age in *Richard III*. The original notion was fifteen-year jumps between the three plays, starting *Henry VI* at fifteen to twenty, *Edward IV* at thirty-five to forty, and *Richard III* at fifty-five or so. The historical Margaret of Anjou was fifty-three when she died, but she did not return from France after the defeat at Tewkesbury. Shakespeare brings her back and is here playing a double time scheme; it is only three months since the battle, but the prince (then unborn) and his brother are shortly to appear as about ten years old. Playing Margaret I needed to decide where I was coming from. When she walks on in the third scene of *Richard III* it is as if she brings with her all the memories of everybody's blackest deeds in the battles of the past, all that they've tried to sweep under the carpet. There is a certain detachment and wry humour about her in this scene, a sense that she is really enjoying being there. I more or less decided that she had not been back to France, but that she had been in a little garret somewhere in somebody's castle with an old retainer to bring her food – except that she doesn't eat, she just walks, night and day, reciting the catechism of hate. When we started work on the scene in rehearsals the thing I wanted, more even than trying to create the sense of Margaret's age, was to have the audience understand what I was talking about, to bring the images of the past to them as fresh as possible, to make the history as specific as I could, especially for those who were seeing *Richard III* without the other plays. We talked a lot about age, too, of course; fifty-five became seventy-five, which wasn't a lot of use to me as a 34-year-old. Then finally Adrian Noble came up with the idea that she is 200 years old and of course that provided the key to it and one could see her as this ageless figure of moral nemesis, who brings on to the stage the entire Wars of the Roses and who has herself been purified by suffering to play this final moral role.

Her cursing speeches in this first scene follow such a rhythm that I found I had to work hard on my breathing. You have to push through to the end, take four-line thoughts on one breath, or it won't make sense. The speeches felt like arias to me, and if you take on board their energy you are sustained by it. There was an odd thing that came up in rehearsal one day: Richard reminds Margaret of what she did to his father, and I couldn't re Then he brings in Rutland, and it comes back to her; she remembers York's curse on her for Rutland's death and now she asks 'Did York's dread curse prevail so much with heaven?' (I.iii.190). It is as though Richard, in reminding her of York's curse, has admitted that cursing works:

> Can curses pierce the clouds and enter heaven?
> Why then, give way, dull clouds, to my quick curses!        (I.iii.194–5)

She heard and now remembers York's curse and it has come true for her. People have to *hear* the curse if it is to work: no amount of pacing round the garret will help. Like an aborigine pointing the bone – you have to believe you are going to die if you are going to die. And the fact is that they all do believe in these curses, none more so than Richard. What we were looking for in the scene was a logical progression: not that she came in with a ready-made plan to curse them all, but that she has responded to what happens in the scene which then moves in a moment-to-moment way. We found, I hope, a narrative journey within the scene – otherwise it ends up as just this silly old bag-woman. Margaret has been depraved; she has also been brave. She has caused suffering and she has suffered. Here, as she

19   Queen Margaret in *Richard III*

stands, 200 years old, calling down curses on them all, there is something tribal, something prehistoric, about her. To mark this, for the last of her curses, on Buckingham, on the line 'O princely Buckingham, I'll kiss thy hand' (line 279), I took his hand and put it on my breast. Since Oliver Cotton, playing Buckingham, had also played Suffolk, this gave a resonance back through the trilogy and gave me the vaguely tribal feeling I wanted for this moment.

Margaret's second scene in *Richard III*, her last appearance in the cycle of plays, is with Queen Elizabeth and the Duchess of York, three women who have carried the emotional weight of events and whose suffering now gives them the right to function as a kind of moral chorus. We talked endlessly about this scene and how to play it until Joanne Pearce (Queen Elizabeth) came up with the idea of refugees, of women in black wandering round Europe after the last war. It seemed appropriate that there might be this mass exit of women from Richard III's London, with Elizabeth and the Duchess of York being joined by Margaret. Interestingly she is not going to stay to the end, to see all her curses come true:

> I am hungry for revenge,
> And now I cloy me with beholding it. (IV.iv.61–2)

I used to get a sort of buzz in rehearsal as I heard her prophecies come true – Rivers and Vaughan, Stanley, Buckingham – a sense of Margaret ticking them all off on her list. So why does she not stay to see Richard's doom? Why is she 'cloyed' with revenge?

One of our aims in this scene was to avoid its becoming just an impersonal commentary. The formal structures of the writing must be used, the repetitions of names, of rhythms, of line beginnings, of questions and answers. It was exquisite to play, provided one didn't get in the way of it. But one did have to find some sense of personal need to be part of the scene. Why does Margaret stop to speak to them, to join their lament? Their grief is now, hers is much older; in a sense she is elevated by her grief and by her satisfaction that, incredibly, all the things she predicted have come to pass. She has a need to relish that, to show them she was right. But there's a growing sense, now, that it's all empty: 'Bear with me, for I am hungry', she says – it's as near as she ever gets to an apology. On some occasions audiences would laugh as the names were listed – 'I had an Edward, till Richard killed him . . . I had a Richard too . . . I had a Rutland . . .'. These were laughs of recognition, recognition of the events of the past and of the terrible absurdity of it all, of what people, including these three women, have done to each other. During the scene, Elizabeth wakes up and the Duchess of York with her. They are both so earth-bound at the beginning: 'What can we do, we are in such pain?', they seem to ask. Margaret comes in and, in a curious way, by the time she leaves the stage they are on their feet, ready to face up to Richard. She uses a remarkable series of animal images for Richard – 'bottled spider', 'bunch-backed toad' – and Elizabeth starts to pick them up. Together they recall the past: 'I called thee then vain flourish of my fortune' (line 82); 'Ah, yes, I was really witty that day', she seems to say and Elizabeth remembers. And in a strange way they become one. That whole long speech beginning 'I called thee then' leads up inevitably and in one movement to its conclusion. 'Thus hath the course of justice wheeled about' (line 105) and 'Now thy proud neck bears half my burdened yoke' (line 111). Then she passes it all to Elizabeth:

> From which even here I slip my weary head
> And leave the burden of it all on thee.          (lines 112–13)

That is where she leaves; the transference has occurred. If you break up the speech you might as well not say it at all; it all leads in one sweep to this moment. She passes the burden to the next woman whose babies are also dead; everybody's dead, and in some way Margaret is free. The speech has an eerie quality; it's hard to touch it lightly enough without destroying the quality of it. It is a wonderful piece of writing and as it progresses it gets more double in its focus, so that she is talking simultaneously about herself and about Elizabeth. And then at the end she passes it all over. She's tired, she's free, and now she can leave.

Elizabeth pulls her back and asks her, to 'teach me how to curse mine enemies' (line 117) – 'you can't just leave like that'. There's something about Margaret's reply which says 'Ah, yes, but you weren't at the Somme', but she tells her 'This is what you do, for all the good it's going to do you. But you have to do it, because we all have to':

> Forbear to sleep the nights, and fast the days;
> Compare dead happiness with living woe;
> Think that thy babes were sweeter than they were.          (lines 117–19)

It's a detached, objective, ironic shopping-list, and she knows – I'm sure she knows – that it's somehow empty. As she leaves the stage she leaves her whole spirit with these women; and they actually get up and are ready to turn on Richard. She walks off and goes back to France, or at least she says that she is going back to France, though it always seemed to me that she just disappears into the ether.

'O, you're playing mad Margaret' people would say to me when I was cast. I spent a lot of time scraping away the preconceptions, coming up against the huge ideas of the mind that created this part, this enormous arc of a role that moves from one play to the next. I know that I had to discover more of myself in taking on the role of this woman who tells us so much about things universal through her particular journey. Surely it is one of the greatest parts ever written.

# Richard of Gloucester in
# *Henry VI* and *Richard III*

## ANTON LESSER

ANTON LESSER played Richard of Gloucester in Adrian Noble's production of the adaptation of the three parts of *Henry VI* with *Richard III*,
titled *The Plantagenets*, at the Royal Shakespeare Theatre in 1988 and at
the Barbican the following year. He had first appeared for the RSC in 1977
as Richard of Gloucester in Terry Hands's production of the *Henry VI*
trilogy. Earlier Shakespeare roles for the RSC had included Romeo (in
1980–81) and Troilus (in 1985–86) and more recently he has played Bol-
ingbroke in *Richard II* (1990–91) and in 1992 Petruccio in *The Taming of
the Shrew* and Ford in *The Merry Wives of Windsor*. Among other roles for
the RSC have been Michael in *The Sons of Light*, Allan in *The Dance of
Death*, Montezuma in *Melons*, Bill Howell in *Principia Scriptorum*, Joe
Taylor in *Some Americans Abroad*, and Edwin Forrest in *Two Shakespearean Actors*. A range of work for other theatre companies has included
such major Shakespearian roles as Hamlet, Feste in *Twelfth Night*, and
Mark Antony in *Julius Caesar*. Among his television roles have been parts
in *The Mill on the Floss*, *The Cherry Orchard*, *Anna of the Five Towns*,
*Freud*, *Stanley Spencer*, *The Strauss Dynasty*, as well as *Troilus and
Cressida* and *King Lear*.

Ten years before *The Plantagenets* I had played Richard of Gloucester in
Terry Hands's production of the *Henry VI* trilogy. There was talk then –
from the critics, at least – of my doing a Richard III. It turned out to be
quite a long wait. Playing the Richard of *Henry VI* again showed me how
much I had changed over the years. Saying those same lines, ten years on,
shows you how far you've come, or not come, as an individual. It's a
curious experience, perhaps unique to acting – artists, after all, don't
usually come back years later to paint a picture again. In fact, I don't
believe the performances bore much relationship to each other, except in
the obvious point of physical appearance. I tried to wipe that last version
from my memory and approach the new one afresh. I was working with a

different director and a set of different actors, so nearly everything had changed. I didn't feel pressure never to repeat things from the last version, though I suspect that almost nothing remained.

To do *Richard III* as part of the cycle was of enormous assistance. On its own the play inevitably requires a central pyrotechnic performance of great magnetism and theatrical invention. It requires that because, as a play on its own, it is full of people whose relationships with each other are baffling. If you go to see *Richard III* without knowing the text, who is Margaret, who is this woman who rushes around cursing everybody? Who are they talking about; who was it that was crowned with a paper crown, on a molehill? And who was this person called Rutland? All these names keep coming up, but they seem to serve only to create a strange nightmarish environment for a Hitler-like character to have his three hours' fretful play. The virtue of doing the play in sequence in *The Plantagenets* was that, by the time you got to *Richard III*, you knew exactly who everybody was; you knew why Margaret is mad and why she is still around the court; you knew the relationships between Hastings and Richard, and Rivers and Grey, and you stopped pretending 'Ah yes,' in response to all those Shakespearian-sounding names that mean nothing. The great virtue of this new situation was that I didn't have to try to make up for these short-comings by doing some sort of extraordinary one-man show. And that, for me, was fine. Instead I had to build a real person, not a two-dimensional figure of evil, but a person whose seeds I found in the play we called *Henry VI* (our version of Shakespeare's 1 *Henry VI* and the first half of 2 *Henry VI*), in which Richard does not even appear. His beginnings are neverthe-less to be found, I think, in that post-chivalric world which degenerates into the anarchic, iconoclastic state which is the England in which the young Richard operates. This is a much more interesting journey, I believe, and it means that by the time I got to *Richard III* there was no need for a one-man show. I felt the truth of this very strongly on those occasions (and the schedule imposed some of them) when we did *Richard III* on its own, outside the sequence of *The Plantagenets*. No doubt if he had been doing *Richard III* alone Adrian Noble would have directed it very dif-ferently, though in what ways one couldn't tell from my position inside the production we created. Conceived as it was as Part 3 of a nine-hour play, I know what a struggle it was, when we did the play alone, to engage the audience in the early stages; by the second scene the process was often only just starting. To do the play in the sequence of the trilogy was to feel the audience carrying you forward on a wave of familiarity and understanding.

The great advantage of this was that I could treat Richard III as one would treat any Shakespearian character, such as Hamlet. As an actor I looked at him not as a one-man show but as a part that contains something of the complexity, the psychological nuance, that Hamlet does. Obviously Richard as a role is much less fully developed than Hamlet: a sketch in comparison. But it can still be looked at in the same way to produce something more like a real man than a 'symbol of evil' – which is not an idea that interests me. You let the audience off the hook if you only present them with their preconceptions, with the embodiment of evil they think they have come to see; it is much more interesting to challenge them, to show them the embodiment of evil looking rather vulnerable in a certain situation, or as continuing to say 'I have neither pity, love, nor fear' while patently revealing all three. In treating him as I would any other part – as a real character to get hold of – I hope it made those parts of the man visible to the audience. I felt that if I could find such moments and make them resonate for the audience they would, perhaps, have a richer experience than if I gave them the strutting, black-leather-clad, club-footed, hump-backed goblin of their preconceptions.

Another advantage of doing the whole cycle was that you saw the emergence of the figure from history – in the same way that Hitler didn't just turn up out of the blue in 1939. It is as if the searchlight of history pans round and you catch a glimpse of this young man; and then it goes to him again and we see he is in minor office; and later he's got a movement together and is beginning to be influential. Then we see him more and more as the light keeps going back to him until he's in the middle of the stage and the light stays on him constantly. He's responsible for the making and shaping of history, but when we first saw him he was just one of the crowd. That, I think, is interesting.

A rather more practical effect of doing Richard in the three-play cycle was the effect it had on the usual RSC working methods. The eighteen-week space from the start of rehearsal until the first preview meant that when we began no set or costume designs were fixed (as they usually have to be if they are to be made in time); one was thus spared that peculiar struggle, as an actor, of trying to find a fresh, original, organically inspired character within so many already rigidly fixed parameters. Here the designer, Bob Crowley, was with us from the start at rehearsal and his deadline for submitting designs to the workshops was some weeks ahead. We were thus free to explore, to discover, to make our own suggestions, and ideas came from everybody. The production was thus a synthesis of everyone who worked on it – which is rare, and rewarding. The one constraint we did have was one of time: Adrian Noble made it clear, on the first day of rehearsal, that from forty-one actors, some hundreds of thousands of words of Shakespeare, no preconceptions about set or costume, we were to make nine hours of theatre – but *only* nine hours, three three-hour shows, not one of them to overrun a minute, since on some days we were to play all three, and time had to be allowed for changeovers. The text thus had to be cut ruthlessly – from *Richard III*, for example, something approaching a third of the lines was omitted. This was a heavy sacrifice, but I hope that the gains of thus being able to offer the whole cycle, the whole movement, outweighed the losses.

And so I came to Richard, not without foreknowledge, but in a production in which from the first I was allowed great freedom of exploration, as well as a determination to engage the audience, to draw them in, to make them think, to challenge them; and to make the simple complex, to make the obvious not obvious. If people came with preconceptions I hope that I sent them home saying, 'I don't know whether I think that any more about that character.' And this, of course, is the constant quality of Shakespeare, the infinite variety of the roles, always amenable to new lines of attack from actors, constantly malleable.

What one plays in Richard is a man destined for power, though not himself aware of that, I think, in the early stages. At first he is just helping to sustain the cause of the House of York; the savagery and killing are legitimized by that dynastic context; the change from political vendetta, from butchery in pursuit of the rights of the family, to the personal paranoia of the yearning for absolute power, is very sharp. I greatly enjoyed my first entry in the play we called *Edward IV* (based on the second half of 2 *Henry VI* and the whole of 3 *Henry VI*). When York returns from Ireland with his three sons, we strode down in lights and with music, my first time on the stage, and with nothing to say. And there was my father looking wonderful and saying quite simply 'Right, here's what this play is about': 'From Ireland thus comes York to claim his right' (v.i.1). We included at this point a briefer version of the genealogy from earlier in 2 *Henry VI* (II.2) and this was wonderful for me, since I could never understand the family tree and to this day its complexities elude me. But when David Calder came on as York in that stirring scene and asked 'What plain proceedings is more plain than this?' (II.ii.53) I was completely convinced: 'Yes. Great. *Now* I understand.' And there I was, silent, but one of the family, part of the team. This is where Richard comes from; he

20   Anton Lesser as Richard of Gloucester in *Edward IV* on the steps of the throne just seized by his father the Duke of York (*Henry VI, Part III*, 1.i)

doesn't just step out from nowhere with 'Now is the winter of our dis-
content'. If the audience has seen the origins, the reasons and the motives,
perhaps they can be more sympathetic. To stand on the stage and hear a
really good actor, like David Calder here, or Ralph Fiennes at other points
in *Edward IV*, and to try to listen afresh each time, is very important. If
you allow what you hear to affect you afresh there is some chance that when
you come to speak it will not come out the same as it did on the last thirty
occasions.

As part of the York team Richard is primarily a fighter. *The Plantagenets*
was full of fights and our fight director, Malcolm Ranson, worked hard to
give these variety, and a sense of progression. We decided from the start
that Richard's fights in *Edward IV* (there are none in *Richard III* until the
final, fateful encounter at Bosworth) should look easy. In the field of battle,
if nowhere else, he has transcended his disabilities: here he is the fastest,
moves with the greatest alacrity, is the most lethal, and yet the effort takes
less toll of him than of anyone else. The fight with Somerset showed
Somerset having a terrible time and Richard making it all look so easy,
anticipating every blow. The fighting, of course, degenerates as the
sequence progresses. The last honourable fight is that between York and
Old Clifford, pausing to admire each other's prowess – 'With thy brave
bearing should I be in love / But that thou art so fast mine enemy' (*Part
II*, v.ii.20) – before they go to it again. And then, immediately after,
Richard fights Somerset, with Somerset very clear that he's drawn the
short straw with Richard, and chivalry nowhere to be seen as butchery and
massacre take over from the last remnants of honour in battle.

It is, then, as part of this fighting team that we first see Richard
operating, pursuing the legitimate (to him) cause of York, with no personal
ambition involved while his father remains alive. The first explosive
expression of that ambition after his brother's betrothal to Elizabeth
Woodville does not, however, come from nowhere. The idea has been
festering away, not even articulated to himself, but expressed in non-verbal
communication, possibilities, little thoughts, winks, to himself. The stir-
rings begin, I think, with the vision of the three suns after the York boys
receive the news of their father's death. It is an apocalyptic vision that
means something different for each of them. For Edward it suggests that
'the sons of brave Plantagenet' should 'over-shine the earth as this the
world'. I decided that for Richard it might imply 'this could mean royal
possibilities for me', so that when Edward concludes his response with the
words

> Whate'er it bodes, henceforward will I bear
> Upon my target three fair-shining suns      (*Part 3*, II.i.39–40)

I thought 'Don't have any sons, for Christ's sake' as Richard says 'Nay, bear three daughters.' Edward's glance meant 'What?' and Richard rapidly makes a joke of it – 'You love the breeder better than the male' (line 42). This is where he first admits the possibility to himself, this is its beginning, but it does not really find its expression until it emerges that Edward is about to get married and the avenues are therefore closing.

Then, suddenly, the latent possibilities, the secret, festering thoughts explode into expression:

> Ay, Edward will use women honourably.
> Would he were wasted, marrow, bones, and all,
> That from his loins no hopeful branch may spring,
> To cross me from the golden time I look for!      (*Part 3*, III.ii.124–7)

It's become urgent, essential to speak out; the secret has to be shared with the audience; it's got to be *now*. The way I approached it, far from its being a long history of Machiavellian plotting which happens to be expressed at this point, it was an embryonic idea that had been seething away which suddenly, irresistibly, found expression. The expression is at hitherto unprecedented length for Richard, as if he has suddenly found his voice, just as Queen Elizabeth finds her voice in the scene when Richard woos her for her daughter. There are moments when characters *have* to speak, and when they speak it all comes out; this is Richard's moment, and he desperately needs to speak and to have the audience share it, and the language comes rushing out, driven by the energy of being so long pent up, a wonderful surprise to the audience, and to Richard. 'It's time for me; I want this *now*.' He starts his move upward at this point, and so long as he's going upward he continues to thrive; it's when he gets there that he loses his grip. His craving for the throne sustains him. His world has been one of hacking his way through, first as defender of the York cause, then as seeker of his own fulfilment. When all there is to do is to sustain an achieved position, he loses his impetus.

That search for his own fulfilment finds its most violent expression at Tewkesbury. Yet it is not so much personal ambition as reaction against the arrogance of young Edward that fuels his violence there. The scorn in which he (and his brothers) are held by this arrogant young man induces a 'let's clear them all up' feeling. Margaret's 'O kill me too' would be readily agreed to by Richard – 'Yes, good idea.' Edward stops that, but Richard's

'Why should she live to fill the world with words?' (v.v.44) has a sort of prophetic quality. Something has happened in him: he feels the Lancastrians must now be completely rooted up, because if they fail to do this, if they don't get the roots out, they'll come up everywhere. Children will keep appearing all over the place; Prince Edward is the representative of all the youth that can get in his way, so that, when he's stopped from killing Margaret, he decides to go to the root, the main root. It suddenly becomes very important, absolutely vital. And off he goes to the Tower. 'He's sudden if a thing comes in his head' (line 86).

The scene of the killing of Henry VI is a moment of truth for Richard. He listens to Henry going on at length about his past; it is when he turns to the future that Richard silences him. 'And if the rest be true which I have heard, / Thou camest ... ' (v.vi.55). Richard decides he has had enough at the prospect of being told the significance of his own presence in the world. This is something that must not be uttered – like having the future read, even having one's fortune told. To know one's future destroys the sanctity of unknown destiny and for Richard (certainly the way I played him) his running condition depends upon experiencing the eternal now: every minute is fresh and full of possibilities. Prophecy always panics him – as with Queen Margaret in the next play. He suffers from the fear that someone who has vision, by uttering what that vision is, can make it happen – and, of course, it does. Henry's switch from past to future triggers that reaction. Richard kills him and utters one of his most remarkable statements of self-awareness and of present-tense self-assertion:

> I have no brother, I am like no brother;
> And this word 'love', which greybeards call divine,
> Be resident in men like one another
> And not in me; I am myself alone.           (*Part 3*, v.vi.80–3)

Richard's fear of the future, observed here, and his fear of children, seen in his response to Edward's marriage, come together in the final scene of *Henry VI* when Edward has picked up his new baby. 'Young Ned', he calls him, and shows him to Richard. 'Ah, lovely', is supposed to be his reaction, but it's a wonderful juxtaposition, because we know what is going on in him, that he knows that the little bundle, that little baby, focuses all Richard's fears, everything that could obstruct what he wants. And so to see him cooing over it, kissing it, is to be aware of the huge space between the public and the private Richard. 'Sound drums and trumpets! Farewell sour annoy! / For here, I hope, begins our lasting joy' says Edward (v.vii.45), and the audience at once perceives the irony of that hope. Quite late in rehearsal we decided that I would end the play with the first syllable of *Richard III* – 'Now' – pointing that irony by answering Edward's hope with Richard's plans. Adrian wanted to overlap the plays, to give a sort of cliff-hanger feel to each of them – one nine-hour play, rather than three separate pieces. He thus ended the first with a long glance of recognition and understanding between Margaret and Henry, since the next phase will be so dominated by their relationship, and here the second part ended with my 'Now', looking forward to the immediacy of Richard in *Richard III*. If we got it right (if the audience didn't start to applaud too soon), the rhythm of the moment caught people unawares just as they were winding down on what was apparently the final couplet.

On stage at that moment was a Yorkist party. There they all were, the victors. And the party still seemed to be going on at the beginning of *Richard III*, more or less the same group. From this group Richard emerged for the famous first soliloquy. We started the third play where we ended the second. The world of Edward is the world of the cessation of war, the reign of the Sun King, peace, 'mirthful comic shows' and 'farewell sour annoy'. It's VE Day, tickertape, and people dancing in the street; the Wars of the Roses are all over and in rehearsal it was at first much more riotous than it became. Having left that world at the end of *Edward IV*, and anxious to find ways of linking the pieces, we did not want to start *Richard III* with the black-moustache-twirling Machiavel alone downstage saying 'Aha!'. We wanted to build into the change. When I looked closely at the speech I felt that the first part was potentially very positive. Obviously you can do it in a thousand ways, but to me the first section shows another aspect of Richard – that, if his energies had gone in another way, he could have been an inspiring statesman with the capacity to appreciate light, goodness, splendour, ceremony, peace. 'Now are our brows bound with victorious wreaths' (i.i.5) – yes, we have achieved something, we have achieved peace, and now we can have a good time, enjoy ourselves. This is it! So this first section of the speech was addressed to the assembled company, with Richard almost as spokesman for the celebration, with 'son of York' addressed to Edward and 'in the deep bosom of the ocean buried' ironically directed to Clarence. Syntactically, too, these first thirteen lines make a unit, revolving around the word 'now'.

Then there is a change. 'Good; now how do I operate in this new world that we've created? I can't, can I?' And so we started playing with ways of expressing that change – again reflected in the syntax, with *I* replacing *now* as the key word. And so I came downstage while the party froze behind me:

'But I, that am not shaped for sportive tricks' (line 14), and a few moments later flung my champagne bottle to smash it against the golden sun of York behind the party. The pattern is repeated through the play, with Richard creating environments which he can then most effectively destroy. He sets up situations only to reverse them.

That beginning in ensemble followed immediately by isolation reflects another important pattern. To play Richard within *The Plantagenets* had, as I have already said, important repercussions on the role in *Richard III*. When we first opened for previews I was, I think, still depending too much on the sense of ensemble. Richard must emerge from that into isolation and dominance, and after a few performances I was told off in no uncertain terms by Adrian for my failure to drive the piece. In *Richard III* Richard must take hold of the play and drive it along; because of my anxiety that it should not become a one-man show I had erred too far on the other side, and disappeared into the ensemble, so that the third play became an anticlimax. It seemed that I was about to let the whole show down by being over-generous. After that I endeavoured to be thoroughly selfish every night – for the good of the company!

The extraordinary number of soliloquies that Richard has to deliver inevitably imposes this sort of responsibility on the actor. Soliloquies are a hefty part of playing Shakespeare, and yet the convention is not altogether easy, the whole notion of how you set about communicating thoughts to an audience offering many choices to the actor: to step forward and talk to the audience as if they were eavesdroppers, or confidants, or as if they had access to your subconscious is a difficult process. When Hamlet comes and asks 'Do I kill myself, or don't I kill myself' you could present the speech in such a way that the audience is drawn in to eavesdrop and to meditate on the man's inner state, or you could go down to them and ask directly 'what am I going to do? To be or not to be?', making direct contact with them, forcing them to think, so that they feel uncertain, worried: 'Oh, I don't know.' And between the two extremes there is obviously a whole spectrum of possibilities, as one tries to involve the audience, to make them think, without intimidating them, or alienating them, and making them so uncomfortable that they stop listening.

Finding the right balance for Richard within this range of choices was vital. After three or four previews Adrian said to me (and it helped me to find a workable convention) 'you *need* the audience; Richard needs them'. Now whether Richard is happy about needing them or not is another question, which gives the relationship an extra dimension; but there are times when he has an irresistible urge to speak, and there is no one in the play on his wavelength, so he has to turn to the audience and say 'Listen! Listen to this … '. This feeling was summed up for me (ironically enough in a remark we had transferred to Richard from the Scrivener) in the moment when Richard has sent Buckingham off to organize the citizens, and he's sitting there in front of Hastings's head and a table of food and he turns to the audience and asks:

> Who is so gross
> That cannot see this palpable device?
> Yet who's so bold but says he sees it not?
> (*Richard III*, III.vi.10–13)

There is a certain pattern to the soliloquies of Richard when one looks at the whole movement from 'Ay, Edward will use women honourably' to the final soliloquy before Bosworth. At first there is a quality of introspection, of the audience eavesdropping on his thoughts: 'Well, what's left for me then?' This returns at the end, though the introspection is now on a much deeper level. In between, many of the soliloquies are obviously vigorous direct address, with Richard using the audience sometimes almost as he uses other characters in the play, to surprise, to shock, to puzzle – for I don't believe that we can say with confidence that Richard is all the time simply 'being himself', not 'acting', in the soliloquies. Obviously after the ghosts he reaches something like rock-bottom – 'I shall despair. There is no creature loves me' (v.iii.201) – but earlier in *Richard III* there is a strong element of display, of performance to the audience, in the soliloquies: 'Did you see that? Watch this then! Was ever woman in this humour wooed?' So often the audience is denied the role of eavesdropper, of secret observer, and forced into involvement, into a mood of uncomfortable collusion:

> Upon my life, she finds, although I cannot,
> Myself to be a marvellous proper man.
> I'll be at charges for a looking-glass
> And entertain a score or two of tailors
> To study fashions to adorn my body.          (I.ii.253–7)

Again the audience is confronted and challenged: 'What do you think about that then? Hm? Like to go out with a man with a hump?'

The wooing of Lady Anne is a remarkable episode with which to begin the final play of the group, for it reveals a great deal about Richard. At an important level, obviously, his motivation here is political: Anne is Warwick's daughter, and to control the Nevilles is to control political (and no doubt financial) power in England. More than that, however, is the challenge that the enterprise presents to him:

> For then I'll marry Warwick's youngest daughter.
> What though I killed her husband and her father?
> The readiest way to make the wench amends
> Is to become her husband and her father,
> The which will I – not all so much for love
> As ...                                    (1.i.153–8)

And then he decides not to tell us (and they say soliloquies are for characters to tell the truth to the audience!):

> As for another secret close intent
> By marrying her which I must reach unto.        (lines 158–9)

The 'secret' motives are, perhaps, largely to do with political wheeling and dealing, but 'not all so much for *love*' seems to imply that he wants it because he wants it, because it is almost impossible, because he thrives on the feeling that 'were it farther off' he'd 'pluck it down'. He seems consciously to decide to make the stakes ridiculous. There are to be no letters of explanation, no attempts to excuse his behaviour on the basis of the necessities of war; he will simply take a situation where her hatred for him is at its most extreme and still succeed. The outrageous, exorbitant determination to achieve what he wants is important to him; he has found that shifting into such a mode releases his energy: the energy that makes it possible for him to achieve what he wants. He has realized, probably by accident, that he operates best in total adversity, that he is galvanized, in some way, by it. So that, although the underlying motive may be political necessity, he discovers early in the scene that this in no way impedes his enjoyment of the process. Indeed, the whole thing becomes necessary for *him*, as a kind of self-fulfilment. There is, I think, no thought of founding his own dynasty in this decision to marry. He is quite unlike Macbeth in this; the whole enterprise begins with Richard and ends with him – and that, of course, is his problem, for once he achieves power it becomes a matter of trying to sustain it and then of realizing that he, too, is mortal.

One aspect of the wooing scene that became clearer as we played it was that Richard must not be seen by Anne to be 'acting'. The more she is confused about how genuine his feelings are, the more unbalancing it will be for her. If she is constantly wondering 'is he really ... has my beauty really had such a profound effect ... is he really crying?', the more, in short, that the player of Richard makes it difficult to know whether he is performing, or genuinely feeling, emotion, the more interesting are the questions that the scene raises. Richard bases his strategy on attack: everything she accuses him of he accepts, with the proviso that everything he has done he has done for her. He makes her, quite specifically, an 'accessory':

> This hand, which for thy love did kill thy love,
> Shall for thy love kill a far truer love;
> To both their deaths shalt thou be accessory.    (I.ii.189–91)

He shifts the blame which, for a Christian person in the terrible straits where Anne Neville now finds herself, is the ultimate means of producing a sense of guilt. Having loaded her with all that, he can feel quite confident when he says 'Take up the sword again, or take up me' (line 183); either kill this so-called sinner or forgive him. The dilemma that he places her in at this moment is the turning-point of the scene; Geraldine Alexander always took her time at this moment, allowing the audience absolutely to share her sense of indecision, before succumbing: 'Arise dissembler.' His offer to kill himself is accompanied by reminders that it was 'her beauty' that provoked him, so that she is forced into the belief that it was her body, her physicality, all that she as a devout Christian is trying to rise above, which provoked his behaviour. The idea we were aiming for was that guilt about her own sexuality, rather than any particular attraction towards his, is what governs her behaviour here.

The exuberance of the wooing scene shows Richard at the height of his powers and I think we found a coherent way of playing it. The 'prayer book' scene with the Lord Mayor was always more difficult. There are so many options here: one could decide to go completely burlesque and to make no concession to reality, to present merely a pantomime. Or one could go the other way and have Richard take great pains to try to convince his auditors of the power of his performance as a pious monarch, from the same mould as Henry VI. We had difficulty in finding the right note on which to play this scene. In the end our decision was to make it as clear as we could that Richard and Buckingham are merely seeking to fulfil a formula: it must be *recorded*, in the annals, that on such-and-such a date, under duress of the people, Richard accepted the crown. The news is then immediately disseminated by messengers, and arrival at that point, however it is reached, was always our main objective in the scene.

The people's acceptance achieved, precariously, Richard moves to the throne. We wanted to offer a strong image of Richard's relationship to the throne as a physical object, very different from the stillness and quietness with which Henry had sat upon it. The idea for presenting this emerged not long into rehearsals, and I don't think we ever really needed to analyse it very much. We had early decided that Act Four Scene Two should begin with a 'coronation walk down' – a little procession to the front of the stage with the throne upstage behind us. At first I tried simply walking back to the throne, sitting down on it and saying 'Stand all apart' (IV.ii.1), but it didn't work because it didn't seem to have the right dynamic. It struck me, as we worked on the scene, that the first half of the play is entirely concerned with getting, getting, getting: 'Many lives stand between me and home … '. The thorny wood bars his way from what he wants, which is to sit on that throne. Then he gets there and the question immediately becomes 'Hm. What do I do now?' This point, therefore, is in every sense a pivot and must be strongly marked; this is his zenith, from which he can only descend. At this point he is like the child who has all along been saying 'I want that, I want that' and then 'I've got it, I've got it … Oh, I'm bored now.' So I decided to rush to the throne with a scream of possessive delight and to leap into it; having done that once in rehearsal, with the director's approval, it stayed in. And the leap of mad delight into that enormous throne was immediately followed by the realization that all that is now left is to try to stay there. He dismisses them all – 'Get out. Everyone get out': 'Stand all apart' – and they all go and just leave him sitting there on his own in a throne that is miles too big for him, his legs dangling down like a little child's, quite unable to reach the floor. The pathos of that image is important at this pivotal point in the play, the wild excitement of leaping into that seat followed in a second or two by the loneliness and stillness of the little figure dwarfed by it.

From this scene in which he first sits on the throne to the end of the play it is clear, at least in retrospect, that Richard is losing power. An important stage in this process is the confrontation with his mother (IV.iv) who 'intercepts' him in his 'expedition' against Buckingham's rebellion. God knows what the relationship between Richard and his mother has been like; clearly the conduit which should allow love to flow naturally between mother and child got bunged-up somewhere, and for Richard it seems it never operated at all. From his emergence from the womb the see-saw effect of alienation and defence, attack and self-protection, created a thick wall of isolation from his mother, driving him towards the superficial comradeship of his brothers, their roles as warriors bringing them into spurious unity as a 'pack', though not to any real sort of love. I think the only real affection for Richard was from and for his father. Perhaps that did

153

have a genuine quality, though no doubt rarely finding expression, since the father would have been too distant a figure. With his mother, however, there is nothing and when she curses him she is expressing that absolute need to speak which we see several characters in the play confronting at certain points. She needs to express her horror at what she has given birth to, to crystallize it, to make it terminal. 'I shall never speak to thee again', she says (IV.iv.182), and Richard thinks 'Exactly – because you never loved me anyway.' In our production Richard's response was punctuated by his rhythmically wounding himself in the hand with his dagger. The idea I wanted to express was that he feels he must hurt, must mutilate himself because if he doesn't he will kill his mother in his rage at what, in his eyes, she has been responsible for. She has prevented the progress of his war, has literally stood in the way of the war machine, and he needs to find a way of releasing the energy that has built up while she goes on and on. And he wounds himself in the hand – the first time in all three plays that we have seen him wounded. He had asked her to be 'brief, good mother, for I am in haste' (line 162), and then she hits him with all those emotionally painful memories, and it rattles him more than he had expected; there being nothing he can do he wounds himself and the moment is ominous, looking forward to the final soliloquy.

He turns from his mother to Queen Elizabeth – 'Ah, I want to speak to her. Now this is going to be easier' – and he seems to think it has been: 'Relenting fool, and shallow, changing woman' (line 431). But she, like the Duchess of York (following their conversation with Queen Margaret), has also found her voice, and begins to prove a match for him. The exchange is very disconcerting; it throws him, though he tries to convince himself he's handled it with his usual dexterity. If the scene is done well, however, the audience should see the huge gap between what happened, and what he tells himself: she has not been shallow and she is not a fool. His failure of perception is part of the process of crumbling which we watch here. He has started to crack, and we see the cracks appearing wider and wider now as the news comes in of all the rats leaving the sinking ship. It started when Buckingham went cold on him and the cracks are getting wider and now he is losing his grip. He knows that and he tries to shore himself up. 'The King's name is a tower of strength' he will say, hopefully, a few scenes later (V.iii.12). 'We'll be all right ... Let's keep positive, that's how I've always operated, on energy ... Another obstacle? – Great, that's how I thrive.' But actually he is going down the slope very fast and subconsciously he knows it.

The subconscious asserts itself, of course, in the dream during the night before Bosworth. As we talked about this scene in the early stages, one of the things I knew I did not want to do was to give a demonstration of Richard's terror during the nightmare. I didn't want him thrashing about in fear because what is often extraordinary about nightmares is that you experience the horror of what you have dreamed only when you wake up and recollect it: 'O my God, that was awful.' Frequently while you are in the nightmare you are just so fascinated by the extraordinary juxta-positions of weird things – talking to John Lennon on a 42 bus while he's dead – and yet while you are asleep the crazy conjunctions of elements are somehow acceptable and you are not necessarily in a state of terror. Then you come back to waking consciousness and start to assess what has happened and it becomes very frightening – and frequently very dramatic. This is evidenced by Richard's speech as he wakes up: 'O coward con-science, how dost thou afflict me' (v.iii.180) ... 'My God, what's happen-ing to me?' 'I fear, I fear,' he says to Ratcliffe and for one moment in the play it is clear that he is not acting. That was what I wanted to get from the ghosts. He had been fascinated by them: 'Clarence, what are you doing here?'; 'Henry, where ... you're dead.' He is in that altered state of consciousness and then he has to assess it afterwards and to consider its implications for his own vulnerability. In the process comes the awful realization that 'if I die, no soul will pity me' (line 202). That was the progression I wanted to get from the ghosts to the soliloquy that followed. As we worked on the scene the idea emerged that Richard might try to talk to some of the ghosts. It was an intuitive feeling that Richard would want to talk to some of them, not only, as it were, to try to explain, or to come to some sort of arrangement or understanding, but more generally to try to make some logical sense out of this illogical crazy thing that was happen-ing. The goblet in which Ratcliff brought the wine is still there and the shock of seeing it has its effect. One does not need to be too specific about its meaning, but it has something of symbolic potency for Richard in his dream, so that the cup of wine becomes the communion cup, the blood of Christ; whatever the audience brings to Richard's responses, here is a symbol of retribution, deliverance, sin, forgiveness, ceremony, final judge-ment. There it is on the table and now Anne is walking in; but she's dead and Richard has something to expiate, to make her understand, just something he has to say to her. At such moments I wanted to listen very intently to what they were saying, though the full realization of their curses does not come until later: 'I shall despair' (line 201). I did not, of course, want to sit there and react specifically to every one of them; there are a lot of them, a long list. What I felt was needed was an explanation of why his reaction to them is delayed. They are telling him extraordinary and terrible things, but at the time he does not take them in because he is just thinking 'O come back. O God, I'm sure I had to tell you something about why I'm here ... and why ... ?' Then, when he snaps back into consciousness, and realizes it was all a dream, the power of all those curses hits him: 'I shall despair' – and die. The impact of that was increased, we felt, by having Richard also hear what is said to Richmond. It does not affect him so much while it's happening, he is in a state of too much confusion for that, but when he wakes it adds to the realization of despair.

The soliloquy that follows the dream seemed to me a major turning-point. Unlike his earlier soliloquies, he does not invite the audience in. They simply overhear. During it he continues verbally the action of stabbing himself which, in our production, had followed his mother's curse. He pins himself like a butterfly to a board. 'Fool, of thyself speak well,' he says (line 193), but he cannot escape the truth: 'You've murdered, you've perjured, you're a villain, you've done it, you've done it. Look, look, look.' Like a pin through a butterfly, the words go home. It is an elusive and exciting speech for an actor, and presents many opportunities: a speech which for me varied from performance to performance. It was important, I thought, to be as specific as possible about the speech in the actual moment after the dream. There is a remarkable clarity about the speech, something like the stillness after a great storm. It is as though a veil has been taken away from Richard; he has been in a state of deep illusion, not just through the dream but through his life, and the curtain has now been drawn back and he looks in the mirror and sees every line on his own face – like the picture of Dorian Gray. It's very clear, and he tries to face it: 'I am a villain.' This present moment, this, is the bottom line: 'There is no creature loves me.' There is a terribly simple but profound understanding here; this is it, this is how it's going to be. Of course he has to try to move beyond it, to find a way of shoring up the situation, to find a way forward. But the perspective has changed. The Richard that he was before this night was 99.9 per cent certain of himself as a winner, with no real element of doubt. The possibility of doubt had its birth in him when Elizabeth and his mother found their voices, but it takes the dream to make him realize, to show him the truth. His belief, his excuse, has been that the world owed him a living because he'd been dealt some rotten cards; but he has been seeking fulfilment in a direction that is now revealed to him as quite simply

21   Anton Lesser as Richard III at the battle of Bosworth

the *wrong* way. He is his own judge and prosecution at what he calls the 'bar', and he sees his predicament with a terrible clarity.

All his experience, however, his patterning, his conditioning, have made him a fighter and he has no choice but to be a fighter to the end. He has seen that there is no escape from the situation to which his own actions have led, but being the man he is he has to take that on board and continue. It is as though he, like everyone else, has a momentum that his previous life has created; something – usually suffering, bereavement, grief – may temporarily halt that and in a moment of great emotional extremity the real self may appear. And yet that experience, which will never allow you to be the same again, does not alter the conditioning, and the momentum goes on. So Richard must continue as a fighter; it's all he has, in spite of his recognition of its futility. The prophetic power of the dream, however, informs a sort of degeneration, a paranoia, that affects him and communicates itself to Ratcliff, Catesby, and Norfolk. It was felt a little before the dream, perhaps the effect of his interview with his mother: 'But where tomorrow? Well, all's one for that' (v.iii.8); but now, you feel the sense of all the things we are not going to talk about, and the sun will not shine, and there's a feeling that things are disintegrating. There is the Henry V style in the oration to his soldiers – 'What shall I say' – but now it is all visibly a waste of time.

We kept the full impact of the dream and the ghosts, however, for the final battle scene. We decided to stage the battle so that the audience might think that perhaps Richard was going to win, that Richmond was about to get it. We devised the final fight to show Richard about to kill Richmond until some of the ghosts returned to utter 'Despair and die.' They stopped him in the course of his succeeding and that was when he was seen to be completely drained of his power. In a sense the moment suggested a supernatural intervention, though it could be interpreted as the audience wished: have the ghosts actually appeared to him on the battlefield or are they a metaphor for the awakening of conscience, of the fact that in times of extreme stress we become open to an area of ourselves that is in touch with some vast reservoir of power or prophecy? We tried to keep the moment ambiguous: the ghosts' appearance behind Richmond meant that only Richard could be aware of their presence. Perhaps if they had been in front of Richmond he wouldn't have seen them either – after all, *he* has never said anything about his dream, only that he slept remarkably well. For Richard, however, the moment was crucial and he surrendered the fight.

We devised a particularly striking – and not always easy to execute – death blow. Richmond's spear actually pierced Richard through the hump, from which blood and matter gushed out as he fell. Finding the hole in the hump with the spear caused us some entertainingly anxious moments, but the image was, I think, a powerful and effective one. The sequence of *The Plantagenets* had been full of battles, though there are none in *Richard III* until Bosworth itself. We felt that we wanted a final, strong martial image to end the play and that we should not cheat the audience with something perfunctory. I wanted to fight with a flag on my spear, to make a big final picture, a last megalomanic statement, and the fight director, Malcolm Ranson, thought of adding the image of the spear piercing Richard's deformity. We were not, I think, consciously trying to present the idea of the evils of the past being concentrated in that deformity, and thus purged in the final ritualistic slaughter, but that notion came to be a part of the moment. The threads of destruction, and evil, explored through three plays, have come together, have come to a final point, and suddenly it's all over.

One of the things I wanted to avoid with Richard was falling into the trap of constantly presenting a Machiavel who knew exactly what he was going to do ten steps ahead, a man of moustache-twirling knowingness and unrelieved cleverness. I wanted his intelligence, and his Machiavellian quality, to be earned, to grow and to develop from the young Richard who responds precisely to the moment, who is always right here and now. 'This world is no good for me,' he says; 'how am I going to make the best of this?' 'Well, I can do this, and I can do that ... ' 'Wet my face with artificial tears ... change colours with the chameleon' (*Part Three*, III.ii.184–91). He makes the moment absolutely his, he snatches it, the perfect opportunist. And, preferably for him, he does so in terribly adverse circumstances, thriving when things are *most* difficult, as with the wooing of Lady Anne. He sets things up for himself in order to go beyond them. Right through the plays, to the conscience speech before Bosworth, he is responding to the moment in this way. Then he meets that other form of here-and-nowness, the realization of his past, something with an absolute quality to it, something he cannot manipulate. And the journey from there to the end is very brief.

People usually come to Shakespeare with preconceptions. What is interesting in the theatre is to send them home saying 'I don't know whether I think that any more.'

# Thersites in
# *Troilus and Cressida*

## SIMON RUSSELL BEALE

SIMON RUSSELL BEALE played Thersites in Sam Mendes's production of *Troilus and Cressida* at the Swan Theatre, Stratford in 1990 and the following season in the Pit Theatre at the Barbican. In the same seasons he played the title role in Marlowe's *Edward II*, Konstantin in *The Seagull*, and the King of Navarre in *Love's Labour's Lost*. A wide range of earlier work for the RSC had included only one other Shakespearian role, that of the Young Shepherd in *The Winter's Tale*, in 1986–87. Among other parts for the Company, many of them, like Thersites, in productions conceived for the Swan, have been Oliver in *The Art of Success*, Ed Kno'well in *Every Man in his Humour*, Fawcett in *The Fair Maid of the West*, Lord Are in *Restoration*, Clincher Senior in *The Constant Couple*, and Sir Fopling Flutter in *The Man of Mode*. In 1992–93, again directed by Sam Mendes, he played the title role in *Richard III* in Stratford and on a regional tour.

To be honest, I didn't have a great deal of enthusiasm for Thersites to begin with. Although I recognized that the man's vocabulary was of a dazzling range and that his intelligence probably outstripped anyone else's on the stage – with the possible exception of Ulysses – I experienced the same despondency when I read the part that I felt when, a few years ago, I first approached the Clown in *The Winter's Tale*. Shakespeare's clown/fool figures are, of course, as varied as one would expect, but all of them seem to require what I suppose we could call a 'personality actor' – an actor, in other words, whose own characteristics can rise above the limitations of the part he is playing. The element of theatricality, of performance, as opposed to the detailed realization of a character, seems to be of paramount import-ance. Astonishing as it seems to me now, Thersites, like the Clown, didn't seem to offer a particularly interesting emotional or intellectual exercise, and if the Royal Shakespeare Company wanted a star-turn, then quite definitely I was not the man for the job.

Thersites also, quite obviously, had to be funny and I was frightened that I would be unable to lift the script off the page and make an audience laugh. I suppose most actors worry that after so many weeks of rehearsal, they will still have failed to find the key to a character's comic life, and Thersites, with his extraordinary baroque use of language, presented a particularly acute challenge. As I read the part, I kept remembering Joe Melia's advice when we were both doing *The Winter's Tale* – actually during a rehearsal of the famous, but very long, pastoral scene in Act Four. He said to me that so long as I sounded as if I was saying something funny, so long as I used a recognizably comic rhythm, I would get a response regardless of whether the majority of the audience immediately understood the words. He called it 'adopting a confident vernacular tone'. It sounds, I know, very reductive, and I admit that it's born out of desperation, but it's an approach that has its value, principally because it recognizes the simple physical power of Shakespeare's language – its sounds and its rhythms – considered independently from its meaning. Like any great writer, Shakespeare understood comic rhythms and those rhythms are to be trusted. Indeed, the first principles of prose performance in Shakespeare are of course not dissimilar to those required for verse, but, unlike verse, there is no history of technical blueprints, no easy-to-follow guides for making archaic prose sound funny.

Too little has been written about the performance of Shakespeare's prose as opposed to the performance of his verse – probably because the added comic and therefore idiosyncratic ingredient is rather difficult to define, because analyses of the clowns rely so heavily on their being seen and cannot, as I implied earlier, be fully discussed apart from particular performances. So, for an actor, constructing a Shakespearian clown is a leap in the dark.

I accepted the part – despite my misgivings – for a series of reasons. I wanted to work with this new director – Sam Mendes – whom I'd heard so much about; I wanted to do some more Shakespeare – I have done so little; and, finally, *Troilus and Cressida* is a play that I had admired for a long time. To my enormous relief and delight I found that, once I had started working, Thersites was genuinely, fluidly funny and, even better, psychologically complex.

To plot his development from the first read-through to the last performance is actually very difficult. I started, not surprisingly, by asking basic questions and by trying to challenge my own admittedly limited preconceptions of the part – a rather academic approach. By the time we opened in Stratford I had constructed a series of what I assumed to be watertight arguments – sure and essential foundations for my performance. Through the year and more of playing, however, all those arguments were challenged and now, to be perfectly honest, I'm not quite sure where I am. What *is* certain is that I realize that Thersites is a movable feast, that his function in the play was determined as much by audience response and by my own state of mind at the time of playing as it was by the work I did in rehearsal. I also realize that, since Thersites's function is essentially choric – he plays no part in the admittedly slender plot-line of *Troilus and Cressida* – it is in his gift to push the audience's response in the direction he chooses. Equally, it is the responsibility of the actor playing him to make sure that Thersites's views do not imperceptibly come to appear as those of Shakespeare. He must not become the voice of the playwright. At one point during the run, I remember, I had got into the habit of delivering one of Thersites's lines – 'The sun borrows of the moon when Diomed keeps his word' (v.i.89) – with a sort of breathy high seriousness. I thought it was rather exciting until Sam Mendes came up to me after a performance and said, 'For God's sake, stop saying that line as if it's the meaning of the play.' It was a salutary reminder not to make Thersites too self-important. It would be arrogant and presumptuous of me to say that Thersites holds the balance of the play in his hands, but his job is unquestionably to keep the audience on its toes, to stop any easy judgements being made. It is important that, despite his theatrical power, Thersites is not necessarily to be trusted. If he is trusted without question, then the play becomes complacently reductive. On the other hand, if his views are ignored or dismissed as merely the result of his unfortunate situation, then a challenging voice is lost. That is both the joy and the difficulty of the part.

If the function of Thersites is to question the motives of the characters in the story and to make the audience question those motives, then his own history must be as clear as possible – and that history must be developed from a calm and unprejudiced reading of the text. The questions I began by asking sound rather obvious now. Does Thersites have to be specifically of a lower class than the other characters in the play? What if he looks hideous but speaks rather beautifully? Why can't, or doesn't, he fight? Is it because of his class or is it because of something else, like deformity? Or, perhaps, does he *choose* not to fight? Why is he so embittered? What, precisely, is his function in the Greek camp?

The last of these questions was the easiest to answer but the most difficult to do anything about. Achilles calls Thersites 'a privileged man' – in other words, a licensed fool. This is the only *direct* reference to Thersites's job; but it is a job that has little or no resonance for me or, I suspect, for an audience. In fact, I associate the figure of the jester only with negative things – a prejudice of mine that the director eventually used. What was worked out by Sam Mendes and me was the result of meeting the jester cliché head on. I decided to use a conventional joker's stick – with bells and all – and it came to serve as a reminder to Thersites of the role he had been asked, for whatever reason, to fulfil – a role that he hates but which pays the rent. The more conventionally jolly the stick, we thought, the more painful the reminder to someone as intelligent and cynical as Thersites of his position as an entertainer and his exclusion from the circle of protagonists.

His other function in the play – although it is never stated clearly – seems to be as a sort of batman to Ajax; a job that Thersites insists he took up voluntarily. Of course, he soon leaves Ajax – at the end of his very first scene, indeed (Act Two, Scene One) – and so his role as batman is not fully explored by the playwright. For the rest of the play, the audience sees Thersites principally as a sidekick to Achilles and Patroclus. As one of the few statements offered by Thersites about his position in the Greek camp, however, this comment that his work as a servant is 'voluntary' is very important – important as a first clue, as it were. It also prompts Achilles to reply: 'Your last service was suff'rance, 'twas not voluntary; no man is beaten voluntary. Ajax was here the voluntary, and you as under an impress' (II.i.95–7). It's not a very good joke – as Thersites appreciates – but Achilles does not directly deny the truth of Thersites's statement. All he does is to point out, rather feebly, that no man enjoys being beaten. There doesn't seem to be any implication that Thersites was dragged over the sea to serve a particular master, or, indeed, any master. It occurred to me, therefore, that perhaps the difference between the great warriors and Thersites is not one based on class. Might it not be the case (given also that all the characters in *Troilus and Cressida* enjoy the same articulacy) that the warriors and Thersites share the same world, that Thersites speaks as an insider? The answer to that question led to the idea that Thersites should speak with the elaborate precision of a school swot in a rather sporty public school. It has to be said that this argument came as rather a relief to me, since I've always found work on accents very difficult and I could now use a voice that was very close to my own. More seriously, the fact that we decided that Thersites should speak like those around him gave him a power and, oddly, an individuality that was very useful.

Quite by chance, the notion of Thersites as Ajax's batman threw up the idea of wearing surgical gloves – a part of my costume that I enjoyed immensely because they were both gruesome and funny. Richard Ridings, who was playing Ajax, had developed in rehearsal a character already absurdly obsessed with his own physical magnificence and, in consequence, rigorously health-conscious. In contrast, I had been playing around with the idea that Thersites had, at some time or other, contracted almost every disease under the sun. The scene between Ajax and Thersites started, in our version, with Thersites's bringing on Ajax's breakfast and I felt that Ajax would probably insist on his batman wearing gloves. I started originally with white butler's gloves – which I would then discard for later scenes – but felt that they looked too much like the trappings of a conventional clown. I then remembered a friend of mine at prep school, who used to wear plastic bags over his feet because he had some debilitating and painful skin disorder. It was humiliating for him, and once I had used the idea as a way of covering Thersites's hands, it became a particularly humiliating and repulsive feature of his costume. The surgical gloves also had a practical use. Putting make-up on your hands is obviously very tricky, since it's always coming off and needs constant reapplication. I wanted to give the impression, in whatever way, that Thersites's hands were diseased. The gloves solved the problem of constant reapplication of make-up as well as adding a rather unpleasant air of mystery to the question of what precise diseases Thersites had contracted.

Actually, Shakespeare doesn't specifically say in the text that Thersites has any disease or deformity. Of course, many comments are made about the fact that he is ugly: Achilles calls him a 'crusty botch of nature' (v.i.5), for example, but no particular disfigurement is mentioned. Homer obviously regards him as one of the most unpleasant men to come over to Troy, and I think I'm right that in Homer he's a fighting man with direct access to the generals. In Shakespeare, he's obviously not a fighting man. The hunched back and the bad leg that I used, and to some extent the skin disorder, came from the fact that I wanted to make sure that Thersites couldn't have fought even if he had wanted to. I had already decided, rightly or wrongly, that he wasn't prevented from fighting because he was born into the wrong class. The other obvious option seemed to be that he is physically incapable of fighting. It is very painful to watch a man who can blame only God, or the gods, for the fact that physically he is a mess and unable to enter into or enjoy fully the world in which he has chosen to work.

It seems odd, I realize, to put forward the idea that somehow Thersites might *want* to fight; but it is an idea that leads us to an answer to the most important question of all: why is he so embittered? It struck me that his voluntary association with this futile war allowed for the apparently absurd possibility that in different circumstances (and with a different body) Thersites might have followed the same noble and courageous path as a Hector, for instance. His cynicism could be the result of a distorted romanticism and, like all cynics, the delight he feels in being proved right is tempered with a numbing disappointment in the behaviour of his fellow human beings. It is a sentimental argument, but it developed to provide a firm psychological basis for Thersites's consistently reductive analyses. It is also the argument that was the first to be challenged by the demands of audiences over the period of playing. Because Thersites's commentary is so funny, it became tempting to play his cynicism as some sort of 'given', not rooted in any particular pain. I began to care less about why Thersites is the sort of man he is than about the fact that he is a brilliant performer – to care less about causes than symptoms, as it were. This simpler approach had two effects: it allowed Thersites to become less human and more diabolical, and it pushed the play into much darker, more destructive areas. What I lost was a whole set of complex reasons behind Thersites's actions – the reasons, for example, for his extreme reaction to Cressida's betrayal of Troilus and his unexpectedly harsh loathing of Diomedes. I also lost the reasons behind his apparently arbitrary but devastating attacks on Patroclus. This was a shame, because Thersites's relationship with Patroclus lay at the root of my original conception of the character.

Patroclus becomes Thersites's victim not just because he is one of the weaker members of the Greek camp. Thersites admires Achilles, I think, and lashes out at him only because of his debilitating relationship with Patroclus; the latter consequently receives the full flow of Thersites's invective. If Achilles were to fulfil his potential (a possibility that provides a major component of the story of the play) then something, at least, would be gained in the fighting of a ridiculous and seemingly endless war. It was for this reason that I wanted Thersites to be present at Hector's death. The death of Patroclus spurs Achilles into action and is therefore a god-sent, if distressing, opportunity for Achilles to prove himself and to reveal those qualities for which he is so admired by his fellow officers and, I suspect, by Thersites. What Achilles does in the end is to kill Hector, the noblest warrior of them all, in a way that is cowardly and despicable. In our production, Thersites screamed as he watched Hector's death. In the complex, sentimental version of Thersites that I started with, it was a scream of pain; later, in the simpler, blacker version, it was a scream of triumph. Actually, more often than not, it was a mixture of the two, triumph and pain, and perhaps that is the most satisfactory option of all. Perhaps the source of this character's pain should remain a mystery.

Thersites has very little stage time. He is only one of many characters who make up the front line in a play where the responsibility is spread very widely. Indeed, he doesn't become a dominant figure until the fifth act, a fact which means that his first three appearances (spread over the long period of the first four acts) must be precisely played and carefully thought through. They must also, it seems to me, be strongly coloured, since, although all three scenes are short, they set the agenda for the internal debate within the character. In other words, the complexity and delicacy of Thersites's commentary in the last act cannot come through unless the audience has a clear picture of the character to look back to and to use.

Thersites's first scene (Act Two, Scene One) is, at its simplest, a scene of comic relief slotted between two of the most difficult debates that Shakespeare ever wrote. It is also a violent scene. I began to wonder, rather late in the run of the play, whether the sight of a huge and powerful warrior beating a smaller and apparently defenceless servant somehow restricted the audience's enjoyment of the scene. But it was important to establish that violence is a regular and expected part of Thersites's life, that it is wearying and boring as well as painful, and that far from being defenceless, Thersites has plenty of his own effective ammunition. The danger of trying to show this sense of a tired, unhappy, brutal relationship was that the beating of Thersites by Ajax tended to look a little pat, a little staged. At its best, the scene showed a neat balance of spontaneous, precise violence and dance-like predictability.

So, until Achilles and Patroclus arrive, the scene is a battle between two surprisingly equal combatants. There are, however, clues for the actor playing Thersites that he is not merely a mouthpiece for savage character assassination. For instance, there is something pathetic about his indirect appeal to Ajax – 'Dost thou think I have no sense, thou strikest me thus?' (II.i.21) – although in performance one has to be careful to avoid introducing self-pity into the character's make-up. Similarly, given that I had decided that Thersites should have 'boils, full, all over, generally' (II.i.2), his first comment in the play, where he imagines Agamemnon in the same condition, has a grim, self-hating bite.

Further clues to the difficulties of Thersites's position in the Greek camp can be found in the reason for the argument between the two

166

characters. On reading the scene, we decided that the proclamation should be seen on stage in the form of a letter – as if Agamemnon and his council had sent an identical memorandum to all the principal officers in the camp. So, instead of Thersites's being beaten simply because he has heard some information which he is refusing to impart, either he has stolen the letter and is refusing to give it back (an option unlikely to deter the much stronger Ajax) or, more interestingly, he is able to read and therefore understand the proclamation and Ajax is not. It was this latter option that we chose – that Ajax is illiterate and needs the otherwise revolting Thersites to read his letters for him – and it served subtly to alter the balance of the scene. Instead of being a rather traditional master–servant scene, it became, despite outward appearances, a scene between equals.

When Achilles and Patroclus enter, the scene changes pace. The physical fight seems to be over and consequently Thersites's tongue can run riot. Indeed, although we decided in rehearsal that Ajax would stop fighting in such a demeaning way as soon as the immensely impressive Achilles enters the scene, Thersites seems to display no hesitation in turning his attention to Patroclus and, more surprisingly, to Achilles. Achilles himself seems to be surprised that Thersites has the nerve to attack him: 'What, with me, too, Thersites?' (II.i.102). The reasons for this lack of discrimination are difficult to determine. It is, of course, obvious by the end of the play that Thersites's desire to lash out at everyone stems from a deep-rooted and universally applied disgust. At this early stage, however, his anger must be seen to be more localized, a reaction to Ajax's stupidity and need to resort to physical violence, to Achilles's self-centred complacency and to Patroclus's mistimed attempt to stop the argument. It seems to me that at this point it is important to establish the fact that to criticize so powerful a person to his face takes some courage – or some extreme sense of desperation – and that, in order to prevent this character becoming merely a function, it is essential to determine the exact nature of each individual insult. In other words, an insult directed to Achilles requires a different motive to one directed at, say, Patroclus, and an insult muttered in private has a different tone to one meant to be heard by another character.

Act Two, Scene One ends with Thersites's leaving Ajax's tent and his statement that he will never return – unusual for a man who never, elsewhere, seems to take firm action over anything:

I will see you hanged like clotpolls ere I come any more to your tents; I will keep where there is wit stirring, and leave the faction of fools.

(II.i.116–18)

167

In order to leave employment, whether 'voluntary' or not, Thersites must be very angry and he seems here to be uncharacteristically expressing his anger quite directly and openly. The insults, although witty, have none of the bantering, game-playing tone that he employs later in his scenes with Achilles and Patroclus. It seems that once he loses his considerable ability for producing disinterested invective, the only option for Thersites is to leave the scene.

His first soliloquy (in the third scene of Act Two) is, in essence, a statement of intent – a result of the character's sense that up until this point his anger has been purposeless: 'How now, Thersites! What, lost in the labyrinth of thy fury?' (II.iii.1). His desire for a solution, bitterly expressed, lies at the centre of this speech: 'Sfoot, I'll learn to conjure and raise devils, but I'll see some issue of my spiteful execrations' (line 5). As I said earlier, it is very rare to hear Thersites speaking without a gloss of self-irony, and indeed, even here, there is a hint of self-mockery in the idea of 'raising devils'; but the tone is, I think, serious. And one can go further. Part of the mystery of this extraordinary character lies in the fact that, although he is essentially passive, he displays, especially in the last act, an alchemist's ability to transform what he sees in front of him, to distort or to reveal the motives of other characters. In other words, he does, despite the powerlessness of his position, 'conjure and raise devils'. What is fascinating for the actor is the question of whether the 'issue' – the last scenes of betrayal and pusillanimity – delights or disgusts Thersites. Once the roots of a hypocritical society are exposed, then the first and principal reaction, even for a radical commentator, is surely one of despair.

At this point the soliloquy changes course. In Sam Mendes's production, I played this speech in front of the tent in which the audience saw Achilles and Patroclus relaxing, and, in the middle of the speech, the sound of jazz from a radio woke Thersites out of his rather self-absorbed analysis. His wit is then employed, more characteristically, in a delicate process of character assassination, including a line that I thought of as one of the funniest in the play: 'If Troy be not taken till these two undermine it, the walls will stand till they fall of themselves' (line 8). Although, at the beginning of the run, this line got the response I wanted, I suspect that, later on, I fell into that dreadful and common trap of enjoying it too much. The audience instinctively guessed that I found the line a great deal funnier than they did and remained resolutely silent.

Once Patroclus and Achilles appear, Thersites sets his mind on the seduction of the two warriors – or rather on the seduction of Achilles.

22   Simon Russell Beale as Thersites mimics Ajax, watched by Patroclus
(Patterson Joseph) 'He stalks up and down like a peacock' (III.iii.251)

Given that he desperately needs employment, it is odd that the butt of his
rather tired routine is Patroclus – Achilles's lover and therefore a man, one
would think, of considerable influence. It says a great deal about Patroclus's status in the camp, Achilles's egoism, and Thersites's understanding

of just how far he can go, how much vitriol he can employ so long as it is hidden behind a mask of game-playing. Thersites even calls Achilles 'a fool' to his face (albeit fleetingly) and, since Achilles does not respond, we must assume that Thersites knows that he is safe. What is unusual about the game, however, is that the audience knows that Thersites, unlike most clowns, can employ his wit in a more incisive and virtuosic way, and knows too that any game seems to be used by Thersites as a form of self-censorship. Of course, the game, although not a particularly dazzling display, is successful in that Achilles invites Thersites to join him; but, in his final address to the audience in this scene, it seems to me that Thersites is talking as much about himself as about Achilles and Patroclus: 'Here is such patchery, such jiggling, and such knavery!' (line 70). It is a speech full of the weariness of someone absurdly over-qualified for his job, and the final curse – a curse that is repeated later in the play with immeasurably greater force – is, at this stage, merely petulant. It seems that Thersites is still waiting for events to live up to his savage expectations.

I have to confess to having found the scene of Thersites's next appearance (Act Three, Scene Three), very difficult, and I have been trying to work out why this was so. I think there are three principal reasons. First, the scene is placed immediately after a very beautiful, but static and demanding, sequence with Ulysses, Achilles and Patroclus, and it is therefore obvious that, as in Act Two, Scene One, Thersites is being employed by the playwright as a necessary comic turn; so, there's the old pressure of *having* to be funny. Secondly, Thersites starts a game that should ideally be played by someone with some skill in mimicry – not one of my strong points. (I solved this problem by imitating the very deep voice that Richard Ridings used in his performance of Ajax, with a series of long and loud burps. It was the decision of a desperate man at the end of a long day of rehearsals, but it worked well enough.) And, thirdly, Thersites seems to be in an unusually good mood; his description of Ajax is almost affectionate and his willingness to play with Patroclus without an aggressive, ulterior motive comes as a bit of a surprise. In other words, Thersites simply wants to entertain. Even his final speech doesn't entirely redress the balance, although it does include the wonderful line 'I had rather be a tick in a sheep than such a valiant ignorance' (line 311). We have to wait until later in the play to see Thersites finally shed his function as fool and find a new role as commentator, answerable to no one but himself and the audience.

During Act Five, Thersites barely leaves the stage. He moves from the side-lines of the story into the centre and his commentary becomes more complex. In a play about the pressures of inactivity it is very exciting that at the point when those pressures lead to two great acts of treachery (Cressida's betrayal of Troilus and Achilles's killing of Hector), it should be an essentially passive figure that is dominant. It is this highly theatrical contradiction – a still, choric figure at the centre of hysterical activity – that allows Shakespeare to reveal some of Thersites's humanity while simultaneously giving him a role that has a diabolical dimension. Despite his doing nothing, Thersites appears to be in control of the events he witnesses. It is as if his vision of the world has finally come to light.

The last act also allows us to see Thersites at his most triumphant and his most despairing. It begins with a savage attack on Patroclus. It is, of course, important that Achilles is temporarily occupied with a letter from Queen Hecuba's daughter, since only with him out of the way can Thersites let his tongue run wild, and what we hear is a remarkable display. It is, I think, fundamentally different from the game-playing of previous scenes in that the desire to amuse is considerably less important than the need to wound. Consequently, Thersites seems to employ a new voice, the result of an elegant deployment of weaponry in a verbal battle that he knows he will win. This was why Sam Mendes and I decided to use the longer list of diseases, since we felt it was good to see Thersites indulging himself. There is something about the list of diseases, and the list of animals in the later soliloquy, that allows Thersites to display his control of, as well as his delight in, language. The mistake that Patroclus makes is to play a game with rules laid down by Thersites and, of course, he loses.

The soliloquy that follows this scene is threaded through with this new style of self-confidence – a self-confidence based less on a need to be heard in spite of the limits imposed by his position in the hierarchy than on a delight in his own virtuosity. The requirement that he should amuse other characters, that he should hide his real abilities behind the mask of a professional fool, is no longer evident and the result is a palpable pride in his own intelligence and the surest statement of his faith in himself: 'Ask me not what I would be, if I were not Thersites' (v.i.60). It is almost an introspective line (unusual for Thersites) and he quickly turns back to the main thrust of his argument: 'I care not to be the louse of a lazar so I were not Menelaus' (line 61). Menelaus, a shadowy figure in the play, is the man whose collapsed marriage is the primary cause of the Trojan war and is therefore a character for whom Thersites feels nothing but contempt. What is extraordinary about the speech, however, is the way that it shows Thersites's ability to personalize an issue. It is Menelaus that he attacks,

23 Thersites during the final battle ('Soft, here comes sleeve, and t'other', v.iv.18)

but it is the war that he finds so ridiculous, and it is his idiosyncratic and unforgiving vision that allows him to pin his frustrations on a character that Shakespeare presents as having little or no personality. Such is the power of the language employed that in performance this long and intricate soliloquy seemed to require no effort. Thersites is now in control and it is this dangerously comfortable relationship with the audience that he almost exclusively exploits for the rest of the play.

The danger in having a character like Thersites as a clown is most clearly evident in the scene in which Cressida betrays Troilus (Act Five, Scene Two). An argument over Cressida's motives is unfortunately beyond the scope of this essay. What can be said here is that the difficulties of the scene are many. Perhaps Shakespeare meant us to believe Thersites when he calls Cressida a whore. It is obviously impossible to know, and since, for a modern audience, her behaviour is, at worst, pragmatic then the question of what Shakespeare thought is probably irrelevant. What is clear to me is that Cressida leaves Troilus only at some emotional cost and that Thersites, in his analysis of her behaviour, is unnecessarily harsh. This poisonous reaction comes as something of a shock. It seems as if Thersites finds this act of lechery more difficult to deal with than anything else in the play. When faced with the grotesque male egoism of Achilles or Ajax, for example, he can maintain some detachment. Watching Cressida reduces him quickly to silence, and when he does speak, after her final speech, it is, for the first and only time, in verse:

> A proof of strength she could not publish more,
> Unless she say 'My mind is now turned whore.'   (IV.ii.115–16)

This is, of course, significant and it signals a change of tone. Thersites is locating the dark heart of the play – where his vision of 'wars and lechery' has been vindicated. Consequently, I felt that it was important that his final speech in this scene should not be a shout of triumph but a single statement of fact. It's as if there is nothing more to say:

Lechery, lechery, still wars and lechery; nothing else holds fashion! A burning devil take them!   (lines 197–8)

The explosion of activity that follows this scene – the battle and the death of Hector – is, in Thersites's eyes, no more than the inevitable result of a communal despair. In our production, the battle was presented by Thersites as a deadly circus act. It seemed the logical way to play it. War, both in the play and in our world, is a mechanistic but dangerously addictive game. We performed *Troilus and Cressida* in Stratford on the night that war was declared in the Gulf and I was powerfully aware then that Thersites's despair was shared by everyone in the theatre. Shakespeare's discussion of institutionalized machismo seemed more powerful and more relevant than ever, and I was reminded that it was an enormous privilege to have a part in presenting this great play and this extraordinary character.

# Titus Andronicus

## BRIAN COX

BRIAN COX played the title role in Deborah Warner's production of *Titus Andronicus* at the Swan Theatre, Stratford, in 1987, and the following year in the Pit Theatre at the Barbican; the performance won him the Olivier 'Best Actor in a revival' award. It was his first season in Stratford and his other roles that year were Petruccio in *The Taming of the Shrew* and Paul Cash in *Fashion*, with Vershinin in *Three Sisters* added in the Barbican season. Earlier roles for the RSC in London had been Danton in *The Danton Affair*, John Tarleton in *Misalliance*, and Timothy Bellboys in *A Penny for a Song*. A wide range of earlier work in Edinburgh, Nottingham, Birmingham, Manchester, for the National Theatre, and elsewhere had included Iago in *Othello*, De Flores in *The Changeling*, Orlando in *As You Like It*, Brutus in *Julius Caesar*, the title roles in *Macbeth* and in *Peer Gynt*, Gregers Werle in *The Wild Duck*, Eilert Lovborg in *Hedda Gabler*, as well as many modern plays. More recently he played Buckingham in *Richard III* and the title role in *King Lear* for the National Theatre (London and world tour, 1990–91). A great range of television work includes *Rat in the Skull*, *The Devil's Crown*, *The Cloning of Joanna May*, *Redfox*, *Six Characters in Search of an Author*, and *Inspector Morse*. His more recent films have been *Hidden Agenda*, *Secret Weapon*, and *Shadow in the Sun*. His autobiography (and account of his teaching experiences with students of the Moscow Arts Theatre School) *Salem to Moscow: An Actor's Odyssey* was published in 1991.

*Titus Andronicus* – the most berated of Shakespeare's tragedies. All the debates of scholarship come into play whenever the authorship and value of this apprentice masterpiece are discussed. In this essay I shall not attempt further to grace this debate except to state that in my view *Titus Andronicus* was most assuredly written by William Shakespeare and by William Shakespeare alone.

I describe the play as an 'apprentice masterpiece' in this respect: just as an apprentice carpenter of the period would prepare and create for himself a test piece, thereby attaining his final articles before becoming a fully fledged practitioner of his craft, so in much the same way *Titus Andronicus* was Shakespeare's test piece, a test piece and template for all the great tragedies that were to follow – *Lear, Othello, Hamlet,* and *Macbeth.* Just as the apprentice would create a formula piece, such as an infant's high chair, so Shakespeare's formula was to write within the style and structure of the revenge drama of the time. Performing within this structure one becomes increasingly aware of the genius of the writer. The apprentice carpenter serves his master, but Shakespeare is his own apprentice and his own master. The disciplines he has created for himself are the disciplines which will exercise, and, paradoxically, exorcise, the spirit of his art and the ultimate meaning of the story he wants to tell, the story of Titus Andronicus.

As the apprentice works to create his test piece, his idiosyncratic nature and ability become fused with the practical necessities of the piece itself. So Shakespeare allows each individual scene of *Titus Andronicus* an idiosyncratic movement that beats through from scene to scene, act to act, and adheres quite carefully to the discipline he has imposed upon himself. After all, there are thirteen murders, four mutilations, and one rape during the course of the play. Shakespeare has created a very slender, but strong, tightrope of absurdity between comedy and tragedy – and the performer has to be very careful how he traverses that tightrope.

This understructure to the play seems to me the reason for writing it in the first place. What is it about, what are the deeper implications for the author? *Titus Andronicus* was written when Shakespeare was in his late twenties. The themes are honour, family, chauvinism, justice, cruelty, revenge, rape, and murder – a fairly bilious diet denoting an acute visceral sensibility, the work, I believe, of a very angry young man, a young man disaffected with the society of which he is a member, a young man with a killingly clear grasp of nihilism before the word 'nihilism' was ever thought of.

*Titus Andronicus* has survived grudgingly for four centuries because of the effect on its audiences within any given historical context during those four centuries. The absurdity of the play mirrors the absurdity of man's existence within systems he creates for himself to maintain that existence, and how those systems become a tyranny by which man traps and imprisons himself and which he finally rebels against and destroys; but the replacement systems in time also become a tyranny and thereby a never-ending cycle is created which becomes impossible to break.

In our century the context for this play has never been more powerful. When Peter Brook produced it in 1951 the shadow of totalitarianism was very much upon us: Stalinism and the purges of the thirties, Hitler's Germany and the subsequent revelations of the Nuremburg trials. And now we have the rise of Islamic fundamentalism, the breakdown of social units, the mindless violence of soccer hooliganism, the sectarian violence of Northern Ireland, the disaffection of individuals within society resulting in mass murder sprees, not to mention the ever-increasing rise in rape crimes over the last forty years.

This may seem an over-generalized spectrum of events relating to just one play by Shakespeare, but every one of those incidents has its parallel in *Titus Andronicus*. The nature of barbarous and civilized behaviour is extremely double-edged in the play. The conquered enemy, the Goths, are described as barbarous, yet the first questionable action of a barbarous nature comes from the allegedly civilized Romans, the ritual slaughter of Alarbus, the eldest of Tamora's sons, killed because of his nobility as a warrior. In Titus's view this is a religious sacrifice; in Tamora's it is cruel and irreligious. The parallel is with Irish Catholic versus Irish Protestant, perhaps – one man's civilized behaviour becomes another man's barbarity. This becomes the central question of *Titus Andronicus*: why does man lose his organic connection with his own life-force? I had a letter from someone during our run of the play saying what a chronicle of our age it is, and I know a lot of people felt this. This is why I think the play is so extraordinary now, why it so caught audiences. This was only the third significant production of it in half a century, and perhaps it caught the right moment when we can respond to its terrible laughter without diminishing its horror.

Playing Titus was a unique experience in that the part was relatively uncharted. Actors over the years have put their stamp on many Shakespearian roles, which for each succeeding generation of players then present a new challenge. Olivier marked Richard III's card for a very long time – until Tony Sher came along and invented a wholly new image – as did Gielgud with Richard II and Hamlet. Of course, Titus was successful for Olivier too in Brook's sumptuous production, but the text was cut and reworked and the humour of the play studiously rationalized.

When I was asked to play the role in the 1987–88 season at Stratford I was initially uneasy, before I'd read the play, because of its blood-and-guts reputation – the death-wish of its generation and yet one of the most popular plays of the period – but when I started work on it I began to realize its many hidden values. Its post-war history in Stratford has been a chequered one. After Peter Brook's production in 1951 it was not seen again until 1972 when Trevor Nunn directed a fairly full Roman-pomp production with the late, great, Colin Blakely (who was, I believe, magnificent). Then John Barton directed a heavily cut production which made up part of an ill-conceived double bill with *The Two Gentlemen of Verona* in 1981. In discussions with Terry Hands, the Artistic Director of the RSC, it seemed important that whoever was to direct *Titus Andronicus* this time around needed not to be forced into preconceptual judgements of the play, and that it required someone fresh and fearless who would allow the play its own identity. Such a director was Deborah Warner. In more than twenty years of working in the theatre I have never witnessed such an auspicious beginning. The coolness and authority with which she allowed the play to grow were awesome. Deborah's methods are egalitarian, thereby harnessing the total input of the whole cast. The process is extremely tiring, as democracy can be, but effective, since it creates a responsibility within the ensemble towards the play as a totality and not just to the individual characters, with the result that a lot of the staging ideas came very quickly in rehearsal.

The most significant example of this was the discovery of how to kill Lavinia, which happened at the first read-through. We were sitting in chairs to read and we didn't put a chair out for Lavinia because (obviously) she doesn't have any lines in the later part of the play. But she is supposed to be in the scenes so, naturally, dutifully, the actress playing Lavinia (Sonia Ritter) came in – and found nowhere to sit. So I asked her to sit on my knee and as she was sitting there I realized that this image, this classic image of parent and child, was also an image of vulnerability and of potential brutality. You could do incredible damage, you could poke somebody's eyes out, when they are that close, trusting you as a little child, a little animal, might trust you. It suddenly occurred to me that this would be perfect for breaking her neck, this close and this intimate. There was something about the image that was tender but at the same time ultimately brutal, and I started really from that point. The whole of the creation of Titus came from that one image of a man sitting in a chef's outfit with a little girl on his knee, about to break her neck like a chicken. It contained the world of tragedy and comedy and the whole middle ground of ludicrousness, of man's ludicrous journey through life which seems to me so important in the play. Because, if you think about it, so much of life is ludicrous: it has its high and low points, its points of passion, romance, comedy, tragedy, but for quite a lot of the time – it's ludicrous. And that image, from so early in rehearsal, seemed to catch that.

The play of *Titus Andronicus* is often described as lacking spiritual depth. One of the main facets of Titus's character, however, is that he is a spiritual bankrupt and his journey through the play is to confront and come to terms with this spiritual bankruptcy. Titus is a general, a warrior, a soldier, a trained killer, trained to kill for Rome. His allegiance to Rome has superseded any domestic, social, or personal affiliations he may have had: Rome is the centre of his life. Twenty-five sons and one daughter he has sired. Twenty-one of these sons are already dead, killed in the service of Rome. Through his overweening pride in the victorious dead of his own house we witness a man who has become brutalized and disconnected from a true sense of parental love. The links to his children, particularly Lavinia, are sentimental. He has destroyed the feminine within himself. His pre-occupations are with death, honour, retirement; he is a man who instinctively wants to retire the field while ahead of the game, but who will be forced to pay the price for the self-brutalization of his own nature.

Along with this sense of the brutality and the horror, though, must go that element of the ludicrous. The vaudeville aspect of the part was very important to me, making the character much more accessible than he otherwise would be. He is a consummate actor, putting on, it seems to me, particularly in the early scenes, a wonderful kind of wilful senility: 'O, I'm too old; I don't know' – he does a lot of 'losing the place'. The sense of the vaudevillian in these opening scenes comes largely from the fact that they are played out to the audience, with almost no interplay between characters. It's all addressed out front; the image of Archie Rice is much stronger than the image of Hamlet. The entry to Rome, the great warrior returning, has irresistible undertones of the performer coming back, the famous actor meeting his audience again: 'I'm so tired, and it's so hot, but my public is waiting . . .' – and the public, the audience, is Rome.

Here, at the beginning of the play, we see Titus at the height of his power, the conquering hero returning from a ten-year campaign against the Goths. Born aloft on the yoke of his prisoners, battle-scarred, exhausted, a touch senile, he enters in triumph. For our production this image, too, came from early in the rehearsal process. I felt he should be at his highest point (quite literally) and that the boys, Tamora's boys, his victims, should be trussed up like pieces of meat, so that you didn't know, at first, that they were absolutely debased. Hence that metal ladder on which they carried him in. The process of getting onto that ladder and

24  Brian Cox as Titus is carried onstage by his Gothic prisoners ('Hail,
Rome, victorious in thy mourning weeds', 1.i.70)

sitting on it with the boys' heads sticking through immediately made him a
kind of grandiose figure but also slightly comic as well. This idea comes,
probably, from my own roots, from constantly looking at things through a
slightly comic kaleidoscope. Greatness and absurdity are so constantly
connected. There is the greatest sailor of all time, Nelson on his column in
Trafalgar Square, but the ludicrous thing is that a bird will sit on his head
and shit on it and there's nothing at all he can do about it. That idea seems
to me relevant to Titus. He has done everything for Rome and now he
wants to retire. With twenty-five sons he may not have noticed which ones
were dying, but with only four left he knows well enough now. He wants to
retire, he feels he's had it, but the play is going to make him pay for the life
he has led. One of the first ideas I had was of a statue that had corroded –
the face gone, cracked, bits showing through. This was where the mud
make-up came from: a man caked in mud, like a miner caked in the grime of
his trade, a particular kind of workhouse. Titus has campaigned so much,
has spent so much of his life on the road; he is no longer a human

personality, he has become a kind of machine. That is what is carried in on that ladder in the first scene. He is weary; done-all, seen-all, just waiting to go out to grass.

There is still, however, a price to be paid. Shakespeare insists on that: as a young writer he was particularly moralistic. This man is not going to be let off the hook, not allowed to go out to grass. This shambling statue, this disintegrating edifice, is only the start. The man who has destroyed the feminine in himself must now try to go through a journey of reconnection, of rediscovery of values. His first value was Rome, but Rome has changed – they have moved the goalposts of Titus's Rome a long time before. And so there we see him, sitting on his ladder, in this incredibly vain entry – for I think he is vain, with a powerful sense of his own achievements. At this point he is monstrously egocentric: 'things are done in this way because *I* say so, and we do it for *Rome*'. He has always been a servant, but, like all servants, all butlers, he actually runs the show, knows more about it than the master does. 'Patience, Prince Saturninus', he says (1.i.203), commanding the future emperor without reflecting on it, but the next moment kneeling to him, vowing service. Like all soldiers (RSMs or generals), he needs to serve.

Because of his popularity, Titus's own name is entered in the lists of contenders for empery. He declines the opportunity, self-mockingly stating his age and feebleness as the reasons for his inadequacy. He is also aware of his limitations. He has been a soldier too long, and a successful one. What is a soldier if not a trained killer? For a moment we have echoes (or, rather, pre-echoes) of Macbeth. Both Macbeth and Titus are soldiers, soldiers and generals, Macbeth younger and with more ambition to become king. But soldiery is what he is best at, the job most fitting his sensibilities. After his disastrous kingship Macbeth's moment of glory comes when once again he dons the armour of the soldier warrior and goes to his death as the person he really is and was meant to be, a man who excels at what he does best – being a soldier. The story of Macbeth might be described as that of a man ambitious for the wrong job. So, too, was Titus, but because of his age and experience he avoids taking the wrong job and his path to self-realization is therefore more brutal. Unlike Macbeth he has no aspirations. He is what he is: he knows about campaigning, about the legalized aspects of killing men, for reasons of honour, imperialism, and all the other monstrous values that prompt men to do such things.

Saturninus becomes Emperor and his direct impetuous action is to take Lavinia as his wife, although she is already betrothed to his brother

Bassianus. Titus's condition of servile stoicism complies with this action, which he views only too happily as a reward for his service to the state. Without these codes of behaviour and rules of state he would be lost, and in the next few minutes he will frantically invoke these rules, first with the rebuttal of the just claim of Bassianus to Lavinia; then the callous murder of his youngest son Mutius; then Saturninus's rejection of Lavinia in preference for Tamora, Queen of the Goths; and finally Titus's initial refusal and final submission to having Mutius buried in the family vault. In this rapid sequence of events we watch Titus steadfastly holding on to the book of law and that book being tossed aside by Saturninus to suit his own purposes; Titus's being governed by his own preconditioned allegiance to the state in his imperviousness to his daughter's happiness, and that imperviousness even further magnified in the killing of Mutius. He doesn't even notice that he's killed him, he's not aware of it at first. It is only an impediment that must be removed, like an impediment in war: here are five bridges that must be destroyed; it just happens that there are 1,200 people crossing them at the time, but the impediment must still be removed. That is the soldier mentality, and the horror of it is shot through with the ludicrous, the deeply silly.

Titus has seen it all before and he has long since ceased to be affected by it. He is ripe for a fall. His mistake at the start of the play is the mistake of the arch conservative, a refusal to recognize that the role he was so passionately wedded to has atrophied and no longer exists. A wind of change is needed and he refuses to acknowledge it; hence his holding to the idea of succession by primogeniture and his support for the unstable Saturninus. He has retired and quite clearly abdicated responsibility to the edifice he has helped to maintain, the edifice of Rome. In the course of this first scene his loyalty to a vanished idea of Rome, and to the Emperor he has so foolishly created in deference to it, prompts him to give his daughter away to Saturninus:

> Kind Rome, that hast thus lovingly reserv'd
> The cordial of mine age to glad my heart.　　　　　(I.i.165–6)

Thus he greets Lavinia's arrival; and it's all *me* (and Rome), nothing about Lavinia. And the first thing he does is to treat her like a piece of property in a meat market. Even his brother Marcus protests as he takes her from Bassianus. Brutality and absurdity again combine, again storing up debts which have to be expiated. During the rest of the play we watch him trying to rebuild his connection with his daughter. It has to be a real connection and not a sentimental one, for the sentimental always debases real emotion. (One sees this in *King Lear*, where the danger of sentimentalizing the father–daughter relationship is particularly important.) The real relationship between parent and child is never sentimental; it is something far deeper and more mysterious than that. Titus treats his daughter in this first scene like a piece of property because Roman society permits him to do that. In attempting to remake the relationship Titus will find himself having to examine that society. His daughter is for him an idealized image and the society he has put his faith in, the society he has upheld, allows her to be defiled, to be desecrated; and he must try to come to terms with that.

The stone-like edifice that Titus presents to the world, that is carried in on that ladder at the beginning, must be broken into to discover the tenderness encased within that embossed exterior. This is wonderful; this is where the poetic element of the play takes over. But it is only momentary, this inner discovery. Titus is too far gone, too hardened, too wrong. His capacity for tenderness is too unformed, like a chicken still in the egg, not properly incubated. Nothing in his life has incubated. When he opens himself, therefore, in response to Lavinia's pain, it's too much, too shocking. It was not for nothing that audiences could not always take it: when members of the audience left the performance it was not, I think, because of the horrors of the play; they left because of the man's grief. Nobody can bear that – but he must go through it. That is the price he has to pay; and unfortunately it's too late. Like Ibsen's Brand, his self-discovery comes too late. Shakespeare doesn't save him. In the 'fly scene' (III.ii) there is the hint of a possibility that Titus has found a sort of spiritual communion with Lavinia:

> Speechless complainer, I will learn thy thought;
> In thy dumb action will I be as perfect
> As begging hermits in their holy prayers:
> Thou shalt not sigh, nor hold thy stumps to heaven,
> Nor wink, nor nod, nor kneel, nor make a sign,
> But I of these will wrest an alphabet,
> And by still practice learn to know thy meaning.          (III.ii.39–45)

But even here, we decided, he actually misinterprets her simple desire for a drink – 'She says she drinks no other drink but tears' (line 37) – and the moment of possible communion vanishes into pain and horror again. No, no, the play says, you have to come to terms with what you are, and you have nearly done so through this girl, but what has happened has been too much. For what happens to this girl is the consequence of years and years

25   Titus with Lavinia (Sonia Ritter)

of battering people into the ground; finally someone comes along and batters him. And they get him through his daughter, where he never expected it, and he is pushed over the edge. When he laughs instead of weeping he has gone over the edge and cannot then be saved. 'Why dost thou laugh?', his brother asks him, and he replies:

> Why, I have not another tear to shed:
> Besides, this sorrow is an enemy,
> And would usurp upon my wat'ry eyes,
> And make them blind with tributary tears:
> Then which way shall I find Revenge's cave. (III.i.266–70)

Titus is pushed over the edge and the play becomes a tale of revenge. The horrors have mounted up and up and finally he is totally overwhelmed. There is a sense of him wanting to connect himself with something that is elemental here:

> I am the sea. Hark how her sighs doth blow;
> She is the weeping welkin, I the earth:
> Then must my sea be moved with her sighs;
> Then must my earth with her continual tears
> Become a deluge ... (III.i.225–9)

Here we are at the edge, and he can't take any more, and suddenly he starts to laugh and that laughter becomes a cue (and a clue) to how the next part of the play should take shape. And you need all your skills as an actor here to turn on a sixpence and change direction from the path you were on and take another, the path of gallows humour, of black, nihilistic humour, very twentieth-century in its mood – for in some ways this is the most modern of plays. Once you've made that turn there are immense new rewards to find in the role. Titus becomes a richly potent figure of nihilism, of destruction, of revenge, who keeps searching, searching for a justice he will never find, for justice has been long dead for him.

To say that he goes mad is to oversimplify. He is obviously on the verge of madness when the play starts, but the line between madness and sanity is a very fine one through all of Shakespeare's plays. For me, playing Titus, the mad state is when he is elevated to the point when he sees quite clearly what he has to do. The end is crystal clear, even though he pretends, and gets others to pretend with him, that other avenues (shooting the arrows, for example) should be tried first. After that laughter, after he has said that he has 'not another tear to shed', when the severed hand and heads are brought on, then he dies – in spirit. And he says to himself: 'Oh, I'm dead. I'm a dead man, and I can do whatever I like – because I'm dead.' That is really the cue. When you decide you're dead, nobody can harm you. He still has his pain, and his tasks to finish, of course, things to tidy, the end to achieve, but he is no longer vulnerable.

The fly scene marks this point of arrival in the play, another crossing-point of the tragic and the ludicrous of which the play presents so much, and which differentiates the part so sharply from the English classical tradition of acting. It is more in the tradition of Scottish vaudeville, of the Glasgow comedians with their sharp sense of reality. How can he kill that fly, that 'had a father and a mother'? (III.ii.60); yet two seconds later he is stabbing viciously at the same fly which has become 'like to the empress' Moor' (line 67). Where do I exist in that? How do I deal with that? This is a good thing, this is a bad thing – they are so easily said, but Titus can no longer deal with them and he sinks back into what he knows, the relentless trying to discover who raped his daughter, the only concrete thing for him to connect with. 'Come, take away' at the end of the scene (line 81) means superficially merely 'clear the table', but for me it means also 'get rid of this thing that's driving me to distraction (and to destruction); take it away, lift this burden from me'. There is only revenge left for him to hang on to. The interval in our production was placed here – at what seems to me a real watershed.

The second half of the play sees an accelerating journey towards the realization of revenge. The mud, the dirt, the crap are more obvious as the man neglects everything in pursuit of his end and more extreme images of the ludicrous emerged – a handkerchief on my head, knotted at the corners, like grandpa at the beach, an old string vest like a navvy. I felt that one had to be merciless in one's presentation of Titus here. I was not going to play him as a dear, hard-done-by, charming old man. There is real harshness here and it must be faced. The man has to be dragged over the coals, seen to be over the edge long before the final scene. One could, I suppose, make that last scene a leap, but I felt that one had to see a progression of images, of a man not caring, rolling around in mud, who hasn't washed, hasn't done anything, who's let himself go, as the household has gone, who's become crazy old Titus, locked up in his house. A man who had admitted, who had deliberately said: 'I am disastrous, therefore I shall be disastrous.' Titus punishes himself and these images of squalor were important for me – not least in the making of the final scene, with his clean, white chef's uniform, a sharp contrast for the celebration of revenge.

Through these scenes of madness and squalor, he tries to make himself concentrate, tries to stay with what he should be doing, discovering the identity of the rapists. It is interesting, however, that he has little to do in the scene where the discovery is made. He is merely an observer there; it is all done by Marcus. Titus takes no control – he's gone, away, contemplating the idea of revenge rather than the identity of its victims. The same seems to me true of the scene with the bows and arrows. In theory vengeance should be sought from the gods, so all right, we'll send the letters, and we'll see what happens. Of course he knows that nothing will happen, because the gods don't exist; he knows that, though he doesn't say it. The scene was funny for the audience, funny, but bleak. These were images I felt strongly committed to – the knotted handkerchief, the string vest, the lack of money to give the clown so he steals some from Marcus – all the little jokes that emphasize the bleakness of it all. For Titus is death-bound now; he knows it, and he's ready.

When he is visited by Tamora disguised as Revenge he is continuing the logic of his course, pursuing vengeance through the approved channels of communion with the gods. He is doing it all by the book – and they say he's mad. Of course he's mad; but society does this, his society did those things. 'Who doth molest my contemplation?' he asks (v.ii.9) and we have the most frightening kind of comically logical point of the play.

When Tamora comes in pretending she is Revenge we felt there was no need for the actress (Estelle Kohler) to be disguised. They all think he's mad, so there's no need to pretend. 'I'm revenge,' she says. 'No, you're not, you're Tamora, Queen of the Goths,' he replies.

> Know thou, sad man, I am not Tamora;
> She is thy enemy, and I thy friend.                      (v.ii.28–9)

And he, supposedly mad, ends up humouring her – 'Art thou Revenge?' – which shows the level of his deviousness and the fact that he can suck people up into his energy even while they think he's mad (as Hamlet does with Polonius). Titus is at one and the same time in the middle of the madness and yet capable of steering it, concentrating his energies to seek his ends, while she pushes him further towards the edge. And that energy and singleness of purpose leave him with the boys as his prisoners at the scene's end. Tamora thinks he's far gone. She doesn't understand what she has done in leaving her sons behind; no more do they; no more, really, does Titus, by this point, as the terrible logic of the play makes possible the achievement of his vengeance.

I was aware, as I played the scene with the boys, that members of the audience were thrilled that I had them, thrilled as I gripped their heads to expose their throats, thrilled at the revenge. The scene plays on certain yearnings in people, which is legitimate, truthful, and honest – and frightening. At a time when we seem to be rediscovering Victorian values in censorship, when television is under attack for its violence, the effect of this scene from this old play is extraordinary. You couldn't get anything more violent. We had held back in the production from showing much blood but here blood was spilled, unstintingly. To the horror, and to the delight, of the audience the blood of Demetrius and Chiron gushed into the bowl held between Lavinia's stumps and we moved into the final scene.

The final scene is a celebration, long anticipated for Titus, and there is something of the priestly about his part in it. This is the end, the last, and he sees himself as host: 'Why art thou thus attir'd?' asks Saturninus (v.iii.30) and Titus replies

> Because I would be sure to have all well
> To entertain your highness and your empress.

We felt it needed something celebratory and toyed at first with the idea of balloons. Because of the general spareness of the production it was clear that that wouldn't work and we then had the idea of using the work-song of Deborah Warner's Kick Theatre Company, the *Snow White* dwarves' song, 'Hi-Ho'. At first we intended to sing the words, but that seemed too much, so it was decided that the company should whistle the tune as the banquet is prepared. It was a risk, but I believe one worth taking – once again for its contribution to the play's sense of the ludicrous. It was also unsettling, and at this point it is important to unsettle the audience, to create something from a different space, a different place, a different genre. People attacked it, some have said it's the only thing they disliked in the production, but I thought it was vital. It unsettled the audience and prepared them for what was coming. And then, in full starched white chef's garb, I came in, leaping over the table, with the pie. The world had gone crazy; the audience's embarrassment about serving the boys in the pie was released in laughter – but laughter from which you could cut them off. You could allow another laugh in the welcome:

> Welcome, my lord; welcome, dread Queen;
> Welcome, ye warlike Goths; welcome, Lucius;
> And welcome, *all* ...                                    (v.iii.26–28)

– the last words addressed to the pie. The laugh there, the frisson of it, released the audience, since they immediately started questioning their reactions. The play has constantly walked the borderline between horror and laughter: 'You thought that was funny, well what about this?' – get people to laugh, and then kick them. 'Why, there they are, both baked in this pie; / Whereof their mother daintily hath fed' (v.iii.60). Sometimes that got a laugh, sometimes none at all. And then Tamora laughs in disbelief, and Titus laughs at her disbelief, and the audience is released to laugh again, only to be silenced by the terrible suddenness of the deaths. The real sensation of that was quite extraordinary, the visceral sense of it for the audience. It is so economic, this point of the play, that you have to pull the audience through it, really pull them, as though through the eye of a needle. They're waiting for it, but they don't know when it's going to be. From the greeting to the pie, through the killing of Lavinia, to the astonishing rapidity of the trio of deaths, is all profoundly theatrical, and you've got to go for it and not be afraid of it; be bold and audacious, because you've earned it. You can always be audacious in the theatre if you've earned it. It's as if you know what your cards are, and you've got the best hand, and you keep it, until you finally have the call. That's one of the things I learned from this play; that you can absolutely do that.

*Titus Andronicus* is a brilliant play. The more I did it, the more I discovered in it, and the more it yielded up. There is no final forgiveness for Titus, no final forgiveness in the play. Its last image is of the casting out of Tamora's body for the birds to peck at. All possibility of progress is destroyed by man's capacity for brutalization. Even poor old Marcus is reduced in the end to a kind of avenging figure. The man of integrity and reason, the man who can deal with the horrors of life if he can find a logic to them, discovers that there is no logic, just as there is no logic to the life of Titus. The play is asking deep, almost existential, questions. It is a very profound piece of work and the more I did it the more I realized that. It offers no philosophical weave to its questioning, as do *Hamlet* or *Lear*; it is spare, to the bone. Shakespeare simply sticks to his brief, and within it unfolds his horrific tale. It out-Bonds Bond. It is a cruel play, deliberately cruel. But, as we know from the history of our own century and the events of our own age, its harshness and horror are not incredible, and its ludicrousness tells a fearful truth. The way human life is prized, the value of man and of his destiny – these things have never been as severely under question as they are now. *Titus Andronicus* examines the values by which we live.

# Hamlet

## PHILIP FRANKS

PHILIP FRANKS played the title role in Roger Michell's production of *Hamlet* for the RSC's regional tour in 1987. On the same tour he appeared as the First Merchant in *The Comedy of Errors*. Earlier Shakespearian roles for the company had included, in 1981, Lysander in *A Midsummer Night's Dream* and Bassianus in *Titus Andronicus* and, in 1982–83, Bertram in *All's Well that Ends Well* and Florizel in *The Winter's Tale*. Elsewhere he has played Romeo, Ariel in *The Tempest*, Octavius Caesar in *Antony and Cleopatra*, and Bassanio in *The Merchant of Venice*, as well as the title role in Marlowe's *Edward II*. Other roles for the RSC have been John Darling in *Peter Pan*, Matthew in *Every Man in His Humour*, Henry Fielding in *The Art of Success* and Gaston in *Worlds Apart*. Some of his more recent theatre appearances have been in *The Mad Woman of Chaillot*, *Much Ado About Nothing* (playing Claudio), and Howard Barker's *Seven Lears*. Television work has included *Bleak House*, *To Serve Them All My Days*, *The Darling Buds of May*, and *The Green Man*.

Most of us go through life as living, walking proof that humankind cannot bear very much reality. We do not think 'I can walk, I am walking, my brain is sending a series of signals resulting in complex muscular activity.' We do not think 'I am breathing in through my mouth, my lungs are inflating and in a second they will deflate again as I breathe out through my nose.' If we try thinking like this for more than a minute the action becomes impossible. Similarly we do not think about nuclear war, incurable disease or examples of man's appalling cruelty *all* the time. If we did we would come to a full stop. This is the peculiar state of panicky inertia (a theologian would call it despair) that we spend much of our time avoiding. I used to get it quite a lot when I was playing Hamlet.

The weight of the past of the play is unbearable: globally famous, one of the great cultural icons, 'a hoop' according to Max Beerbohm, 'through which every actor must sooner or later jump' – or even if denied the chance, through which they'd like to jump. There are libraries full of criticism and stage history, countless productions, films, recordings and spinoffs, not forgetting the cigars. Every so often, in rehearsals, in the middle of the night, or most inconveniently of all, waiting to go on for my first entrance, the clouds methought would open and show all this accumulated garbage ready to drop upon me. It's a nasty feeling and I don't recommend it. If you've ever run over a rabbit and caught the expression on its face in the headlights you'll have some idea.

Because it seemed as though my reality block was becoming increasingly flimsy, I devised a series of slaps to the flagging psyche: 'no one can say everything about Hamlet, so don't try. Everyone identifies with him, and so should you – don't try to comment. There are as many Hamlets as there are people – what is unique about yours is that you are you. You can even use this feeling of panic – make it his. Now, stop whining and get on stage.' A reassuring squeeze of the hand from the Ghost and I could pick up my battered leather suitcases and get on.

Unfortunately this feeling didn't leave me once the production was over, although it manifested itself in a different way. When I think about playing Hamlet, I feel a sense of regret, of failure, of opportunity missed and general inadequacy. I gather with some relief that other Hamlets have felt this, and indeed I remember feeling it myself when I played the part as a student. And yet it was the most taxing and rewarding piece of work that I have done and I was and am proud of the production. So why the worry? Usually a part recedes in the memory into a set of images and considered opinions. It is possible to be fairly objective about how and why it was done and how it could have been improved. *Hamlet* is another matter, I suppose because of the unusually high level of personal input that the part demands.

Actor and audience alike have an oddly personal relationship with the part and the play. It seems to identify itself with the particular age and body of the time in which it is being played. Productions are often seen as pinpointing the nature and quality of the day's disaffected youth, though this quality can vary from gentle disappointed fatalism to angry violent nihilism without a word being altered. The actor must be true to himself as well as the play. It is every Hamlet's task to be faithful to the text, to mine it for nuance, to observe its rhythms, to play on the line. It is also his task to pour as much of himself and his experience of loss, doubt, fear, and lack of faith into the operation as possible. Hamlet is the antithesis of a 'character part'. These twin tasks must be equally addressed – to over-emphasize the former will lead to dry commentary or empty histrionics (depending on your approach) and to go all out for the latter will produce four hours or so of meandering self-indulgence, more proper to the analyst's couch.

I started my own relationship with the play at the age of nine. I saw Peter Hall's production at Stratford and resolutely set about making a film of the play as a vehicle for myself. I used a borrowed Super-8 camera (no sound) with my aunt's garden standing in for Elsinore. Casting was pragmatic: Claudius couldn't act but he had a chemistry set and I wanted the poisoned cup to foam and bubble. Various other friends were bullied into standing around self-consciously in makeshift fancy dress as I postured in front of them in an expensive floppy white shirt. Ten years later I played the part again, with words this time, in a modern-dress studio production. It was intense, self-absorbed, emotional and entirely unpoetic; short on humour and theatricality and high on anguish. The third attempt was with Roger Michell directing for the RSC: a tour of England and Northern Ireland with our own portable 500-seater auditorium. We aimed for a fast, witty playing style with a lot of direct address to the audience. Thus even in this tiny footnote to theatrical history there is an example of the shifting nature of the play – from Vehicle to Private Experience to – what? Perhaps I'm still too close to the production (at the time of writing) to define it neatly or reductively.

When I first met Roger to discuss the play we both found that large questions of definition or interpretation were not of much use. We skirted around the usual ones – what is the play saying? Who is Hamlet? Is his madness real or feigned? – and discarded them, with relief, in favour of a detailed and organic approach, a mining of the text and discussion of particular relationships. Thereafter, we hardly ever talked about 'interpretation', only about the choices available within a scene, a speech, a line or a word.

Of course, certain interpretative decisions were taken before a word was spoken in rehearsals. Design parameters were defined: we would perform the play on a carpet with a minimal set, Jacobean costumes and modern props. The props became a source of controversy later on, especially among literal-minded students in seach of symbolism. They were in fact not symbolic of anything but themselves. There is an Elizabethan drawing of a scene from *Titus Andronicus* in which the characters wear sixteenth-century clothes with 'Roman' accessories: a toga, an elaborate crown, various short swords and javelins. The picture says a great deal about the flexibility of the Elizabethan theatre, and suggests that its audiences were able to accept period and locale through shorthand reference. It also shows a visual equivalent for the anachronisms in the writing. Shakespeare is always talking about his own world as well as an historical or invented one. We tried to achieve the same effect with the opposite device. In a world of doublet and hose, Laertes left for France with a Samsonite case and a couple of tennis raquets, Claudius addressed his new court through a microphone and later sat gnawing at his conscience with the aid of a whisky decanter and soda-siphon. I used to take a Polaroid of him in Act One, Scene Two, a photo I could use later for 'look here upon this picture and on this' (III.iv.54). Other examples were many and varied. Almost all of them were found during rehearsals, but the first principle was arrived at early: if there is something we can think of to place a moment, to sharpen an emotional state, to suggest location, climate, or time of day, then rather than an 'Elizabethan' equivalent we will use the thing itself. In the same way that we use electric light and sound-effects to tell a story, not candles and cannonballs, we used any prop that we needed. I found it an exciting idea, both surprising and fun, and appropriate to a play as full of images of the theatre as *Hamlet*. During the run, some of our modern devices became redundant as we increased in confidence – the Polaroid, for instance, bit the dust when we started to discover the tension of the scene through the words. Others remained useful and resonant, and stayed.

The other major pieces of pre-production decision-making were casting and cutting the play. Richard O'Callaghan (Claudius) is a slight, febrile man, worlds away from the booming sensualist of tradition; Maggie Steed (Gertrude) and David Collings (Polonius) are younger, stronger, and more intelligent than is usual, and Bob Goody (the Ghost) is very tall and worryingly thin, so a mighty poleaxe-wielding warrior was out of the question. He was also to treble the part with the Player King and the Gravedigger, providing an opportunity to investigate father-figures in different areas of the play. These are just a few examples: any casting process for any play closes off some avenues and opens others.

Preparing a cut text is a task faced by most directors of *Hamlet*, since the uncut second quarto (the fullest version) would take nearly five hours to play. In our case we had to be fairly fierce – most of our touring venues had demanded an evening of not more than three hours. We never managed this, but it gave us a needed goal. As a general rule of thumb we decided to go largely with the First Folio text, since this would seem to be an acting version. It was not an unbreakable rule but it proved a surprisingly useful one, often sorting out thorny problems of meaning or staging when we were stuck in rehearsal. We tried to cut painlessly – nips and tucks rather than amputation – although there were some major losses, chief amongst which was the soliloquy, 'How all occasions do inform against me' (IV.iv.32). This cut (again following the Folio) was consistent with what emerged as a domestic view of the play, but was no help at all to the Fortinbras plot. Otherwise, cuts were added to and subtracted from during rehearsal and performance. We often worked on material marked as cut in case something could be yielded that we had been too stupid to see. At all times we tried to cut for clarity and efficiency rather than to mould the play to a particular vision. However, as Harold Jenkins says in his introduction to the new Arden text: 'the editor must be eclectic; every variant imposes upon him the inescapable responsibility of choice'.

In an ideal world, or a good rehearsal, there is a synthesis between technical skill, textual fidelity and instinctive personal choice. In the early stages of rehearsal Roger was adept at keeping all three healthy, like a good physiotherapist who will not develop one muscle while another wastes. The first two weeks were thrilling with variety. We sat on a flat roof on top of Sadlers Wells Theatre discussing textual variants and punctuation problems, then downstairs to the rehearsal room for group work and improvisation. This might be followed by two or three of us filling in our own picture of the characters' past history or inner life. The input was threefold, and my own insights and discoveries started to be tempered by those of other people apart from Roger. This was particularly surprising when it came to investigating parental relationships. Bob Goody was creating a crippled, agonised, asthmatic Ghost, doubled up with pain and begging for revenge with, as it were, his last gasp. I had never thought of the part like this, yet suddenly it seemed to make perfect sense. Hamlet constantly refers to the Ghost in compassionate terms: 'Alas, poor ghost', 'ay, thou poor ghost', 'this piteous action', 'tears perchance for blood' – all these phrases leapt into prominence and with them a more complicated set of responses than I had anticipated. To see a strong, authoritative father brought so low and desperate provoked a far deeper unease and guilty responsibility than a mighty armed Commendatore figure would have done. Seeing misery and, more important, weakness in a parent for the first time is profoundly unsettling. I found it a valuable addition to all the other horrors of the scene, and I also found it very moving. Indeed, I was moved to tears by the scene almost every time we played it.

Bob's choice also seemed to fit in miraculously with what I was discovering about the first Act of the play. His appearance combined with his information and appeal to bring Hamlet's doubts and fears into focus.

From the first entrance I felt he was a man in spiritual turmoil, seeing everything and everybody with new and suspicious eyes since his bereavement. The meeting with the Ghost intensifies this need to root out duplicity to the point of neurotic illness. It is fascinating that the first description of Hamlet after this encounter is Ophelia's: 'He falls to such perusal of my face / As 'a would draw it' (II.i.90). As well as intensifying purpose, the Ghost also gives focus to Hamlet's language – never again is it as fragmented and labyrinthine as in the first soliloquy.

I always found this speech far and away the most difficult. The first sentence:

> O that this too too sullied flesh would melt,
> Thaw, and resolve itself into a dew;
> Or that the Everlasting had not fixed
> His canon 'gainst self-slaughter          (I.ii.129–32)

is rolling and sonorous, the thoughts flow unimpeded from line to line and the dominant consonants are 'l's and 'r's, giving a liquid feel, no hesitations. It is as though this is a ready-made thought that has been filling him to the brim and he has simply let it out. Then he starts interrupting himself: 'Oh God, God' and again two lines later, 'fie on't, ah fie' as the real poison of his unhappiness comes to the surface. He compares the world to an 'unweeded garden', a melancholy and domestic image, apparently, which is suddenly subverted and made alarmingly sensual by 'things rank and gross in nature possess it merely'. As the language becomes sensual, so he makes his first reference to his immediate situation: 'That it should come to this – / But two months dead.' Right from the beginning, then, whether we understand it intellectually or feel it subliminally, Hamlet's grief is bound up with a troubled sexuality.

This sets up resonances throughout the play which I was keen to explore, especially in the light of the work Maggie Steed was doing on Gertrude. In my student production the Gertrude was younger than me and uneasy in the part. As a result, we did not explore their relationship very deeply. This time, Maggie was finding a woman radiant in the rediscovery of her sexuality, glowing with well-being and longing to share her happiness. My Hamlet found this happiness appalling and the sexuality traumatic. Their relationship became the single most important one in the play.

Back to the speech: the sentences grow shorter, interruptions come more frequently, and full stops, when they occur, occur in eight out of nine cases in mid-line – a sure sign that thoughts are coming quickly. Shakespeare structures his pauses into his verse: a pause will be indicated for you by an end-stop or an incomplete half-line. Here there are only two, when he tries to put the lid on his feelings with the proverb-like 'Frailty, thy name is woman', and later after his vision of the marriage-bed with its 'incestuous sheets'. Leading up to this, we see the pull between grief and sexual ferment becoming stronger. Claudius is compared to a satyr, with all that creature's priapic associations, while Gertrude is described with increasing prurience: her shoes, her tears, her face, her eyes are all dwelt on; comparing her to a beast ('a beast that wants discourse of reason / Would have mourned longer' (lines 150–1)) links her subliminally with other 'animal' instincts, and the final image of illicit sex ('O, most wicked speed, to post / With such dexterity to incestuous sheets' (lines 156–7)) with its whispering, rustling sounds, demonstrates a more than intellectual involvement. Hamlet then relapses into silence and we are left feeling that there is more than one reason why he must hold his tongue. Like President Nixon, 'I know what I meant', but the speech is fearsomely hard to achieve. Speed of thought without gabbling, torment without tension, confusion without diffusion, and all within minutes of arriving on stage. After a few weeks in performance it struck me that my difficulties are also Hamlet's: he is talking to a group of strangers about a situation he does not fully understand. Later in the play he is able to talk to them with total openness, just as the actor relaxes when the play has got under way.

Parallel to detailed work on individual speeches and long solo calls with Roger, we were beginning to establish a framework for the production and I was slowly plotting a graph of development. We decided to run the play either in chunks or in its entirety much earlier than is usual in a rehearsal period to help me plot the graph accurately – to get some idea of the energy demanded. As an artist will block in a canvas roughly to have an idea of tone and composition before starting on detail, so we would stagger through huge areas of the play. For me, quite apart from giving me a great deal of exercise and much to lose sleep over, these early runs gave me two major objectives: speed of thought and delivery and finding and holding on to Hamlet's wit.

Hamlet is consumed by thought and is driven to speak; his inaction is never an excuse for lethargy. I found myself eaten up by restless energy in and out of rehearsal; my reading speed and my retentive memory both improved considerably. I saw it as my particular task to find and achieve Hamlet's speed of thinking, rather than simply gabbling through the lines: it is, after all, the working of his mind that gives the play its narrative thrust, every bit as much as the actual events of the revenge tragedy.

Every bit as necessary as speed was wit. Roger told me early on that he wanted *Hamlet* to have more laughs than *The Comedy of Errors* (which we toured at the same time) and while we never quite achieved that, the remark was not lightly meant. Hamlet is the only one of Shakespeare's tragic heroes who possesses a sense of humour. Exploring his wit, its quality and seriousness, yielded huge rewards. For one thing, it struck a very personal chord – like many other over-educated Englishmen I have irony in my bones – and for another, it seemed to be the quality that keeps the play buoyant, that prevents Hamlet's negative energy from simply digging a great hole for itself. As Shaw says: '*Hamlet* is a very long play; and it only seems a short one when the high mettled comedy with which it is impregnated from beginning to end leaps out with all the lightness and spring of its wonderful loftiness of temper. *Hamlet* is full of a celestial gaiety and fascination.'

Hamlet's wit must be as vital a part of him as his heart or stomach. To use it does not indicate cheeriness or flippancy – far from it. The Elizabethans saw wit as a common adjunct to the clinical state of melancholy, and Hamlet often jokes about the very things that are causing him the most pain: 'Thrift, thrift, Horatio. The funeral baked meats / Did coldly furnish forth the marriage tables' (1.ii.180–1). Searching for wit whenever and wherever I could kept me, I hope, from sliding into gloom or sentimentality. I even tried to die wittily, to 'prophesy' Fortinbras's succession when the only option is a room full of corpses seemed heavily ironic, and there is even a pun in 'the rest is silence' for someone who talks so compulsively. The wit and speed are of course interrelated: if the intellect is a passionate, engaged and witty one then ideas and feelings can be worked out and expressed at one and the same time: the thought can be contained within the words, and there is no need to elaborate around the edges.

Hamlet's wit is never comfortable and seldom gentle. To explore his cruelty, Roger and I talked at length about the experience of bereavement. Many people seem compelled to 'tell the truth', as they see it, in any situation after the death of a close relative or friend. It is as though the protective life-lies have simply disappeared. This may be emotionally necessary but it is often painful for all concerned. In his obsessive questioning of motive and morality Hamlet is cruel to everyone, and we tried not to shirk this. Only Horatio passes the tests that Hamlet sets him, and their relationship grows and develops accordingly. The quiet, worried, but spiritually fulfilled academic that Malcolm Sinclair was developing worked wonderfully for me here – a still point around which I could be volatile. Yet even Horatio is met with suspicion and rudeness, and the cruelty that Hamlet metes out to Ophelia is, and should be, disgusting. What saves him from alienating the audience's sympathy entirely should be their appreciation of his inner pain and their realization that the person who comes in for the fiercest criticism from Hamlet is himself.

I talked earlier of plotting a graph of energy for the playing of the part. This is easier in theory than in practice, particularly in the first act. This makes huge demands, not least because it is largely reactive – extraordinary things happen to Hamlet which demand extreme responses. I always felt completely wrung out after Act One, Scene Five, yet unable to relax. I had to find ways of keeping hold of all the psychological upheaval and yet be alert and ready for the next huge scene, Act Two, Scene Two. This scene includes dangerous verbal fencing with Polonius (made all the more dangerous by David Collings's eschewing of the doddery buffer in favour of a charming razor-sharp politician), the testing of Rosencrantz and Guildenstern, meeting the Players and finally the 'rogue and peasant slave' soliloquy, the most athletic and pyrotechnic of all the soliloquies. By the time you reach this, you must be firing on all cylinders: wit, anguish, self-laceration, intellectual curiosity, histrionics, rage, and direct contact with the audience are all called into play. To play this speech well, as I know I sometimes did, is the most exciting experience I have had on stage.

Scarcely time to walk round the auditorium from one side to another and Hamlet is straight back on, plunged from the huge positive high of 'the play's the thing' to the introspective depths of 'to be or not to be'. What seems at first reading to be an impossible logical inconsistency becomes in performance a psychological and theatrical masterstroke, rendering it possible for the actor to start another upward arc that culminates in the 'closet' scene (Act Three, Scene Four). The energy needed for this arc is awesome, and even if achieved, terribly difficult to keep under control. It is tempting to allow an explosion to occur in the play scene but this would cause a fatal dip and make the frenzy of the 'closet' scene impossible to reach.

The task, then, was to chart an upward curve from 'to be or not to be' (which I tried to play with the simplicity of utter exhaustion) through the delicacy and gentleness of the first half of the following scene with Ophelia (two ex-lovers finding themselves alone together) which explodes into awful viciousness after the betrayal of 'Where's your father?' . . . 'At home, my lord' (III.i.130–1). There is then a violent gear change into the advice to the Players, informed with a mounting excitement but which needs to be given real moral weight, followed by the mounting hysteria of the play

26   Philip Franks as Hamlet in the play scene (III.ii), the players in the background

scene itself. I was hyperactive – setting furniture, operating lights and smoke machines, and generally leaping about. In the 'recorders' scene after the court has left, I used to have an image of Hamlet as incandescent, lit from within, like a nuclear reactor about to explode, driven towards the promised interview with Gertrude. The 'now might I do it' (III.iii.75) speech over the praying Claudius becomes, then, something of an irrelevance. The violent emotional pull is towards Gertrude's closet, and there is simply no room in Hamlet's soul for killing Claudius at that moment, whatever other reasons he may give. When he reaches Gertrude, the explosion occurs and everything comes pouring out: self-loathing, sexual confusion, loss, need and violence; for the first time, he takes human life, and his 'killing virginity' is lost. It is a traumatic scene to play, for both actors, but a satisfying one too, in that you feel you have arrived at the centre of the play. It marks a point of huge change too, for both of them. Gertrude moves into a mode of introspective sadness and guilt (Maggie would stand washing herself obsessively after I had left the stage, visibly ageing) and Hamlet has purged enough of the debilitating poison from his system to be able to leave Elsinore for England.

The period away, at sea with the pirates, marks a huge growth of maturity for Hamlet. I found the last act of the play to be full of maturity and wisdom. I wanted to show a man who can think and see clearly without making impossible demands on himself or others; who can deal with people with gentleness and grace; who has a direct, non-neurotic relationship with death. There is violence too, and anger, but I never found a revenger's satisfaction in the final bloodbath, only the sadness and irony of inevitability.

This then, roughly, was my graph. It changed and developed, and we tried many alternative choices along the way – a great bitterness and contempt for everything was something we tried in Act Five and discarded, for instance. The world of the court took shape around me, and informed all these choices too. Roger created, along with designer Alex Byrne, a sophisticated and political world, comfortable, efficient and polite, holding up the virtues of the family, brimful of forward-looking self-confidence, and founded on lies and violence. Those looking for contemporary reference would hopefully not be disappointed here, nor perhaps in the society's critic, too bound up in self-doubt and questions of morality to be able to bring it down. The furniture suggested a series of domestic interiors, since *Hamlet* is almost exclusively an indoor play. Ophelia had a bed, with all her letters and keepsakes in a hatbox under it. Gertrude's closet was suggested by a rail of dresses (the arras) and a washstand. Claudius had a whole series of rooms, delineated by a cheval-glass, a low red leather chair with drinks table, or a marquetry chess table – all images of sophistication. These essentially private rooms were framed at the back of the stage by a beautiful, ornately gilded, Victorian-style proscenium arch. This was our visual correlative to the preponderance of theatrical metaphor, and the constant insistence in the play on sincerity and seeming, both in language and situation. The production began and ended with two tableaux of the public face covering up something – a royal wedding group at the start, and Fortinbras triumphant at the end.

Much of what I have described as the rehearsal process is bound up in my mind with the way in which the play grew and changed in performance. It is difficult to be rigorously accurate about what idea came from where and when, especially in a good and happy production. There is another element to it all, however, which it is difficult to talk about without sounding pretentious, and this is the effect of carrying the part around inside you. Sometimes it is as though you are haunted, sometimes you feel that you are in possession of something so precious that you are the luckiest person in the world, and sometimes it is like having a tumour. The experience of *not* playing it is just the same: something has been cut away, perhaps something dangerous and ugly. But something of ineffable value has been lost as well, and after a while you begin to doubt whether you ever had it at all.

# Imogen in
## *Cymbeline*
### HARRIET WALTER

HARRIET WALTER played Imogen in Bill Alexander's production of *Cymbeline* at The Other Place, Stratford, in 1987 and the following year in the Pit Theatre at the Barbican. Her other roles in these seasons were Viola in *Twelfth Night* and Dacha in *A Question of Geography*, with Masha in *Three Sisters* added in the London season, performances for which she won an Olivier award as 'Actress of the Year in a revival'. In 1989–90 she returned to the RSC to play the title role in *The Duchess of Malfi*. In an earlier season (1981–82) with the Company she had been Helena in *A Midsummer Night's Dream*, Constance in *The Twin Rivals*, Winnifred in *The Witch of Edmonton*, Lady Percy in *1* and *2 Henry IV*, Helena in *All's Well that Ends Well*, and Madeline Bray in *Nicholas Nickleby*. Shakespearian roles elsewhere include Ophelia in *Hamlet* and Portia in *The Merchant of Venice*. Other performances have been as Jane in *A Fair Quarrel*, Nina in *The Seagull*, Maria in *The Possessed*, and Julia in *The Lucky Change*. A range of television work includes Harriet Vane in the Dorothy L. Sayers adaptations and roles in *The Men's Room*, *Ashenden*, *Girls on Top*, and *The Cherry Orchard*. Films include *The Good Father*, *Turtle Diary*, and *Reflections*. She has recently accepted a position as an artistic director at the Royal Exchange Theatre, Manchester.

I once heard a joke about an actor in *King Lear* being asked what the play was about; he replied, 'Oh, it's about this doctor who has to tend a sick demented old man who thinks he's King of Britain.' He, of course, was playing the doctor. In Truffaut's film *Day for Night*, there was a similar scene where a journalist interviews the actors on the set of a film: 'Can you tell me the story of the film?' The young man says, 'It's about this young man who falls in love'; the woman says, 'it's about this woman . . .'; the old man says, 'it's about this old man who . . .'. From the moment we are invited to play a part, a mental process gets under way, intended to bridge the gap between me and her/him. Subjectivity begins to set in, and our character becomes the centre of our universe. Consequently there is a sense in which for me *Cymbeline* is about Imogen. As work is beginning, however, we fight to keep our objectivity, to keep doors open, to allow the not-yet-too-subjective insights of fellow actors to throw light on the whole play and our part in it, because, of course, the meaning of the play is revealed through all the characters.

In the early stages of rehearsal, with Bill Alexander directing, we focused on identifying the main themes of *Cymbeline*. We had ambitious talks about politics and world peace, animated discussions about love and sexual jealousy, and so on. It was a time of great sharing and excitement, of inexhaustible questioning and textual exploration, which revealed not only the larger themes but also the echoes for each individual and how the general informed the particular and vice versa. Before the rot of self-centredness could set in, I hoped to root my work firmly in the common ground discovered with the company, and if I succeeded, then anything I now say about the journey of Imogen might help uncover the meaning of the play.

Imogen is a coveted role. It is her range that chiefly appeals. In one evening an actress can play a bit of Desdemona, Juliet, Cordelia, Lady Anne, Rosalind and Cleopatra. In reading up about Imogen, I came across many descriptive adjectives: 'divine', 'enchanting', 'virtuous'. To describe a character is to judge it. The term 'character' acquired the meaning it now has for us relatively recently. Shakespeare himself writes of 'suiting the action to the word, the word to the action', about 'one man in his time plays many parts', and this comes nearer to it for me. As I see it, my preparatory task is to read and read the text and nothing but the text. To attempt to retrace Shakespeare's steps from the word, to the thought, to the motivation, to the heart of Imogen I must understand her choices, inhabit the mind that expresses itself through her imagery and thereby make her 'live'. I can't act 'virtue', 'chastity', 'divine', 'enchanting'; all I can actually do is say her words and perform her actions. At the end of the evening, I will have exposed her to the audience's judgement; that is inevitable, but the big enemy is prejudice or reputation. Luckily, *Cymbeline* not being a much-performed play, Imogen is not well known.

What are the given facts? She is the only daughter of the King of Britain. Her two brothers were stolen in infancy. Her mother is dead. Her father has remarried a scheming woman with designs on the crown, through her son Cloten's marriage to Imogen. Imogen has in fact secretly married Posthumus, an orphan whom her father adopted at birth, and reared as

Imogen's childhood companion. The opening scene of the play establishes what at court is commonly thought of all these people. Imogen and Posthumus are goodies, and reflect one another's worth:

> To his mistress ...
> ... her own price
> Proclaims how she esteem'd him; and his virtue
> By her election may be truly read
> What kind of man he is. (I.i.50–5)

Cloten and the Queen are baddies, and Cymbeline is a potential goody who has lost his way. It is so often the burden of a Shakespearian actress to live up to a lot of laudatory descriptions of her character. More recently I have played Portia in *The Merchant of Venice* who is 'Fair, and, fairer than that word, / Of wondrous virtues' (I.i.162–3) and 'All the world desires her; / From the four corners of the earth they come / To kiss this shrine, this mortal breathing saint' (II.vii.38–40); and Viola in *Twelfth Night* who 'bore a mind that envy could not but call fair' (II.i.26) and, even as a boy, Olivia lists 'this youth's perfections ... thy tongue, thy face, thy limbs, actions and spirit / Do give thee five-fold blazon' (I.v.281–6). How does the actress get behind these 'perfections', and why should an audience take for granted a heroine's virtue on the strength of what some other character says of her? Virtue is not a property that a heroine possesses. It has to be demonstrated by being put through a series of tests. Shakespeare may have intended his heroines to uphold some moral torch, and have redemptive powers, but he also realized that if they were perfect they would be unbelievable and dramatically static. To play a heroine one must look for her faults, her human weaknesses. If a flawed and vulnerable person is seen to be tested, to learn, to change, to make brave choices and to overcome the odds, this puts heroic achievements within our reach and gives us hope for humankind.

In what, then, does Imogen's virtue consist? In much male-centred thinking, virginity would be enough to guarantee her saintly status, for as long as she retained it. But virtue is not passive, it involves knowledge and the choice of what to do with that knowledge. Most virginal heroines have little first-hand knowledge of the world, and even less power of choice. Imogen is different. First, she is a Princess. Secondly, she is not a virgin. She is married. When Posthumus says 'Me of my lawful pleasure she restrain'd, / And pray'd me oft forbearance' (II.iv.161–2), we know the marriage was consummated, but that she sometimes had a headache. Besides, we only have Posthumus's word that she turned him down 'with a pudency so rosy' – maybe she was afraid to get pregnant and blow their cover prematurely. Nor is she obedient. She thwarts her father's wishes by marrying Posthumus, and thereby rebels against her King. I decided she had married impulsively with no great plan in mind, but somehow was instinctively defending herself against the projected marriage to Cloten with a *fait accompli*. When the shit finally hits the fan she'll think again. The clue to this characteristic impetuosity I found in her later lines: 'I see before me, man; nor here, nor here, / Nor what ensues' (III.ii.79–80). She seems to have a defiantly independent version of what is right and she sticks to it. Call it integrity or call it arrogance, her strength and her chief fault are two sides of the same coin. She starts off the play with a strong sense of her own importance, both as lawful wife to Posthumus and as Princess of Britain. Her sense of self is intricately bound up in those two titles and, as the play goes on, she will be rocked in her faith in both.

In the first section of the play, I discovered a quality in Imogen which I could never clearly describe. It was a kind of self-dramatization. It is as though in order to bear her misery, she casts herself in a noble role, and in playing that to the hilt, she cannot be seen to give in or let herself down. She starts by choosing her own roles, but as the play goes on, fate and other people will force her into many disguises. These have a narrative justification and function, but on a deeper level they have the quality of metamorphoses. They are in some way like a series of small deaths and rebirths in another form, and involve giving up some outer trapping of her identity the better to find her true self. Through all these roles she retains her Imogen-ness. Again, I hoped that if I didn't define in advance what that Imogen-ness was and lay it on, but played each situation and role for what it was, the Imogen-ness would take care of itself. It would reveal itself not in spite of, but because of, the disguise. I found it helpful to signpost her journey in terms of these metamorphoses, which simplistically could be labelled thus: Princess/Wife to Princess/Rebel to Franklin's Housewife to Boy/Housewife to Roman Page to Princess/Wife.

*Role 1: Princess/Rebel: 'A wedded lady that hath her husband banished'*

Imogen is under house-arrest. What with Posthumus's banishment, her father's rejection, Cloten's assaults, and the scheming of the Queen, she has a lot to cope with. She yearns to be a 'neat-herd's daughter' (I.ii.80), but recognizes the inevitability of 'most miserable is the desire that's glorious' (I.vii.6). Sensible of her royal status, she draws strength from a knowledge that she isn't just anyone going through a personal tragedy, but that there are subjects out there relying on her to survive with all the values of the Old Britain intact. This sureness of her role gives her the courage to tell her father, 'I am senseless of your wrath' (I.ii.66). He is like the 'tyrannous breathing of the north' that 'shakes all our buds from growing' (I.iii.36). Both David Bradley (Cymbeline) and I wanted to show that theirs was the rage that comes from betrayal of what had been great love between them. This endows Cymbeline with the humanity he will need in the final scene and helps our reconciliation at the end. This was not an intellectual imposition on our part but arose from both of our instinctive responses to the scene as soon as we put it on its feet. There seemed to be something so immediate and intimate in the confrontation between them; a suggested matching of temperaments. It reminded me of other father/ daughter conflicts – Regan and Lear, Juliet and Capulet – that despite the hostility of the moment show quite uncluttered channels of communication, open to great love as well as great antagonism.

Almost from day one David Bradley introduced a whacking great slap on my jaw which seemed absolutely right, as did the equally ferocious embrace which followed it. Like many of these things one cannot quite remember whose idea it was; all I know is that to both of us it seemed physically and neatly to demonstrate the complicated feeling between us. I accepted the slap not because I'm any kind of masochist, but because it was an extremely useful catapult into the next whirlwind of emotion that takes Imogen over for the rest of the scene. David is one of the gentlest, kindest men I know, but he can't half pack a punch! On one occasion after playing the scene I went up to him backstage with a lop-sided jaw and asked him to go a little easier (but not too easy) as I had quite a lot more words to say that night! Offstage relationships do undoubtedly colour onstage ones. Sometimes you can use them, other times you have to suppress them. I *think* it was quite hard for David Bradley to hit me as we were great friends. I may of course be wrong.

Similarly, my friendship with Jim Hooper who played Pisanio blinded me to the obvious. Apart from the loyal Pisanio, whom Posthumus left her as a kind of parting gift, Imogen has no ally. For most of the run in Stratford we emphasized the friendship between Pisanio and Imogen. Actors are often both tactile and insecure (maybe the former because of the latter) so I found myself accompanying every 'good Pisanio' and 'true Pisanio' with a clutch of Jim's wrist or an arm round his shoulder – wrong! He is a servant and she a princess, and when we came to re-rehearse the play for Newcastle, Bill Alexander encouraged me to be more regally distant with Pisanio. To stress this gulf in status pays off later when Imogen must somehow believe Pisanio capable of murdering Posthumus. She has not been reared in an atmosphere of great trust (if Belarius's descriptions of the court are accurate); nor, with her mother dead and the Queen as the only female role-model, has she had much cause to love womankind. In our production (very simply staged at The Other Place) the first scene between Pisanio and Imogen took place in what we imagined to be almost a hidey-hole, lit only by one candle which seemed to symbolize the memory of Posthumus, which we were conspiratorially keeping alive. Some members of the audience were no more than four feet away and we could be heard at a whisper. We inserted cries of 'Imogen' from the Queen down a corridor somewhere and we hoped the dangerous atmosphere would be palpable. Imogen feels almost competitive with Pisanio in her devotion to Posthumus. She interrupts and tops him every time: 'Thou shouldst have made him / As little as a crow ... I would have broke mine eye-strings' (I.iv.14–16). Because she and Posthumus have been brought up together, I imagine their relationship not unlike that of Cathy and Heathcliff. Childhood companions, twin souls sharing secrets, platonic lovers, suddenly become man and wife. Sexual knowledge opens the Pandora's box of jealousy, fear of loss, mistrust and ignorance of the opposite sex. They are parted at a vulnerable stage in their development together. Sex has the power to make them strangers to one another, and it is that power that Iachimo exploits. Imogen betrays early on her suspicions of the 'she's of Italy' (of course in this case it is not just her mistrust of other women, but of Italy in general she is showing), and on parting with Posthumus she (again slightly self-dramatizingly) suggests that Posthumus might 'woo another wife when Imogen is dead' (I.ii.44).

One of the play's themes is 'too ready hearing'. Belarius tells how, with little resistance, Cymbeline believed him to be 'confederate with the Romans' through 'two villains whose false oaths prevail'd / Before my perfect honour' (III.iii.66–7). Posthumus (admittedly with quite tangible 'proof') believes Imogen to be unfaithful, and Imogen succumbs to Iachimo's suggestions of Posthumus's infidelity with what I found in the playing to be disconcerting speed. She soon realizes what she's done and blames herself with 'I do condemn mine ears, / That have so long attended thee' (I.vii.141–2) and, feeling guilty at her momentary lapse of faith, she proceeds to overcompensate Iachimo with her trust, to the point where the next morning, missing her bracelet, and through all the trials that follow, she never once suspects him.

I found the scene when Iachimo first visits her one of the hardest and most exciting to play. With Donald Sumpter and myself the balance each night could be minutely and importantly altered. I had to negotiate subtly, delicately, how much to believe when, and how quickly. Don likes being unpredictable and so do I. One has to keep a sharp vigil, however, lest in the interests of being different for its own sake one sacrifices the credibility for one's fellow player. For instance, if Don were to make Iachimo too smarmy, with Imogen's already strong prejudice against Italians would she not see through him too early on? Likewise I had to give Don/Iachimo just the right ambiguity on 'How should I be revenged?' (line 129) for him to be able to interpret it as a possible lead for his lascivious suggestion. I had to *mean* 'What would *you* know . . . you cannot understand the enormity of this betrayal . . . revenge is so inappropriate' but say the line in such a way that Iachimo would be able to *hear* it as 'I'm at a loss to think of a suitable revenge to match this crime. Have you any ideas?' Interesting. On nights when Don/Iachimo exaggerated his account of Posthumus the Briton reveller creasing up at the sighing French lover, crying 'O can my sides hold, to think that man, who knows . . . what woman is . . . will's free hours languish for assured bondage?' (lines 69–73). I would deliver my line 'will my lord say so?' in an 'oh yeah?' kind of way – if Don played it more delicately I'd say it with a shadow crossing my face, but an attempt at light-heartedness in my voice. These are just a few examples of the kind of fine tuning which kept us on our toes right through the run of the play from November 1987 to February 1989.

In playing Imogen in most of her other scenes, I had the sensation of driving through like a steamroller, raging at her father, overriding Pisanio, letting off volleys of insults at Cloten and the Queen. There was an element of the boxing-ring as I would enter the horseshoe-shaped arena at The Other Place and later the clean open space at The Pit, for a two-hander, head-on contest with Cloten or the King and usually come off best, if only verbally. Here with Iachimo, on the other hand, she is off-footed from the start. She begins with outrage at the intrusion of a stranger, and instantly on learning he comes from Italy and Posthumus she is thrown into the opposite mood of ecstatic excitement. 'Change you madam' is Iachimo's knowing understatement (I.vii.11) and Shakespeare's stage direction, all in one. This volatility of mood where Posthumus is concerned is the key both to her credulity and her over-quick forgiveness of Iachimo. From this point the unconditional warmth and charm she extends to Iachimo as a fellow adorer of Posthumus is misinterpreted by Iachimo. As in *The Winter's Tale* and *Othello* a woman showing open friendship for a man other than her spouse is misunderstood by a misogynist onlooker or a frightened husband through their ignorance of the complex range of a woman's feelings.

Iachimo can undermine Imogen's and Posthumus's faith in one another by the same means as Iago can manipulate Othello. The thing you most prize you most fear losing. Living with that fear, in a world where propaganda perpetuates suspicion between the sexes, can become so unbearable that you break under the strain. You begin to want to believe the worst, in order to alleviate the pressure. Hence Posthumus is driven to say 'No swearing: / If you will swear you have not done't you lie, / And I will kill thee if thou dost deny / Thou'st made me cuckold' (ii.iv.1423–6). Loss of faith in Imogen leads Posthumus to his famous diatribe against her entire gender. It is significant that Imogen herself has imbibed the prevailing misogyny of the world and at worst believes 'some jay of Italy / Whose mother was her painting, hath betrayed him' (iii.iv.49–50).

In The Other Place, windchimes, suspended oil drums, the inside of a piano, stamping feet and human calls, all scored expertly by Ilona Sekacz, provided atmospheric percussion throughout the play. In the bedroom scene, Act Two, Scene Two, a couple of delicate strokes on a windchime instantly conjured up a hot night cooled by a breeze and evoked (for me anyway) the cricket-singing that Iachimo speaks of. A sudden kick of an oil drum makes Imogen jump out of her skin: 'Who's there?' Her woman Helen enters; 'What hour is it? (ii.ii.2). 'Almost midnight, madam' was delivered in such a way as to suggest this is unusually late for Imogen still to be reading. When Helen settles Imogen down for a sleep and is about to blow out the candle, I played up Imogen's nervousness by sudden fitful rhythms on 'Take not away the taper, leave it burning' and 'if thou canst awake by four o'th' clock, / I prithee call me' (lines 5–6). This is followed by her prayer for protection against the 'tempters of the night' and as if for added security I kissed Posthumus's bracelet, so soon to be slipped from my arm by Iachimo, just as she describes herself as having done next day in Act Two, Scene Three. All of this signals a sense of foreboding, a certain disquiet in Imogen that could spring from a deep-down self-recrimination at her earlier behaviour with Iachimo. Again tempted to play on the fine line separating seeming-guilt and innocence, I returned Iachimo's kiss in my sleep. Shakespeare doesn't state that Iachimo does indeed kiss her but

Don quite justifiably took 'one kiss! Rubies unparagon'd, /How dearly they do't' (lines 17–18) to mean that he should. I took the active verb 'do't'at face value, justifying it by knowing she later talks of dreaming of Posthumus every night. Neither Iachimo nor the audience are to know for sure at this point whether it's the kiss of the actual Iachimo or the dreamed-of Posthumus that she is returning so sweetly. Again the proximity of the audience in this studio production gave the scene a terrible intimacy, an almost voyeuristic edge, and for this reason I found the scene to be the ultimate in passive vulnerability, right down to the virginal white nightie. I was literally in Don's hands and very trustworthy he was. (I do remember one night when there was a leak in The Other Place just above where the bed was set in the wings. Lying in a cold rainsoaked bed and trying not to wince or giggle is quite a challenge, believe me!)

If there are hints of Imogen's unease in the bedroom scene, they grow to full-blown dread in the following scene with Cloten. We know she has both the guts and the wit to stick up for herself and make mincemeat of Cloten any day of the week, but on this occasion the loss of her bracelet troubles her so much that she goes too far with the insults and tips Cloten over into a maddened vengeful rage. Is she possibly nagged by some unformed notion of having done something wrong? In all that I read about the play, I never met any criticism of Imogen for believing ill of Posthumus, such as is levelled at Posthumus for believing ill of Imogen. The issue gets confusing, of course, because in Posthumus's case, although Iachimo has presented him with concrete 'proof' of her adultery in the shape of her bracelet, Posthumus goes on to the unforgiveable extreme of ordering Pisanio to kill her.

Another theme which struck me as vitally important was that of 'good service'. I am baffled and disappointed that Shakespeare doesn't reward Pisanio for what I feel to be the most virtuous conduct of all. He is a servant and therefore risks great punishment in disobeying orders. He knows Imogen is true without needing proof. He has been ordered by his master to kill her. He refuses. He thinks on his feet and formulates a plan to save the situation. He was given the power to kill and he didn't use it. Compare his 'If it be so to do good service, never / Let me be counted serviceable' (III.ii.14–15) with a war criminal's 'I was only carrying out orders.' Surely the woman who went against her King/Father's orders when she thought him corrupt would approve of Pisanio's attitude. I felt this so strongly, I even changed a line in Act Five (v.v.401), since no one acknowledges Pisanio's role in the happy outcome of events, and addressed 'And you relieved me to see this gracious season' to Pisanio rather than to Belarius. Pisanio's virtue comes from his sense of honour – 'How look I, / That I should seem to lack humanity / So much as this fact comes to' (III.iii.17–19) – just as Iachimo's capacity for evil comes from his lack of self-love. To a great extent we judge others according to what we know of ourselves. Iachimo refuses to believe in love and fidelity between Posthumus and Imogen because he feels incapable of such feelings himself. This is why Imogen's belief in herself is so important. It feeds her belief in others, which involves faith and hope. Biblically, despair is a sin. Imogen speaks of herself as 'past hope, and in despair, that way past grace' (I.ii.68). To hope requires courage to face the risk of loss. Strength comes from self-knowledge, which in turn is gained through the courage to change and learn – and courage is a quality that Imogen is constantly called on to demonstrate. Even in her scene with Cloten, who could at this point be dismissed as a fool, I laughed in Bruce Alexander's face when Cloten says, 'I'll be revenged' (II.iii.156), and it was a laugh tinged with fear of a more dangerous man beneath.

*Role 2: The Franklin's Housewife: 'I am almost a man already'*

At last comes a release, both for Imogen and for the actress playing her. She receives a letter from Posthumus inviting her to meet him at Milford Haven – 'O, for a horse with wings!' (III.ii.49) – and she almost takes flight. This speech provides an all-too-rare opportunity for vein-bursting joy. The danger for me is that exhilaration runs away with me and my tongue runs away with the words – though it is important, of course, that Pisanio gets no chance to stem the tide and interrupt. To avoid detection in her escape from the palace to Milford Haven, Imogen dresses as a 'franklin's housewife' (III.ii.78). It is an impulsive solution intended 'for the gap / Which we shall make in time, from our hence-going / And our return, to excuse' (lines 63–5). But after the events on her arrival in Wales, that return becomes out of the question. She won't go back. She speaks of 'the perturbed court ... whereunto I never purpose return' (III.iv.106–8). And when Pisanio suggests 'If you'll back to the court ...', she jumps in on him 'No court, no father, nor no more ado ...' (line 132). Maybe subconsciously she knew from the beginning that she was initiating a final break. Here on a Welsh hillside, humbly dressed, she learns of Posthumus's intent to kill her for her adultery. The news as good as kills her at first. She begs Pisanio to obey Posthumus's orders as without Posthumus in her heart there's no point to her life. She never believes that Posthumus actually thinks she's false. Her honour is beyond question: 'I false? Thy conscience witness' (line 46). As she constructs it, he has fallen for someone else and wants her out of the way. She not only confronts literal death by Pisanio's sword, but a death of faith: 'All good seeming, / By thy revolt, O husband, shall be thought / Put on for villainy' (lines 54–6); but Imogen doesn't die that easily. The confrontation brings out the fight in her. At this point things tended to get dangerous. The advantages of the small space here became disadvantages. I found it hard to contain the size of Imogen's emotions within that little wooden 'O'. I wanted to yell from the Welsh mountain tops. When Jim threw his sword away and when I cast Posthumus's love-letters aside, quite often they landed at the audience's feet. Both had to be retrieved during the action and it's hard to conjure up in one's imagination the loneliness of a clearing in a wood near Milford Haven while grovelling among Hush Puppies and handbags! From this point of view things improved in the larger Pit theatre.

Until this point Imogen has identified herself with Britain to such an extent that when Iachimo in Act One, Scene Seven plants doubts in her mind as to Posthumus's fidelity, she says, 'My lord, I fear, has forgot Britain' (line 112). In her book, Cymbeline has also 'forgot Britain'. She protests to him, 'It is your fault that I have lov'd Posthumus: / You bred him as my play-fellow' (I.ii.75–6). And with that it seems as if she is saying 'you taught me my values and now you're reneging on them. It's up to me and Posthumus to carry the flag for all that is good about Britain until you come to your senses and see through that wicked Queen who has led you up the garden path.' Now through the trauma of Act Three, Scene Four she manages to extricate her belief in Posthumus from her belief in herself and both from her belief in Britain:

> Hath Britain all the sun that shines? Day? Night?
> Are they not but in Britain? I' th' world's volume
> Our Britain seems as of it, but not in't:
> In a great pool, a swan's nest: prithee think
> There's livers out of Britain.          (lines 135–9)

In that moment, the 'strain of rareness' she had earlier rather chest-thumpingly declared in herself becomes real. She becomes larger.

Having given up her royal identity, she next gives up her sexual identity. Unlike Rosalind and Portia, Imogen does not volunteer to disguise as a boy. It is Pisanio who advises, 'You must forget to be a woman' (line 155). And unusually, in Imogen's case, maleness does not bring with it authority, but rather it means she must 'change command into obedience', as Pisanio puts it. She is already well along the road to forgiving Posthumus, not a little thanks to Pisanio's constancy. Pisanio's proposal is that she travel to Italy in the service of the Roman General Caius Lucius, where she can at least be near Posthumus, and who knows what might happen then? The Princess who has barely stepped outside her castle bedroom jumps at his suggestion: 'O, for such means, / Though peril to my modesty, not death on't, / I would adventure' (lines 151–3).

The musical movement of this scene is so clearly indicated by Shakespeare that we just had to surrender to his 'stage directions' and, provided we didn't dodge the full force of the emotions, we could then ride it out, so to speak. To begin with, each character describes how the other should be behaving: 'wherefore breaks that sigh from th' inward of thee?' ... 'Put thyself into a 'haviour of less fear' (lines 5–8), etc. Similarly, Imogen says nothing after reading Posthumus's letter and Shakespeare gives Pisanio eight lines aside to cover her silence, beginning with 'What shall I need to draw my sword? the paper / Hath cut her throat already' (lines 32–3). Then Imogen's white-hot anger takes over the scene, leaving Pisanio winded and gasping, until, exhausted, she allows him to speak. He begins tentatively and she still manages to rush in and contradict him until, after insisting that 'some Roman courtesan' has caused Posthumus's treachery, Jim forgot his servant status, grabbed me by the shoulders and fairly shook me on the line 'No, on my life' (line 124). This shocked me first into bewilderment – 'Why, good fellow, what shall I do the while?' – then determination, rejecting all idea of returning to court, and then giving Pisanio the cue 'I am most glad you think of other place ...' (line 141). In a quieter, more compliant, frame of mind she takes on his plan. The scene ended with Pisanio handing me back Posthumus's bundle of letters and my quiet, serious, 'I thank thee' from a finally lucid Imogen.

*Role 3: Boy/Housewife: 'Cook to honest creatures' ... 'He is a man, I'll love him as my brother'*

Dressed as a British page, determined to bear her trials with 'a prince's courage', Imogen is forced to reach a more quintessential definition of herself. She has had to slough off 'Imogen' like an old skin, and underneath she finds 'Fidele', the faithful one. In this state, Shakespeare has prepared her to meet her brothers. The meeting is geographically an outrageous coincidence, but it is spiritually timely. She learns the limitations of her physical courage: 'If mine enemy / But fear the sword like me, he'll scarcely look on't' (III.vi.25–6). But she also learns of her fortitude: 'I should be sick, / But that my resolution helps me' (lines 3–4). In Act One, Scene Seven, she had said 'Had I been thief-stolen, / As my two brothers, happy ... blessed be those, / How mean so e'er, that have their honest wills' (lines 5–8). Now she's testing these sentiments for real and on meeting her brothers and finding them to be 'kind creatures', she can confirm 'what lies I have heard. / Our courtiers say all's savage but at court; / Experience, O, thou disprov'st report' (IV.ii.32–4). The costumes for this production were all drawn from stock, and within a basic framework agreed between Bill Alexander and Alan Watson (Head of Wardrobe), we were free to choose the clothes we felt best fitted our image of the character. My image of Imogen was something of Boudicca and something of Fuchsia in Mervyn Peake's *Gormenghast* – the smutty rebel child grown into wilful adult with amazon potential. I chose a rough simple velvet dress to begin with and on becoming a boy I wore a costume based on the standard 'look' of the other men – velvet jerkin, white shirt, belt, braces, and brown trousers tucked into mid-calf boots. My thick, not-too-groomed red mane got plaited and my gold headband was replaced by a brown one giving me a Viking/Red Indian look. I most decidedly didn't want to wear my own short hair at this point as that was my image for the more gamine Viola which I was still playing, and for my own sake I needed sharply to differentiate between them.

With her boy disguise the pressure is somehow off Imogen and off the player of Imogen. The emotional drive relaxes, and there is more oppor- tunity for comedy and lyricism. Shakespeare even takes her to the very edge of acceptable irony with 'would ... they had been my father's sons' (III.vi.75–6). Here the actress gives in willingly to audience titters, though the character is in earnest. I learned to dare to give a pause after such a line – I say 'dare' because one risks a laugh-less silence and egg on the face. The pause should be just long enough to let the audience know that they can laugh – that I the actress intend the joke, though the character is innocent of it – a challenging knife-edge to tread. The play is riddled with such prescient utterances: either, as in this case, rooted in a character's greatest yearnings, or in their deepest dread, such as 'I hope it be not gone to tell my lord / That I kiss aught but he' (II.iii.148). From the confrontation with Pisanio's sword (which incidentally she forgot to fear at the time) to the first meeting with the cave-dwellers – 'if you kill me for my fault, I should / Have died had I not made it' (III..vii.29–30) – Imogen has felt herself dangerously close to death, the great leveller, and this has led her to 'philosophize': 'clay and clay differs in dignity / Whose dust is both alike' (IV.ii.4–5) and 'falsehood is worse in kings than beggars' (III.vi.13). Not wildly original maybe, but, for a Princess reared in a palace as heir to the throne, quite a leap. Now her sad-sickness prompts her to swallow the drug Pisanio gave her from the Queen, and we next see her lifeless form carried on by Cadwal and lain on the ground as dead.

### 'Thou thy worldly task hast done'

Playing Imogen one spends quite a lot of time 'asleep', listening to the more beautiful passages of poetry in the play. First when Iachimo stalks her bedroom, and then when the two cave-boys speak 'Fear no more the heat of the sun' (IV.ii.258) over her 'dead' body. Incidentally, it is not only the cave-dwellers who believe Imogen's death, but even the audience on occasion are convinced of it – if they happened to doze off when the doctor told them that his drug was harmless and capable merely of 'locking up the spirits a time / To be more fresh, reviving' (I.vi.41–2). I often heard a gasp or even a vocalized 'Oh, no' at the point when I swallowed the drug. This is one of the advantages of a little-known play. We all know about Juliet! To represent Belarius's 'ingenious instrument', Ilona Sekacz had devised a beautiful haunting tune played by the company blowing across bottles behind the scenes. A strip of coloured tape on the bottle marked the point to which it must be filled with water and another label told the note it would then play when blown. A careless sip by a thirsty actor passing the props table could have changed a melodious G to a hideous discordant G flat or worse.

Lying there prone to the floor with my eyes closed, I tried to allow the words to inspire me, in preparation for my most difficult acting task to date. Each time I did it I wondered 'Will I make it? How will I make it? And what will come out of me this time?', and I rarely felt I had succeeded. Something in me resisted fixing that speech. Somehow I needed to depend on the inspiration of the moment. The scene is a minefield of the most fundamental acting problems. First I had to try to imagine a situation way outside my experience and which I hope will remain so. Shakespeare had already imagined the reactions of a woman in such a situation and he had given her the words to express her feelings. I had to bring my imagination into line with his. Secondly, there are two major traps in delivering a highly charged Shakespearian soliloquy: on the one hand, there is the temptation to impose a generalized emotion, to wash the stage with genuine tears, which may touch but certainly won't surprise the audience; and at the other extreme there is a danger of rhetoric, of spouting beautiful words with not a thought in your head because the emotional energy was just not on tap that night. The golden rule is to trust Shakespeare's words. This is why I try not to plan ahead. The audience know you believe the headless corpse lying next to you is Posthumus. They know you will be extremely unhappy about that. What they can't anticipate is how you are going to deal with your grief, whether you will recover, and how you will move on. The soliloquy provides the answers and it should be every bit as dynamic and unpredictable as a scene between two characters. It must never become a question of holding up the action to allow Imogen to let off steam, but rather it must be an exciting spectator event, watching someone come to terms with the unacceptable. How is she going to get out of this? What thought will she have next? The actor has to find the character's need to talk to the audience. I have to admit that Shakespeare is not at his most helpful when he asks me to deliver a panegyric to Posthumus (who the audience know is Cloten) and to weep over his 'martial thigh' and 'brawns of Hercules' (IV.ii.310) with only a stuffed dummy to help me! I'm comforted in the knowledge that both Ellen Terry and Peggy Ashcroft found this speech fearfully difficult. I charted my way through it.

I reminded myself that she is still probably semi-drugged. When she sees the headless corpse of Posthumus (as she supposes) she begins her deranged groping for reason. 'I hope I dream', she begins (line 297). Then when she finally realizes she is awake, 'How should this be?' (line 325). How to explain the unthinkable? She converts grief into rage. She had regained her total belief in Posthumus but has now settled on Pisanio as her husband's murderer. Still seeing herself as the heroine of her own story or 'the madded Hecuba' of a Greek tragedy, she has hitherto believed herself to have a special relationship with the gods. She felt her destiny mattered to them and has allowed Jove to test her. They were feared by her, but she felt their protection. Now, however, 'murder in heaven' has been committed. The gods are against her. From such a viewpoint she can believe even Pisanio is her enemy. She covers her face with Posthumus's blood, united again with him. There is a feeling of 'it's us against the world' in her speech 'that we the horrider may seem to those / That chance to find us' (lines 331–2).

Next she will surrender her nationalistic identity. The woman who had railed against 'drug-damned Italy' and the 'Romish stew' is now ready for

27  Harriet Walter as Imogen and the headless corpse of Cloten, with the
Soothsayer (Arnold Yarrow) and Caius Lucius (Geoffrey Freshwater)
(IV.ii)

her fourth role, as page to a Roman general. She has come even closer to
death. When I slump in tears over the 'corpse', awaiting the arrival of
General Lucius, I truly feel 'thou thy *acting* task hast done'. I can hand
over the stage to Posthumus. Again, another part of Imogen has 'died'. 'I
am nothing', she tells the General (line 367), but still she answers to the
name of Fidele.

*Role 4: The Roman Page: 'I am nothing'*

Having washed my face and donned my Roman jacket for my fleeting,
silent appearance in the battle scene, I then joined the rest of the company
to lend musical aids (the studio production having more or less eschewed
visual aids) to the descent of Jupiter in Posthumus's dream. Bashing piano

216

28  Imogen reconciled to Cymbeline (David Bradley) and Posthumus
    (Nicholas Farrell) (V.V)

wires was the one point of relaxation I had in the evening, and I could listen to Nick Farrell (Posthumus) repenting for having murdered Imogen – 'O Pisanio, every good servant does not all commands' (v.i.5) – and wishing he was dead. Imogen has also expressed a death-wish in 'nothing to be were better' (IV.ii.368). He wanted Imogen dead, but confronted with the bloody cloth which proves his wish has been fulfilled, he can't bear a world without her, and his moral rigidity bends:

> – You married ones,
> If each of you should take this course, how many
> Must murder wives much better than themselves
> For wrying but a little? (v.i.2–5)

In battle he is then given the chance to kill Iachimo and doesn't. Iachimo looks death in the face and is saved. The young princes are at last testing their noble blood in battle and all the characters are being prepared for Act Five, and the unravelling of all their interwoven themes.

If we had planted the right seeds, Act Five worked a treat. The play's characters have to go through some almost impossible suspensions of disbelief – not recognizing people two feet away, spotting rings and birth-marks they never noticed before – as for the next thirty minutes they learn what the audience already knows. In that sense the audience are like the gods and can look on with benign amusement. But in addition, if the play has worked, they will have undergone a journey with the players, had a mirror held up to them, just as the characters have. Imogen looks at Posthumus, Posthumus looks at Iachimo, Cymbeline looks at Belarius and Lucius, and all see some reflection of their own errors. There is a feeling of 'let him that is without sin cast the first stone'. We have seen good Italians and bad, good Britons and bad, good women and bad. The barriers of sex, birth and nation have been broken down. We begin to honour the bonds instead of perpetuating the divisions. Forgiveness is within our range – 'Pardon's the word to all' (v.v.423). On refinding his family, Cymbeline describes himself as 'the mother to the birth of three' (line 370). A society has been purged (admittedly with the help of the gods and the scapegoat Queen) and reborn. Glasnost is given a chance.

### 'The Tune of Imogen'

All the principal characters have been through trial of their faith, confront-ation with death, resurrection and reconciliation, but nowhere is this journey more completely or schematically illustrated than in Imogen's story. Restored to her final role as *Princess/Wife* (with the help of a blow from Posthumus which provides her final re-awakening), Imogen the individual recedes and merges with the whole as in the final image of the play we all kneel in a circle to praise the gods.

# Production credits

Productions have been listed in the order of essays in this volume. With the exception of *Much Ado about Nothing*, which played only in Stratford, and *Hamlet*, which played many venues on a nationwide regional tour, but which was not seen at any of the RSC's usual theatres, all the productions played in Stratford through the season in which they opened and then, during the following year, in Newcastle upon Tyne and at the Barbican Centre in London (the Royal Shakespeare Theatre (RST) productions moving to the Barbican main stage and the two Swan and two Other Place productions moving to the Barbican studio theatre, the Pit). In addition, *Titus Andronicus* followed its London season with a tour of European cities. The date given in each case is that of the first public performance (in Stratford in all instances except *Hamlet*).

MEASURE FOR MEASURE
RST, 5 November 1987
Director: Nicholas Hytner
Design and costumes: Mark Thompson
Music: Jeremy Sams
Lighting: Mark Henderson

MUCH ADO ABOUT NOTHING
RST, 7 April 1988
Director: Di Trevis
Design and costumes: Mark Thompson
Music: Dominic Muldowney
Lighting: Mark Henderson

THE MERCHANT OF VENICE
RST, 23 April 1987
Director: Bill Alexander
Designer: Kit Surrey

Costumes: Andreane Neofitou
Music: Guy Woolfenden
Lighting: Robert Bryan

AS YOU LIKE IT
RST, 8 September 1989
Director: John Caird
Design and costumes: Ultz
Music: Ilona Sekacz
Lighting: Alan Burrett

KING JOHN
The Other Place, 4 May 1988
Director: Deborah Warner
Design and costumes: Sue Blane
Music: Guy Woolfenden
Lighting: Chris Parry

HENRY VI and RICHARD III ('THE PLANTAGENETS')
RST, 29 September 1988
Director: Adrian Noble
Design and costumes: Bob Crowley
Music: Edward Gregson
Lighting: Chris Parry

TROILUS AND CRESSIDA
The Swan Theatre, 18 April 1990
Director: Sam Mendes
Design and costumes: Anthony Ward
Music: Shaun Davey
Lighting: Geraint Pughe

TITUS ANDRONICUS
The Swan Theatre, 28 April 1987
Director: Deborah Warner
Design and costumes: Isabella Bywater
[No music]
Lighting: Wayne Dowdeswell

HAMLET
Burton-upon-Trent, 12 October 1987 (and regional tour)
Director: Roger Michell
Design and costumes: Alexandra Byrne
Music: Jeremy Sams
Lighting: Chris Parry

CYMBELINE
The Other Place, 4 November 1987
Director: Bill Alexander
[No designer]
Costumes: Alan Watson
Music: Ilona Sekacz
Lighting: Clive Morris